MONTH-BY-MONTH GARDENING

TEXAS

First published in 2014 by Cool Springs Press, an imprint of Quarto Publishing Group USA Inc.,
400 First Avenue North, Suite 400, Minneapolis, MN 55401

The information in this book is true and complete to the best of our knowledge. All recommendations are made without any guarantee on the part of the author or Publisher, who also disclaims any liability incurred in connection with the use of this data or specific details.

Cool Springs Press titles are also available at discounts in bulk quantity for industrial or sales-promotional use. For details write to Special Sales Manager at Cool Springs Press, 400 First Avenue North, Suite 400, Minneapolis, MN 55401 USA. To find out more about our books, visit us online at www.coolspringspress.com.

ISBN: 978-1-59186-611-4

Library of Congress Cataloging-in-Publication Data

Richter, Robert "Skip".
Texas month-by-month gardening : what to do each month to have a beautiful garden all year / Robert "Skip" Richter.
pages cm
Includes bibliographical references and index.
ISBN 978-1-59186-611-4 (sc)
1. Gardening--Texas. I. Title.

SB453.2.T4R54 2015
635.09764--dc23

2014021515

Acquisitions Editor: Billie Brownell
Design Manager: Brad Springer
Layout: Kim Winscher

Printed in China
10 9 8 7 6 5 4 3 2 1

MONTH-BY-MONTH GARDENING

TEXAS

**What to Do Each Month to Have
a Beautiful Garden All Year**

SKIP RICHTER

COOL
SPRINGS
PRESS
Home and Garden Experts™

MINNEAPOLIS, MINNESOTA

Dedication

To my wife and children who encouraged me during the months of writing and photography. This book is in large part a result of their encouragement, understanding, love, and support. —*Skip Richter*

Acknowledgments

First and foremost, I am grateful to my God and Creator, whose first idea it was to put mankind in a garden. He has given me a love for gardening and a fascination with the wonders of nature that are a lifelong source of learning and enjoyment.

I am forever a learner and there have been a long line of gardeners and horticulturists from whom I have learned much about gardening. My first garden was a 4-H project, which I built with my mom, an avid gardener. Time spent with gardening neighbors, college professors, coworkers, Master Gardener volunteers, and other gardening friends has made me a better gardener, and I am forever grateful.

Contents

Introduction

WELCOME TO GARDENING IN TEXAS!

Texas is a huge state as any Texan will gladly tell you. Texarkana is closer to Chicago, Illinois, than it is to El Paso. If you live in Dalhart you are only about a half hour farther from Billings, Montana, or Bismarck, North Dakota, than you are from Brownsville. El Paso is closer to Los Angeles than to Beaumont. Well, I think you get the point.

When it comes to gardening we have a greater range of climate and soil conditions than some small countries. That makes writing a book about Texas gardening quite a challenge. A gardener in Dalhart (zone 6) in the Panhandle experiences midwinter lows in the -5 to -10°F range, while Brownsville gardeners in the lower Rio Grande Valley (zones 9 to 10) can expect temperatures in an average winter to drop only a few degrees below freezing or not to freeze at all.

Gardeners in the southeastern corner of Texas average 56 inches of rainfall while their counterparts in the far western tip can count on only 8 inches in an entire year. Soils range from the acidic sands of east Texas to the black gumbo clays of the Houston, Austin, and Dallas areas to the gravelly soils of the Post Oak Belt to some wonderful sandy loam soils across the state.

Perhaps the biggest soil challenge for gardeners is the urban/suburban soils. These have often been turned upside down, scraped away by bulldozers, or hauled in as fill from another location. Add the bed mixes of improved soil that landscapers bring in and you can see that reading a soil map may not tell you much about the soil in your landscape.

Despite the many challenges, Texas is a wonderful place to garden. Wherever you live there is a broad palate of native and adapted plants that will thrive in your soil and climate, as well as many great edibles.

Gardening is a wonderfully enjoyable and rewarding hobby. Our gardens and landscapes are places to exercise, relax, create, and learn. Whether you are a veteran gardener or newbie, you'll find an endless source of pleasure and fulfillment in building and tending your Texas garden.

INTRODUCTION

BUILD YOUR GARDEN FROM THE GROUND UP

Wherever you live and garden, improving your soil is critical to gardening success. When it is time to plant, your chances of success or failure are already largely determined by the location (sun or shade) and soil (pH, nutrient content, and drainage). It makes sense to get this first part right. Successful gardens are literally built from the ground up. Spend a dollar on your soil before you spend a dollar on plants, and you will save money and have a more beautiful and bountiful garden.

It is a good idea to have your soil tested every few years. While there are general guidelines for fertilizing various plants, the best fertilizer recommendations are based on a soil test. That way you can be sure to apply the right amounts of the nutrients that are most needed and avoid adding nutrients already present at high levels.

Your County Extension Office can assist with this and with interpreting the results so you can make the appropriate additions and amendments. Drainage is critical also. Few plants can tolerate soggy wet conditions for extended periods of time. Our rainfall often comes in deluges for days on end. So if drainage is at all in question, it makes sense to build raised beds to keep the plants' roots from drowning due to lack of oxygen in oversaturated soil.

Larger plants, such as ornamental or fruit-bearing shrubs, trees, and woody vines, have more extensive root systems so a small raised bed may not suffice. Check to make sure the area drains well, especially if the species is not adapted to soggy soil conditions. One way is to note how long an area stands in water after a rain. If water remains for longer than a day it may be best to choose another location or bring in a lot of soil to raise the planting area to a depth of 10 to 12 inches or more. To test internal soil drainage dig a hole about 18 to 24 inches deep and fill it with water. Check to see how long it takes to drain. If it drains in a few hours, that's great. If it takes a day, the site is fine. But if it takes longer, consider a different location or a species adapted to wet sites.

Most plants will benefit from such additions as compost to amend the soil. Mixing it down into the soil will improve the root zone of the plants.

Compost makes the best soil amendment because it is already mostly decomposed. Leaves, wood chips, and other undecomposed organic materials can be worked into the soil but will require time to decompose before the area can be planted, and that ties up nitrogen as the matter begins to decompose.

Here in Texas our long, hot growing season coupled with the rain and irrigation needed to wet the soil results in rapid decomposition of organic matter. So we need to add it frequently to maintain a good organic matter content to help a sandy soil hold moisture and nutrients or help a clay soil form a good crumbly structure for better aeration and drainage in the plant's root zone.

That said, when planting native plants, especially more Western types of natives, it isn't as important to add compost, and large amounts can even be detrimental by creating soil conditions that are quite different from those in which the plant will thrive.

Our plants benefit from a layer of mulch applied over the surface of the soil. Mulch protects the surface from forming a hard crust following rain or sprinkler irrigation. It moderates soil temperatures, which is especially helpful during the hottest and coldest months of the year. Mulch also helps deter weed invasions by preventing weed seeds from getting the sunlight they need to germinate and grow. In time mulch decomposes where it comes in contact with the underlying soil, providing composted organic matter for the growing plant roots. The best mulches are made from natural ingredients such as bark chips, shredded tree trimmings, leaves, grass clippings, compost, hay, or pine needles.

START WITH A PLAN

Buying and planting plants is fun! But buying on impulse when we don't have a plot prepared or a plan in place is a recipe for disappointing results. Begin with a general plan. Whether you hire a landscaper to develop a formal plan or just sketch out your landscape and garden yourself, a plan helps you create a design that is aesthetically pleasing throughout the year.

Large sweeping beds, effective use of color, and seasonal changes are all part of a good plan. Stand or sit in the locations where you will view your landscape most often. Imagine the layout of beds and sketch them on a piece of paper. Use a garden hose to outline the shape of landscape beds. Consider the mature height of plants, when they bloom, and what the landscape will look like in all four seasons. Evergreens are a great way to begin, since they provide a foundation for all four seasons.

When we get "gardening fever" it is not uncommon to take on more than we can handle. Whether installing a flower bed or a vegetable garden, or planning a landscape renovation, take it slow. It is better to start small and expand the garden or project over time than to plant more that you can maintain. Remember that every square foot of garden you plant is a square foot to weed, water, and maintain. This is not a plea against large gardens and elaborate landscapes, but rather a word of wisdom to ensure that you get the full enjoyment out of the wonderful hobby of gardening without undue disappointments or frustration.

Color selection truly is an art. It can seem complicated, but basically amounts to choosing colors that look good together. Find a color wheel and note the colors opposite each other on the wheel. These are called complementary colors and look good when combined with each other. Colors that are adjacent to each other on the wheel are called analogous colors. These colors harmonize and blend together well when used in combinations. Light colors brighten a dark area while dark colors are most visible in bright sun. Large swaths of color make a stunning impact and are even attractive when viewed at a distance. Mixes of many colors are interesting when viewed up close but get lost in the mix when seen from a distance.

All this said, my personal rule about gardening is that there are no rules. You do what you want. Plant what pleases you and have fun in the process. Don't lose the excitement and wonder of gardening in concerns about "getting it right." I like to think of gardening like an Etch-A-Sketch®. Remember those? You draw and then just turn it upside down and shake it. Voila! You have a blank slate on which to start over again. In a sense you can't fail at gardening. Just pull the plants out, rototill, and start again.

Every new season is a new start. We gardeners are forever learning, forever experimenting. Jimmy Turner, former director of the Dallas Arboretum and Botanical Garden, put it well by saying, "The success of my garden is built on the compost of my failures!" So learn all you can, don't be afraid to try something new, and then go out there and have a blast.

TEXAS GARDENING SEASONS AND PLANTS

Everyone knows that the calendar has four seasons, each about three months long. In our region the climate doesn't match these well. Winter lasts about one to two months in most of the state, but summer can run from May through September if you let the thermometer mark the season. Our spring and fall seasons are the prime growing seasons for most species of flowers and vegetables.

KNOW YOUR ZONE

There may be 200 to 300 or more frost-free days where you live, but in the midst of these days is that scorching, sweltering summer season that shuts down petunias and causes tomatoes not to set fruit. This means that we have two short growing seasons interrupted by a summer season. We need to choose varieties accordingly.

It is helpful to know your hardiness zone (see page 13). Texas fully spans four hardiness zones, which means that species that do well in one area may not survive farther north. It also affects plant classifications. For example, a shrub in zone 9b may be a perennial in zone 8a, dying back to the ground each winter, and an annual in zone 6 or 7. While hardiness zones are important, so is heat tolerance. Don't just assume if a plant is listed for your hardiness zone that it will grow well in your landscape. Check with local sources as to how heat tolerant it is. As a case in point, there are zones 6, 7, and 8 near the Canadian border in Washington state, but our summers are a world apart.

FLOWERS

In annual flower beds we may change out the spring plants for summer-tough species, and then switch out the color plantings again for fall. During the heat of summer colorful foliage can step in to help out a limited palate of blooming species. Perennial flowers are available that can take the heat. We need to make full use of them to keep the color coming all summer long.

When fall arrives many flowers are spent from the long summer. That is where some exciting late summer- to fall-blooming flowers can step to center stage. Consider where you place these latecomers to provide fall color throughout the landscape.

VEGETABLES

Homegrown vegetables are making a comeback as people become more interested in having a healthy diet and the desire for fresh and local produce becomes mainstream. You can't get more local than your backyard or front porch. If you've not tried growing vegetables due to a lack of space, consider including them in and among landscape plants or in containers around the landscape. Many are quite ornamental and there's nothing like fresh homegrown produce.

In one sense Texas gardeners enjoy a long growing season with some areas suitable for gardening year-round. In another sense when it comes to vegetables we have a short spring season and a short fall season, with a few fire-proof species able to withstand the blast furnace of summer. Many of our favorite vegetables, including tomatoes, peppers, cucumbers, and squash, tend not to set fruit well once the weather heats up in summer.

Therefore varieties that are popular "up north" where the growing season is short may be great for us also. Varieties well suited to the midsections of the country (where there is a long growing season and summer is not quite as hot, for not quite as long) may take too long to mature here, thus providing lower yields. Choose varieties with shorter days-to-harvest intervals to allow for the most productivity in the time between the last frost and the arrival of hot weather.

Winters are mild enough in much of Texas to keep growing flowers and vegetables. In some areas subtropical plants can even survive winter, greatly opening up the possibilities for an exciting palette of ornamental and fruit plants.

WOODY ORNAMENTALS

There are a dozen or so common shrubs that are the staple of our landscapes. There are many others that deserve to be planted and would help break up the cookie cutter mold that is so common to suburbia. Visit botanical gardens and learn about some underutilized trees and shrubs.

Small blooming trees are a great way to add seasonal interest to your home place. They are great for shading a patio or providing an accent to a landscape bed. Blooming shrubs and shrubs with colorful foliage are another way to break up the "sea of green" that is all too common throughout the region. Think and dream outside the box and make your place both beautiful and unique.

NATIVE PLANTS

A word about native plants is in order. Native plants have a track record of surviving and thriving, despite the vicissitudes of nature and challenging soils of your area. But we should consider what is a "Texas native plant." In Tyler or Beaumont a plant from the southeastern United States would likely be better adapted than one from San Angelo or Austin. Make sure that a native plant you are considering is native to your area.

There are other areas of the world with similar climates, which can offer some very well-adapted plants, although they are far from native. The Hill Country or Edward's Plateau is similar in climate to much of the Mediterranean region, and plants from this region do well in areas like Austin and San Antonio. Ask rosemary about whether it is a native plant and it will tell you, "I'm not a native Texan, but I got here as fast as I could!" So while natives are a super option, don't let state lines define the term and don't overlook many other very well-adapted plants.

FRUIT PLANTS

You need not have space for a backyard orchard to grow fruit. They can be integrated into the landscape among other ornamental plants. The spring blooms of fruit trees such as peaches, plums, apples, and pears earn them a space in an ornamental landscape. Citrus planted in large containers on a patio or next to an outdoor sitting area perfume the air with their wonderfully fragrant blooms. Persimmons hang on the tree like ornaments in the fall, long after the leaves turn color and drop. Grapes make an arbor tasty as well as a source of shade. Strawberries can line a garden bed or pathway, or adorn containers on a deck.

BUILDING YOUR OUTDOOR LIVINGSCAPE

We have a lot of opportunities to enjoy the outdoors for most months of the year provided we build our outdoor living areas to suit our climate. Make your outdoor area an inviting place to gather and to play. Lawns and groundcovers are the carpets of our landscape. Vines and hedges form the walls. Trees and arbors are our ceilings. Think about that when you are planning your plantings.

A vine or tree shading a western wall can really help reduce your cooling costs. An arbor can provide much needed shade extending the time you'll want to be outdoors with family and friends. Choose your trees wisely so that the species you plant are long lived and fit the space available to them. A stately old tree adds resale value to your home and enjoyment value to the outdoor livingscape.

Consider textures when designing outdoor areas. Bold broad foliage as well as narrow, fine-textured foliage makes a great contrast. The movement of ornamental grasses in the breeze or the rain-like sound of a clumping bamboo as the wind moves the papery foliage are a nice added touch.

We can plant container-grown plants twelve months out of the year, if we are prepared to provide the care they need. This is especially important when planting in the summer, as post-planting care involves the balance of watering enough but not too much to help the plants become well established despite the heat. Perennial flowers, herbs, and ornamental grasses, and woody ornamental shrubs, trees, and vines are best planted or transplanted in the fall. Spring is the second best time. Fall planting gives the plants months to establish an extensive root system before the demands of summer heat and drought arrive. Spring planting is fine, but try to take some of that "spring fever" and transfer it to fall, the "second spring" here in Texas. Your gardening endeavors will be more successful if you make fall a prime planting season.

MANAGING PESTS

We are not the only ones that love our landscape and garden plants. There are many pests and diseases that can become a problem at times. The key to effective pest and disease control is not to spray the problems away. Rather, start with naturally resistant plant species and varieties. Provide the soil and cultural practices that keep plants strong and healthy. Don't crowd disease-prone plants and don't wet the foliage when you can avoid it to minimize disease outbreaks.

Recognize that a few pests are just part of nature and minor damage is no reason to resort to spraying. A few pests here and there can often attract beneficial insects, which in turn can help prevent a pest outbreak. When you have a few of the "good guys" around they tend to keep pest populations down to acceptable levels.

If you were to wipe out all insects on your property, the first result would be a pest outbreak because your unprotected "salad bar" is too tempting to resist. After the pests have had time to start their population explosion, then beneficials will begin to show up since their food source is now present. This takes time, and so it is better to have a few of both types around to help maintain a balance of nature.

Attract beneficial insects to your landscape and gardens by providing sources of nectar and pollen for the adults of some species and allowing a few pests to remain present as food for adults and larvae of other species.

When you have to spray, choose products that are low in toxicity and more targeted instead of broad spectrum. It is the difference between an arrow and a grenade. One hits the target without collateral damage while the other kills everything in the area. For example, Bacillus thuringiensis (B.t.) kills caterpillar larvae but not other types of insects, so it would not destroy lady beetles, lacewings, or other beneficials. Insecticidal soap or horticultural oil both work on small, soft-bodied insects but don't kill by poisoning pests. After soap or oil sprays dry they no longer pose a significant threat to beneficial insects.

MORE HELP IS AVAILABLE

In addition to this book, there is a lot of help available to gardeners in Texas. Each of the state's 254 counties has access to the Texas A & M AgriLife Extension Service and its County Agents. The national eXtension online program, "Ask an Expert" (ask.extension.org/ask) allows you to submit questions and digital photos to your local Extension experts free of charge. There are approximately eighty-eight Master Gardener programs across the state in which Extension-trained volunteers assist the public with their gardening questions. Many areas have local botanical gardens, and there are a multitude of plant societies with experts in a wide variety of species. So help is never far away. Take advantage of the many opportunities to get assistance and become more successful in your gardening activities.

HOW TO USE THIS BOOK

Texas Month-by-Month Gardening is designed to help you plant and care for your landscape and garden throughout the year. Think of it as an "owner's manual." Each month is divided into the major tasks involved in establishing and maintaining a healthy, attractive, and productive garden and landscape. This includes the basics of gardening: planning, planting, plant care, watering, fertilizing, and problem-solving. The goal is to create an easy-to-use, year-round reference both for people new to gardening and for those with years of experience.

Within each of the major activities is specific advice for any of these major plant groups:

- **Annuals** provide fast and easy color to our landscapes. They are usually planted in a series of transitions through the year to keep the color coming in spring, summer, fall, and winter. Learn when and how to start them as transplants indoors, plant them outdoors, manage pests, and keep them healthy and blooming their best throughout the growing season.

- **Edibles** include vegetables, herbs, and fruits. Interest in growing your own food is rising with the increased interest in healthy eating. These plants need not have their own section of the landscape but can be used in an "edible landscaping" scheme, interspersing them among other plants. Learn when and how to plant and care for your garden and fruit plants to ensure a bountiful, flavorful harvest of healthy eating.

- **Lawns** are the carpet of the landscape. They help moderate temperature and provide a

recreational setting for the family. Learn the best times to establish and care for a lawn to create dense, healthy turf without wasting water or having to treat for weeds.

- **Perennials & Ornamental Grasses** include herbaceous perennials, subshrubs, bulbs, and ornamental grasses. Perennial plants each have their moment in the spotlight, some for months, where they provide eye-catching appeal. Perennials provide a good return on investment, coming back each year for another seasonal display. Learn how to select perennials for the season, keep them healthy and attractive, and use them as part of an overall landscape plan that has year-round interest.

- **Roses** are the queen of the landscape flowers. They seem to have the power to enthrall us with their magical beauty and lovely fragrance. Learn how to select, when to plant, and care for roses in ways that minimize pest and disease problems and maximize blooming dividends on your time and money.

- **Shrubs** provide outdoor walls and focal points in the landscape plan. They are part of the skeleton of the landscape around which other plants are woven to create a beautiful setting. Learn timing for proper planting and care, including pruning to ensure your shrubs achieve your goals, whether to provide privacy or to display a bounty of blooms.

- **Trees** are another skeletal element around which we build a landscape. They can be a wall to hide a view, a ceiling for shade, or a feature plant that offers a seasonal display of flowers. Learn to select, plant, and prune them properly for strong, attractive structure, and so they grow more valuable through the years.

- **Vines & Groundcovers** provide floors, walls, and ceilings for our outdoor living spaces. Groundcovers can be a great alternative in areas where a lawn is not wanted or cannot thrive. Vines can help save on cooling costs and shade us on a hot summer day. Learn how to select, when to plant, and care for these versatile plants.

USDA COLD HARDINESS ZONES FOR TEXAS

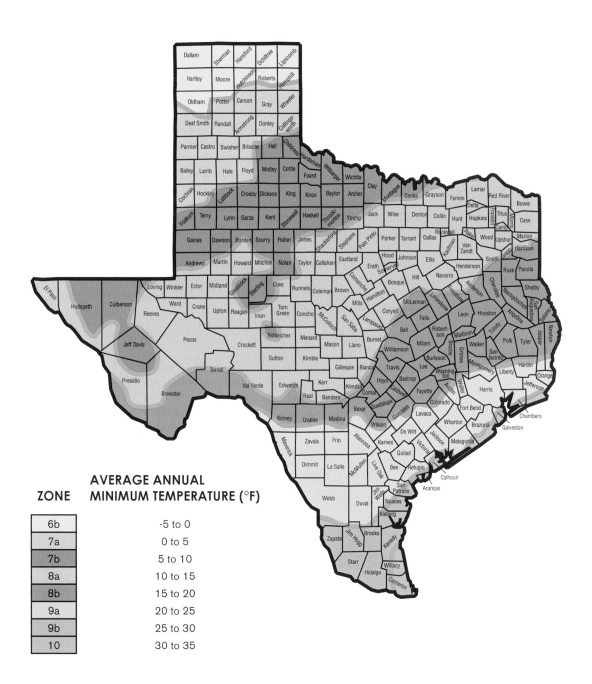

ZONE	AVERAGE ANNUAL MINIMUM TEMPERATURE (°F)
6b	-5 to 0
7a	0 to 5
7b	5 to 10
8a	10 to 15
8b	15 to 20
9a	20 to 25
9b	25 to 30
10	30 to 35

■ *USDA Plant Hardiness Zone Map, 2012. Agricultural Research Service, U.S. Department of Agriculture. Accessed from http://planthardiness.ars.usda.gov*

January

The new year is upon us and seed catalogues are arriving in the mail. It's exciting to check out their descriptions and photos of gorgeous flowers and delectable vegetables. Start with some tried-and-true species and varieties to ensure a successful outcome, but also experiment with new-and-improved ones too.

Warning: Spring fever is just around the corner. Common symptoms include impulse purchases, a lack of soil preparation, and failure to plan before you plant. Take advantage of bad weather days to think through changes to your landscape and garden beds. What site preparations are needed? Which plants will thrive in a location? Are there species and varieties with natural disease or pest resistance? How will the planting look in spring, summer, fall, and winter? Prepare for "fever season" and enjoy the beauty and bounty of a well-planned garden and landscape.

Although this is the dormant season we have plenty of mild winter days when it warms up enough to begin some important tasks such as soil preparation. A beautiful and productive garden, lawn, or landscape is built on a foundation of good soil. Now is a great time to have your soil tested so you can make any necessary changes indicated by the test results in time for late winter and spring planting.

Late winter is pruning season so when weather keeps you indoors use the opportunity to sharpen and oil your pruning tools. Sharp tools are easier to use and make clean cuts that heal faster. Check your pruning saws and if the blades are not sharp it may be time to purchase a new one.

It is important to sharpen the gardener also. Gardening classes are available in many communities. Magazines and books are another way to brush up on your knowledge and skills. Contact your local Extension office, garden centers, and botanical gardens to inquire about classes offered in late winter and spring. A bonus of local classes is that in addition to locally applicable information, you get to meet new gardening friends.

PLAN

ALL

Start the new year off right by creating a system for keeping track of what you planted, when, how it performed, pest and disease problems, and other observations. Think about using a garden journal, calendar, or other means as a way to keep your notes.

If you are gardening in a new area or have not had the soil in your garden tested in the past few years, now is a great time to do so. That way you can get the results back in time to make the necessary amendments for spring planting. Once you have your soil test results, spread the prescribed fertilizer nutrients over the soil surface, add an inch of compost, and mix it all in with a spade or rototiller to a depth of about 6 inches to blend them throughout the soil. In new garden areas add 3 inches of compost instead of just 1 inch. Compost helps sandy soil hold water and nutrients and will help a clay soil form a looser structure and drain better.

Build up raised planting beds by adding a blend of soil and compost, known as a bed mix, in areas with poor drainage. Purchase a quality bed mix from a local supplier. A good bed mix contains compost that's well decomposed and screened, with some topsoil or sand mixed in. Some suppliers add ingredients such as decomposed bark or branch trimmings to provide a coarser structure to prevent the bed mix from being poorly aerated.

■ *Count back from the last average frost date to determine when to start seeds of flower and vegetable transplants.*

Expanded shale (or haydite) may also be added for the same purpose.

Mix a few inches of the bed mix into the surface of the soil where the bed will be built to create a more gradual transition between the bed mix and the soil. Then add more bed mix until the bed is 8 to 12 inches high, since it will settle over time. Your plants will thank you when a period of heavy rainfall leaves the area standing in water, since most plants can't tolerate soggy conditions for extended periods of time.

ANNUALS, PERENNIALS & ORNAMENTAL GRASSES

Grab those seed catalogues that you've been dreaming over these past weeks and place your orders for a spring, summer, and fall garden filled with flowers. The earlier you order the better as popular selections may soon be out of stock. You can also visit the seed racks at a local garden center to make your selections. While shopping, pick up some seed-starting trays and a growing medium designed for starting seeds. Also pick up some labels for identifying the variety of flower, herb, or vegetable and the date the seeds were planted. If your budget allows, a seed-starting mat is a great way to ensure good germination and seedling growth.

Local garden centers often will still have a stock of bulbs (See October, What Is a Bulb?) left from the preceding fall season. Consider which ones might deserve a spot in your landscape and purchase some for planting as soon as you have a spot prepared.

Make notes in your garden journal (See page 23, Here's How to Keep Track of Your Gardening Activities) of the dates when the various flower species you want to grow should be planted. For species that are best set out as transplants note instructions on the seed packet to find the days or weeks needed to grow from planting to a size appropriate for transplanting. Count back from that recommended outdoor planting date and mark your calendar for when you need to start the seeds in transplant trays. Allow a little extra time from seeding to transplanting as often our home-growing conditions are less than ideal, and seedlings may take longer to reach the size they need before they are moved outdoors. (Of course, you can buy many transplants, but it's fun to grow your own.)

EDIBLES

The time to start transplants of warm-season vegetables for the spring garden begins this month for gardeners in zones 8 and 9. Before purchasing seeds do some research to determine the best varieties for your area. Your County Extension Office offers free publications on the best varieties and times to plant for your area. Local gardeners are another good source for proven varieties that do well in the soil and climate where you live.

Check Frost-Freeze Data for Texas Cities on page 214 to determine when it is safe to plant cold-tender vegetables outdoors. Count back the appropriate number of weeks indicated on the seed packet for starting your own transplants, and make a note in your garden journal or on your calendar.

January is prime planting season for bare-root fruit and nut plants. Depending on where you live in Texas, your area may receive as few as 200 or well over 1,000 hours of what is termed "chilling hours". Choose fruit plants according to their chilling hour needs and how that relates to your locale if you hope to enjoy a bountiful harvest in years to come. Just because a fruit plant is for sale in your area doesn't mean that it is well adapted or will be productive in your area. Also, as you investigate the best plants note which species require or benefit from having more than one variety for cross-pollination, and plan accordingly as you design your planting.

LAWNS

Evaluate your lawn for areas that are performing poorly. Turf beneath the shade of a large tree may lack sufficient light to stay dense and healthy. Make a note about doing some minor pruning to thin the canopy of the tree late this month or next to allow more light to reach the turf grass.

Now is a good time to redesign areas where your turf grass isn't thriving because of a lack of sunlight or where full sun and sandy soil conditions make it especially drought prone. Make plans now to renovate the area into a planting of species

appropriate to the soil and sun exposure of the site. Examples include groundcovers, shrubs, ornamental grasses, perennials, or an outdoor sitting area with mulched soil and steppingstones.

VINES & GROUNDCOVERS

Groundcovers make a low-care option for areas where foot traffic is minimal and a few steppingstones can provide pedestrian access. Groundcovers' low-growth habit won't block a view and many offer blooms or colorful foliage. Plan makeovers of areas where shade or sun create a challenge for most other plants by designing a bed of sun-loving, shade-loving, or drought-tolerant groundcovers. (See July, Great Groundcover Alternatives to Turf.)

Woody vines add a great structural element to landscapes when planted on an arbor or trained to a wall as an espalier or simply to form a vertical wall. Choose one that fits your aesthetic preferences and make plans to get it planted prior to the end of winter so it has a head start on summer heat.

ROSES, SHRUBS & TREES

Winter is a good time to evaluate woody ornamental plantings. Grab a cup of coffee, hot tea, or cocoa and take a stroll through your landscape with an eye for where some new woody ornamental plants such as roses, shrubs, small trees, and woody vines could provide an aesthetic addition. Would a tree be helpful to shade the west side of your home to help reduce cooling bills? Would some additional evergreen plants make the winter landscape more attractive? Where would some berry-producing plants provide a nice addition?

Evaluate your landscape regarding what blooms and when. Where would a spring- or summer-blooming rose or a flowering shrub or tree be a great bonus? How about installing a lattice with blooming vines on the west side of that deck or patio, or an arbor to make the area more hospitable on warm days? Woody ornamentals are best established when the weather is still cool, so a little planning now will pay off in better new plant survival and a landscape that is beautiful all four seasons of the year.

HERE'S HOW

TO ESTIMATE HOW MUCH SOIL OR MULCH IS NEEDED

How large is the area (square feet)?	How deep (inches) do you want to cover the area?				
	1 inch	3 inches	6 inches	8 inches	12 inches
50	4 cu. ft.	½ yd.	1 yd.	1¼ yd.	2 yd.
100	8 cu. ft.	1 yd.	2 yd.	2½ yd.	4 yd.
500	1½ yd.	4½ yd.	9¼ yd.	12⅓ yd.	18½ yd.
1,000	3 yd.	9¼ yd.	18½ yd.	24¾ yd.	37 yd.

Here's how to do the math for an exact amount:

Area to cover (in square feet)	x	Desired depth of mulch or soil (in inches)	x	0.0031	=	Cubic yards of mulch or soil required

PLANT

ANNUALS

Gardeners in zones 7b to 9 can continue to plant transplants of cool-season annual flowers out in the landscape. The color plants best able to withstand colder temperatures are pansies, violas, ornamental cabbages, and ornamental kale. Not too far behind them are dianthus, stock, and snapdragons. Dusty miller, although not grown for its blooms, makes an attractive and cold-hardy addition with its silvery foliage. As you move south across the state into zone 9, the cool-season color options expand to include nasturtium, alyssum, and calendula.

Seeds of sweet peas, poppies, and larkspur *can* still be planted if done so early in the month, but they perform best if sown in the fall. These flowers, like our beloved bluebonnets, will sprout in the fall, form small plants, and sit out the winter ready for a burst of growth and blooms in early to mid-spring.

Start seeds of alyssum, nasturtium, and calendula indoors in zones 7 (late in the month) and 8 (early in the month) for transplanting outdoors six to eight weeks later when the danger of a hard freeze is less and the plants will be strong enough to establish out in the landscape.

EDIBLES

The family of vegetables known as "cole crops," which includes cabbage, broccoli, Brussels sprouts, kohlrabi, kale, mustard, and collards, is quite cold hardy. Gardeners in zones 8 and 9 can plant them as transplants now for a late winter harvest that will extend into spring. Water new transplants with a water-soluble fertilizer solution or a mix of fish emulsion and seaweed.

Gardeners in zones 6 and 7 can still start cole crop transplants in early January for setting out in the garden 4 to 6 weeks later. Provide growing transplants plenty of light and avoid overwatering, as soggy growing media can promote root-rot diseases.

Plant seeds of cool-season greens, including lettuce, spinach, arugula, mache (corn salad), mustard, kale, and various Asian greens, into the garden in zones 8b and 9, but be ready to cover the young seedlings if a freeze is forecast.

Another option for cool-season greens is to start them as transplants to set out in the garden when they are three or four weeks old. Starting them as transplants helps hedge against a freeze or period of rainy weather outdoors that may damage sprouting seeds. It also makes better use of garden

TO BUILD A SEED-STARTING LIGHT STAND

Materials

2 – 10-foot sections of ½-inch PVC pipe
8 – ½-inch PVC "L" fittings
6 – ½-inch PVC "T" fittings
2 – 4-inch shop light fixtures
2 – Warm white fluorescent tubes
2 – Cool white fluorescent tubes
Chain or String to suspend the shop lights

Steps

Cut the first 10-foot section of PVC pipe into:
      2 – 39-inch pieces
      4 – 1½-inch pieces
      2 – 7¼-inch pieces
      2 – 10½-inch pieces

Cut the second 10-foot section of PVC pipe into:
      1 – 39-inch piece
      2 – 7¼-inch pieces
      4 – 16½-inch pieces

Assemble the pieces as shown in the accompanying photos.

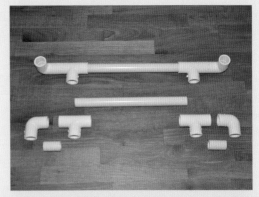

space by avoiding the gaps in a planting bed that can result from poor germination or damage to tender seedlings.

Bare-root fruit and nut plants, including peaches, plums, pears, apples, persimmons, pecans, blackberries, and grapes, are available in local garden centers in January or early February. The sooner you plant the more time the roots have to grow and establish into the surrounding soil, which makes the plant more resilient when hot weather arrives. When planting bare-root fruit and nut plants follow the same procedures as described in Here's How to Plant a Bare-Root Plant on page 36 in February. Although bare-root plants are more economical they are only available for planting in mid- to late winter. Container-grown fruit and nut plants can be established now or anytime. Don't put fertilizer in the planting hole when planting fruit trees or pecans. The roots won't need supplemental nutrients as they begin growth and some fertilizers can burn tender new roots.

■ *Finish planting any spring-flowering bulbs still on hand, such as these Johnson's amaryllis.*

PERENNIALS

Plant any spring-flowering bulbs that you still have on hand as soon as possible. This includes tulip and hyacinth bulbs in refrigerated storage and other spring bloomers such as bearded iris (*Iris germanica*), white cemetery iris (*Iris albicans*),

HERE'S HOW

TO GROW YOUR OWN TRANSPLANTS

Starting your own transplants from seeds is fun and can be more economical than purchasing transplants. Here are some basic tips to get your seedlings off to a good start:

1. Choose a fresh growing media designed for starting seeds. Used potting soil may contain diseases that will play "Paul Bunyan" with your new crop of tender seedlings. Seed-starting media is finer textured than potting soil, making it easier to plant seeds at the exact depth you want while providing good seed-to-soil contact for successful germination. A mix should hold moisture well but also drain away excess moisture to avoid staying oversaturated.

2. If the mix is dry, moisten it *before* planting. Dry growing media repels water, making it difficult to wet it thoroughly. Premoistened media will be much easier to wet thoroughly after planting.

3. Plant seeds at the depth prescribed on the seed packet. Gently press the media into contact with the seeds. Some seed, such as lettuce, impatiens, nicotiana, and snapdragons, need light to germinate and should be pressed into the soil surface or at most covered with a ⅛-inch layer of fine vermiculite.

HERE'S HOW CONTINUED

4. Mist the trays after planting to avoid dislodging the seeds with a blast of water. Another technique, called "bottom watering," is to set the tray of planted seeds in a container with ½ inch of water in it and allow the water to wick up into the mix. Once the mix is moistened remove the tray and set it where any excess water can drain away.

5. Cover seeded trays with a clear plastic cover to hold in moisture during the germination period. Remove the cover after seeds sprout.

6. Place the trays in a location where the temperature is close to the ideal germination temperature range for the plant species. Most seeds germinate well at about 70°F. Some seeds prefer it a bit warmer or cooler. There are special mats that can be purchased to provide bottom heat; the top of a refrigerator is usually a little warmer location.

7. Provide seedlings with plenty of light to keep them stocky and strong. Low light levels result in spindly, weak growth. (See Here's How to Build a Seed-Starting Light Stand on page 19.)

8. Fertilize *very lightly* with a diluted solution after the seedlings develop their first true leaves. Don't overdo it; excessive fertilizing can result in lanky, succulent growth and seedlings that don't establish well out in the garden.

9. Brush your seedlings every day or two once they are up and growing. Take a pencil or dowel and gently move it across the top of the seedlings. This movement will cause the seeds to develop sturdier stems than if they were growing in perfectly still conditions.

10. Begin to "harden off" seedlings a couple of weeks before planting outdoors. The shock of moving from a warm, cozy seed-starting spot to cold nights and windy conditions out in the garden can be too much if they are not gradually acclimated to the outdoor conditions. Move them outside to a part-sun spot during the day for a few hours, gradually leaving them out longer and moving them into full sun over the course of a week or two.

■ *Set roses, shrubs, and trees at the same depth they were growing in the container. Check the soil level using the handle of a shovel or similar tool.*

Johnson's amaryllis (*Hippeastrum* x *johnsonii*), Byzantine gladiolus (*Gladiolus byzantinus*), and spring starflower (*Ipheion uniflorum*).

You can also plant summer- or fall-blooming bulbs now such as rain lilies (*Zephyranthus* spp.), copper lilies (*Habranthus* spp.), schoolhouse or oxblood lilies (*Rhodophiala bifida*), montbretia (*Crocosmia pottsii*), milk and wine lilies (*Crinum* spp.), daylilies (*Hemerocallis* spp.), Texas spider lilies (*Hymenocallis liriosme*), cannas (*Canna* × *generalis*), red spider lilies (*Lycoris radiata*), Philippine lilies (*Lilium formosanum*), and gladiolus.

Start setting out transplants of hardy perennial flowers in zones 8 and 9. This includes the many great perennial salvias such as Mexican bush sage (*Salvia leucantha*), cherry sage (*Salvia greggii*), blue anise sage (*Salvia guaranitica*), and *Salvia* 'Indigo Spires' and 'Mystic Spires'. Firm the soil in around the plant roots and water the new transplants in well using a dilute water-soluble fertilizer solution.

ROSES, SHRUBS & TREES

You need not wait for February to plant roses. Our winters are mild enough to plant anytime from fall to early spring, and the sooner you plant, the more time the rose bushes will have to establish roots in preparation for the hot weather ahead. The same is true for other woody ornamental plants such as flowering shrubs and trees, evergreens, shade trees, and woody vines.

Garden centers have bare-root roses available for planting this month and next. (See February, Here's How to Plant a Bare-Root Plant.) It is best not to purchase bare-root plants until the planting site has been prepared. However, if you have the plants and still need to prepare the soil, pot them up in a container of potting mix and focus on getting the soil ready. Potted up bare-root roses can be held for several months if needed.

If you purchased a living Christmas tree this holiday season, get it outside into better light as soon as possible. Plant it like you would any other woody ornamental, but take extra care to loosen and unwind any circling roots, as they will grow in diameter as the trunk grows and end up strangling the plant about ten years after planting if they're not unwound. Dig the hole to fit the unwound roots. If necessary, cut any roots you cannot unwind, but limit this to one or two cuts at most.

Plant container-grown woody ornamentals in a hole no deeper than the rootball. Lay the container on its side and bump the sides and bottom to help loosen the plant so it will slide out of the container. Set the plant in the hole and check the surrounding soil level to make sure that it is not set deeper than it was previously growing. Fill the hole with soil, adding water as you do to settle the soil around the rootball.

Don't put fertilizer into a planting hole. While slow-release fertilizers won't harm plants, fast-release fertilizers are salt-based products and if used in excess can "burn" tender emerging roots. Plants will have plenty of nutrition to get started and won't need any supplemental fertilizing until the weather warms and they are growing rapidly. Finish with a berm of soil for watering during the first critical spring and summer season. The Texas Forest Service has a wealth of helpful, indepth information on tree planting and care on their web page, texastreeplanting.tamu.edu.

HERE'S HOW

TO KEEP TRACK OF YOUR GARDENING ACTIVITIES

Four ideas, from old school to high tech:

1. **Paper Calendar**—*an "old school," low-tech option that is simple and easy.*
    Use a blank calendar dedicated to "all things garden" to record future planting dates, when to start transplants, pests encountered, harvest dates and amounts, frost and freeze dates, fertilizers and sprays applied, and upcoming gardening classes, plant sales, and other events.

2. **Gardening Journal**—*easy, handy, and even elegant and beautiful.*
    Gardening journals can be as simple as a blank spiral notebook or paper moleskin booklet or as elegant as a cloth- or leather-bound journal designed for gardening. Choose lined or blank paper, with or without monthly tabs. If you go with the simple paper style store it, along with some pencils, in a mailbox you set up out in your garden so it will always be handy for a quick note.

3. **3-Ring Binder**—*old school for the scholar who wants to build a living book.*
    A binder can do all a journal can. Plus you can add gardening publications, magazine and newspaper articles, printed digital photos, and more to create a great reference and historical record of your gardening activities.

4. **Software and Smart Phone Apps**—*high tech, super versatile, and powerful.* The sky's the limit. I prefer an app that syncs from my smartphone or tablet to the computer. The Evernote app, for example, will allow you to take photos in the app (a beautiful rose you want to purchase, information on a plant tag or seed packet, design ideas from another landscape or a botanical garden, or some

new insect to be identified), or record sound (a lecture or your own observations about a plant), and even "clip" articles and photos from the Web. All these along with your typed notes can be filed in various gardening folders you create.

VINES & GROUNDCOVERS

Plant groundcovers in shady or sunny spots to provide a low-care carpet over the soil. Mix 2 to 3 inches of compost into the soil and rototill or spade it into the surface to a depth of 3 to 4 inches. If tree roots prevent deep rototilling, work it in around roots as deep as is practical with a spading fork. Even a little amending helps. (See July, Great Groundcover Alternatives to Turf.)

Plant woody vines this month and next. (See January, Woody Vines for Landscapes.) Amend the soil in as wide an area as is practical by mixing in a few inches of compost and then digging the hole as deep as the rootball in the container. Firm the soil around the rootball and provide a good soaking to water the new plant in well. Finish by building a circular berm of soil a few inches wider than the rootball and 4 inches high. This will help by providing a place to allow deep soaking of the roots after planting and again weekly until the weather warms. Then water two or three times a week to support the top growth and the establishing root system.

CARE

ANNUALS

Mulches protect the soil in flowerbeds from erosion and deter cool-season weeds. In zones 6 and 7, where temperatures can be bitter cold, a mulch cover in winter can minimize cold injury to a plant's crown and roots.

When the forecast indicates that temperatures will drop into the mid- to low 20s, provide a protective cover over annual flowers. A dense row-cover fabric or even some bed sheets will help hold in some of the soil's warmth and can make a big difference for the plants. Even if the plants can survive the temperatures being forecast, the protection will prevent them from being set back and result in a better display of blooms in the weeks to come. Remove the covers during the day to allow the sun to warm the plants and soil. Wait until late in the day when the sun is setting to replace the cover if another hard freeze is on the way.

EDIBLES

Check fruit trees for any dried fruit still hanging on the tree from the previous season. These "mummies" often contain disease spores and are likely to increase disease problems in the coming crop if not removed from the area. Also pick up any fallen fruit beneath the trees. Discard mummies and fallen fruit in the trash.

You can begin pruning your fruit plants now if you have quite a few and need to get an early

■ *Prune ornamental grasses to remove old growth for a more attractive plant when the new growth emerges in spring.*

start. Otherwise wait until early February to do your pruning. (See February for advice on pruning fruit plants.)

LAWNS

In the warmer areas of the state, deciduous trees often hold onto their foliage past the fall season, dropping them in early- to midwinter. Remove fallen tree leaves from the lawn to allow light to reach the soil. St. Augustine turf is not fully dormant and will benefit from sunlight on mild winter days to replenish its carbohydrate reserves. For turf growing beneath the shade of a deciduous tree, this winter sun exposure can mean the difference between growing denser or declining over time.

PERENNIALS & ORNAMENTAL GRASSES

Cut back perennials that have been killed by cold weather to about 2 to 4 inches above the ground to remove the dead growth and tidy up the planting area. Add a few inches of mulch over the plants' base to protect them from cold and to deter cool-season weeds. Maintain 6 to 8 inches of leaf mulch over perennials that are marginally hardy in your area of the state to help protect the plants' crowns and roots on an especially cold night.

Trim ornamental grasses back to about 6 to 10 inches above ground in zones 8 and 9 to remove the old growth. A sharp pair of hand or lopper pruners will cut through the dead grass material a little at a time. Pampas grass has sharp, serrated edges so be careful when trimming it back. This is a tough grass and pruning is not easy to do but is needed nevertheless. In spring, ornamental grasses will send out fresh new growth, resulting in a more attractive plant. Chop up the trimmings to recycle in the compost pile or use as mulch.

Divide summer- and fall-blooming perennial flowering plants and ornamental grasses in zone 9 gardens. (See February for a list of plants that bloom in summer and in fall.)

SHRUBS & TREES

Mid- to late winter is pruning time for shrubs and trees. Gardeners in zone 9 should complete this

Remove guy wires and stakes from trees that have been in the ground for more than six months to prevent them from damaging the trunk or branches.

dormant season pruning now prior to the arrival of new spring growth. Pruning wounds heal the fastest in spring but very slowly in summer. Therefore, complete your pruning tasks at the end of winter for fastest wound closure, which minimizes the time the interior wood is left exposed to moisture and organisms that cause decay.

Remove guy wires and stakes on trees that were planted six to twelve months ago. These supports have done their job and a tree's roots are established well enough to anchor the tree. Leaving such supports longer risks damaging the branches by strangling them as they grow larger.

VINES & GROUNDCOVERS

This month is a good time to clean up groundcover plants in zones 8 and 9. Use shears, a string trimmer, or the lawn mower set on the highest setting to mow over liriope and remove all the old growth. Fresh, healthy new growth will emerge as the weather warms, making the groundcover area much more attractive.

Areas of ivy or jasmine with old growth that has become diseased or looks unsightly can be mowed or trimmed with a string trimmer or mower. Apply an inch of compost over the area after cutting it back to deter weed seeds from sprouting and to gradually feed the new emerging growth over the coming months.

ROSES

Roses that repeat bloom through the season are pruned in winter, prior to the arrival of their new spring growth. If you live in zone 9, where spring arrives early, now is a good time to start pruning your roses. Gardeners in zones 7 and 8 who have a lot of pruning to do around their landscape can also start pruning their roses now. Otherwise it is fine to delay pruning until February. Wait to prune roses that *only bloom in the spring* until *after* they bloom.

WATER

ALL

The winter season is cooler with more frequent rainfall in most parts of the state. This rain, along with less intense sunlight and periods of cloudy weather, dramatically reduces the need for watering outdoor plantings. However, unseasonably warm spells, sunny locations, sandy soils, and an ongoing drought can combine to create dry soil conditions that necessitate supplemental watering.

ANNUALS

If it hasn't rained at least ½ inch in the past two or three weeks, check the soil in cool-season color beds, including pansies, violas, snapdragons, stock, alyssum, dianthus, and foliage plants, such as dusty miller, ornamental cabbage, and ornamental kale. Water if the soil is dry to the touch two inches below the surface.

In south Texas, where winters remain very mild, you may need to water color beds every seven to ten days in the absence of rainfall. Sandy soils and coarse-textured bed mixes may require more supplemental watering than clay or loam soils.

Seedlings growing indoors need to be checked daily and watered when the surface of the growing media begins to dry. The goal is to keep the growing mix *moist* but not constantly saturated. Soggy root conditions create favorable conditions for diseases that can wipe out tender seedlings. Use a fine mist sprayer or bottom watering to avoid knocking tender seedlings over with a blast of water.

EDIBLES

Although our cool-season vegetables such as lettuce, spinach, and other greens or broccoli and its blue-leaved cousins are using less water now, they still need moderate soil moisture to stay healthy and productive. If it hasn't rained, you should water as the plants' needs dictate in order to maintain moderate soil moisture. Feel the soil a few inches deep, and you will be able to tell if it is moist or getting a bit too dry.

Perennial herbs need less water as they are in a more dormant state, and they are often from regions of the world with fairly dry winter weather. If the soil remains too wet in winter, the plants can be lost to root and crown rots. Rosemary, oregano, and thyme are herbs that prefer to remain on the dry side in the cool season. If you live in the eastern parts of Texas where rainfall is more plentiful, soggy winter conditions can be a challenge for these plants if they are not planted in well-drained raised beds or containers.

LAWNS

Unless a drought is underway, lawn watering is seldom required in the winter except in the dry, western areas of the state and the southernmost areas where temperatures stay mild most of the winter. In the absence of rainfall, watering every two to three weeks will usually suffice in such conditions.

Lawns that were overseeded with a winter grass such as ryegrass will often need some winter watering to keep the cool-season ryegrass in good condition. The same can be said for groundcovers, including Asian jasmine, English ivy, mondograss, liriope, ajuga, marlberry (*Ardisia japonica*), and wedelia (*Wedelia trilobata*).

PERENNIALS & ORNAMENTAL GRASSES

Perennials and ornamental grasses often have deeper root systems and are in a more dormant state than cool-season annual flowers. Therefore they seldom require winter watering. If you are unsure, dig down 3 to 4 inches, feel the soil, and water if it is dry to the touch. Many of our landscape perennials are not fond of sitting in soggy conditions during the cool season and prefer to dry out a bit before receiving more water.

If you are starting seeds of perennial flowers, such as monarda, echinacea, or verbena, take care to keep the soil moist but not soggy wet as described in annuals.

ROSES, SHRUBS & TREES

Check the soil moisture a few inches below the surface around the root zone of woody ornamentals that were planted the previous fall or winter if it hasn't rained for a few weeks. If it is dry, give them a good soaking; with any luck, natural rainfall will take over the task of maintaining moderate soil moisture.

Established woody ornamental plants should not need any midwinter watering. Evergreens are an exception since they retain their leaves through the winter and continue to need water, although at a much lower rate. As a result they may need a "rescue watering" every few weeks in the absence of rain.

If you have roses, boxwoods, hollies, and other woody shrubs growing in containers, they will need more frequent watering, depending on the daily temperatures and their sun exposure. Be ready to water container plants carrying foliage through the winter once a week if the weather is mild where you live.

VINES & GROUNDCOVERS

Some winter watering is needed to keep groundcovers in good shape, and that includes Asian jasmine (*Trachelospermum asiaticum*), English ivy (*Hedera helix*), mondograss (*Ophiopogon japonicus*), liriope (*Liriope muscari*), ajuga (*Ajuga reptans*), marlberry (*Ardisia japonica*), and wedelia (*Wedelia trilobata*).

However, some groundcovers (and low-growing subshrubs used as groundcovers), including woolly stemodia (*Stemodia tomentosa*), santolina or

lavender cotton (*Santolina chamaecyparissus*), lamb's ear (*Stachys byzantine*), and silver ponyfoot (*Dichondra argentea*) are especially unhappy when kept too wet. As a general guide, if it is a drought-tolerant plant with silvery gray foliage, it doesn't want to be kept too wet, especially in the winter. Likewise most succulents including sedums and heartleaf ice plant (*Aptenia cordifolia*) don't like wet soil, especially in winter.

Perennial vines and woody vines shouldn't need any supplemental watering unless your area has been in a drought over the last few months. If you are not sure about the need for watering, dig down into the soil a few inches and feel how much soil moisture there is. Water only if it is dry.

FERTILIZE

ANNUALS

If you haven't fertilized your cool-season color beds in the past month, sprinkle a complete fertilizer around the plants at moderate rate. (See April, Here's How to Fertilize Flowers, Ornamental Grasses, and Vegetables.) Gently scratch it into the surface inch of soil with a hand cultivation tool, and then water the area well to start the process of releasing the nutrients to the growing plants. This added nutrient boost can help keep the plants strong and ready to produce more blooms during mild winter weather.

EDIBLES

Fertilize cole crops and leafy greens, including broccoli, cabbage, cauliflower, kohlrabi, Brussels sprouts, collards, kale, lettuce, spinach, arugula, and Swiss chard (if you live far enough south to grow it in winter) every four to six weeks to provide optimum nutrition for best production. Use a fertilizer that is higher in nitrogen, such as many products sold for the lawn. (For application rates, see April, Here's How to Fertilize Flowers, Ornamental Grasses, and Vegetables.) If you choose an organic or natural product, *double* the application rate because the concentration of nutrients is generally lower in organic fertilizers, and it takes more time for them to break down and release nutrients in cool soil conditions.

■ *Fertilize cool-season vegetables every few weeks to provide plenty of nutrition for the growing plants.*

Don't fertilize cool-season peas as they produce their own nitrogen in nodules on their roots and excessive nitrogen will decrease yields. Root crops such as radishes, turnips, beets, and carrots also need less nitrogen, so hold off on fertilizing them this month.

If you have access to a source of well-decomposed manure, you can spread it about an inch deep beneath the branch spread of fruit trees, and then cover it with a mulch. Check to make sure the manure is from livestock that didn't feed on herbicide-treated pastures, as some weed-and-brush control products are persistent enough to go through an animal's digestive system and still be present (which could harm some plants).

Well-decomposed manure can also be rototilled or spaded into garden beds that won't be planted until early summer. The manure will continue to decompose over time, releasing nutrients to the growing trees over the coming months. Don't use fresh manure in gardens as it can contain microbes that could contaminate the harvest.

LAWNS
Our warm-season lawn grasses need no fertilization this month. If your lawn is overseeded with ryegrass, a light fertilization may be helpful in keeping the overseeded grass a healthy green color. Use a rate about one-half of what is on the label for regular season lawn fertilizing. (See April, Here's How to Fertilize a Lawn.)

PERENNIALS & ORNAMENTAL GRASSES
Most perennials and ornamental grasses are dormant across the state and won't benefit from fertilizing at this time of the year.

ROSES, SHRUBS & TREES

Newly planted woody ornamentals don't need to be fertilized yet. Established plants likewise won't need fertilizer. However, applying an inch of compost or well-rotted manure to the soil surface will be helpful in providing nutrients as the weather warms up in spring and the plants begin active growth. Cover the compost or manure with a 2- to 3-inch mulch of leaves.

PROBLEM-SOLVE

ALL

New seedlings being started indoors for transplanting out into the garden should be checked frequently to monitor their condition. Diseases, lack of adequate light, and temperature extremes can cause a new tray of transplants to perform poorly. (See February, Here's How to Identify Problems with Germinating Seeds.)

Cold protection is a challenge for many parts of the state. We love to grow things that are a little outside their preferred hardiness zone. If you have annuals, perennials, shrubs, or small trees that are threatened by a cold snap, take measures to protect them using sheets, blankets, tarps, and if necessary, a source of heat beneath the cover. (See October, Here's How to Protect Plants From a Freeze.)

ANNUALS

In the state's warmest areas winter days are often mild enough for some insect pests to become active. Check flowering annuals for aphids and caterpillars. These pests won't usually be present in enough numbers to warrant control. If an infestation appears to be growing, a quick spray of insecticidal soap or another labeled remedy for aphids, or a product containing *Bacillus thuringiensis* for the caterpillars, will reduce their populations significantly.

Freeze burn on flowers and foliage often follows a significant freeze. There is nothing to do after the fact, except wait for the weather to warm up a bit so they will resume growth and fill back in with more healthy foliage and blooms.

EDIBLES

Check your cool-season vegetable plants for pests. In warmer areas of the state a few aphids and caterpillars may be getting the idea that they should visit what we call our vegetable garden and they call a salad bar. A spray of insecticidal soap for aphids or *Bacillus thuringiensis* for caterpillars can keep our produce relatively free of these pests.

Patches of small, white flakes or "bumps" on a fruit tree's trunk or branches, which can easily be scraped off with a fingernail, may be scale insects. If you are not sure if what you are seeing is scale, take a scraping of the pests or a section of branch with the symptoms to your County Extension Office for assistance. When you apply dormant oil at the end of the winter season make sure to treat those areas thoroughly to shut down the pests.

LAWNS

Cool-season weeds are about to make their big push of growth in zones 8b and 9. Now is a good time to hand-pull them if there are not too many in the lawn. You can cover a lot of ground in a fairly short time and avoid using post-emergence weedkillers. Once these weeds start to flower and set seeds in the coming month or two such products won't be effective anyway.

PERENNIALS & ORNAMENTAL GRASSES

Perennials that never reappear after winter may have been killed by either soggy wet soil conditions or a lack of cold hardiness. If the soil stays too saturated in a cold, wet winter season you may need to build up a higher raised planting bed before replanting with your favorite perennials. A thick blanket of mulch will help hold in the soil's warmth and increase a plant's chance of surviving cold.

SHRUBS & TREES

Check for signs of scale insects on the branches of shrubs and trees. Some woody ornamental plants that are often targets of scale insects include American beautyberry, hollies, camellias, and euonymus. Note any plants that have scale so you can treat them next month with dormant oil.

WOODY VINES FOR LANDSCAPES

Vine	Texas Zones	Climbing Structure	Characteristics
Boston ivy (*Parthenocissus tricuspidata*)		Attaches	Very vigorous, semi-evergreen with insignificant blooms followed by dark blue berries.
Bougainvillea (*Bougainvillea* spp.)	9	Non-climbing*	Clusters of flowers in cycles throughout growing season in shades of red, coral, orange, pink, fuchsia, yellow/gold, and white.
Cape honeysuckle (*Tecomaria capensis*)	8b–9	Non-climbing*	Bright orange-red (or yellow) tubular flowers from late summer to fall.
Carolina jessamine (*Gelsemium sempervirens*)	6–8	Twining	Yellow blooms in late winter to early spring.
Cat's claw vine (*Macfadyena unguis-cati*)		Tendrils	Yellow trumpet flowers in spring. Very vigorous.
Clematis (*Clematis* spp.)	6–9a	Twining	Large colorful blooms in late spring to summer. Smaller, native types also available.
Clematis, sweet autumn (*Clematis terniflora*)	6–9	Twining	Clusters of small, fragrant white blooms in late summer to fall.
Climbing roses	6–9	Non-climbing*	Usually "spring-only" blooms. 'Lady Banks' is thornless.
Creeping fig (*Ficus pumila*)	8b–9	Attaches	Evergreen foliage; stays very close to wall.
Crossvine (*Bignonia capreolata*)	6–9	Attaches	Yellow-brick red (native) or coral-orange ('Tangerine Beauty') trumpets in early to mid-spring.
Jasmine, Confederate star (*Trachelospermum jasminoides*)	8–9	Twining	Fragrant white blooms in mid-spring to summer.
Jasmine, Sambac (*Jasminum* sp.)	8b–9	Twining	Fragrant white blooms in summer to fall.
Pink jasmine (*Jasminum polyanthum*)	8–9	Twining	Fragrant white blooms in early spring.
Potato vine (*Solanum jasminoides*)	8–9	Twining	Clusters of white, 1-inch, star-shaped blooms in spring and summer.
Trumpet creeper (*Campsis radicans*)	6–9	Attaches	Orange-red trumpets in summer. Very vigorous.
Trumpet honeysuckle (*Lonicera sempervirens*)	6–8	Twining	Coral/orange/pink blooms in early to late spring.

Vine	Texas Zones	Climbing Structure	Characteristics
Wisteria (*Wisteria* spp.)	7b–8 6–9	Non-climbing*	Purple, lavender, or white blooms in mid- to late spring.
Wisteria evergreen (*Millettia reticulata*)	7b–9	Twining	Dark burgundy flower clusters in summer to fall.
Yellow orchid vine (*Mascagnia macroptera*)	8b–9	Twining	Clusters of yellow flowers late spring to fall followed by seedpods that resemble butterflies.
Yunnan bauhinia (*Bauhinia yunnanensis*)	8b–9	Tendrils	Pale pink and purple orchid-like blooms in late summer to fall.

* Must be woven into or tied to trellis for support.

■ *'Tangerine Beauty' crossvine is a beautiful spring-blooming vine. Plant woody vines such as crossvine early this month to provide time for the plants to establish prior to the onset of spring growth.*

February

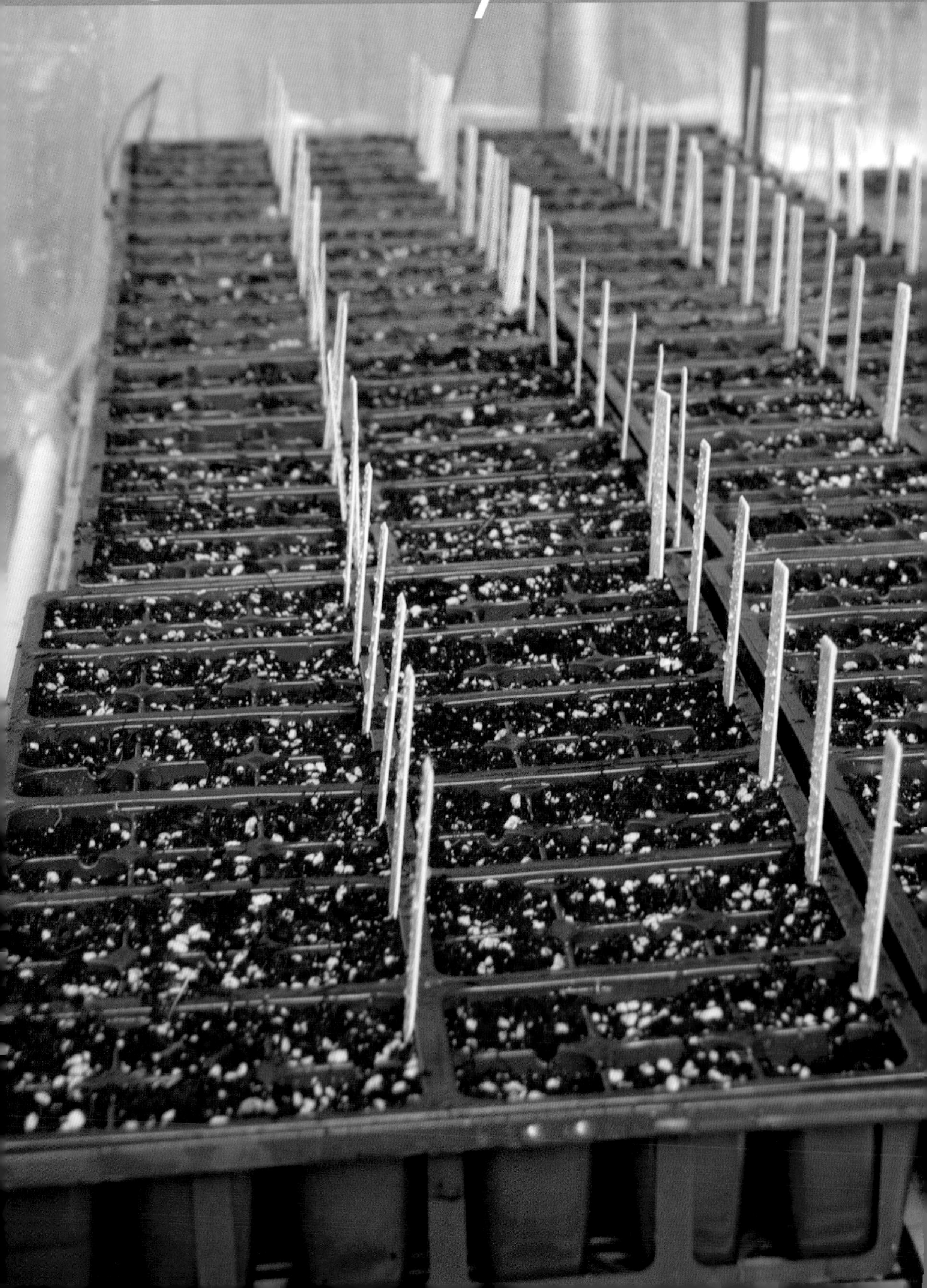

This is a busy month in the gardens and landscapes in most of Texas. Gardeners are busy indoors caring for warm-season transplants, which were planted in good faith that spring is coming, while they make another planting of cool-season vegetables and flowers outdoors. Seed catalogues sit waiting for bad weather days when we can peruse them with their promises of the most bountiful gardening year ever. I am never a better gardener than I am in my late winter plans and dreams.

Gardeners in north Texas are facing periods of bitter cold and occasional snow this month while in south Texas the weather is mild and many plants seem to believe that winter has come to an end.

February is also a month for gardening hope. We can almost smell spring and all our activities are done in the hope of a successful new gardening year. Gardening fever is epidemic and even nongardeners are getting the itch to plant *something*. That makes planning even more important. Grab a cup of coffee, cocoa, or hot tea and take an afternoon stroll through the garden. Make some mental notes of things you'd like to change. Where are more evergreens needed? Where would some extra color be nice? How have the existing plants performed? What would be a good sunny spot for growing some vegetables this spring?

Pruning season has arrived in the landscape and home orchard. Proper training of young plants and pruning of older plants builds strong structure and ensures better blooming and, in the case of fruit trees, more bountiful production. Take time to learn about pruning before you head outside with shears in hand. These plants are long-term investments in your landscape and it makes sense to do it right from the start.

Take a class or attend a gardening lecture. Gardening is an ever-learning endeavor. There are always new and rediscovered plants, cultural practices, and growing techniques to learn about. Thomas Jefferson said it well, "Though I am an old man, I am but a new gardener."

PLAN

ANNUALS

Now is a good time to lay out your color beds and order the compost or bed mix needed for building up the soil. Purchase seeds of heat-tolerant species such as zinnias, marigolds, and sunflowers if you plan to grow your own transplants or to direct seed in the beds a month or two from now.

Check with your local botanical garden and Master Gardener group for area plant sales. These are fun and often provide a chance to purchase species and varieties not commonly available in your area. They are also very educational and you get to meet other gardening enthusiasts.

EDIBLES

The time for planting warm-season vegetables is arriving in zone 9 and just around the corner in zones 7 and 8. Make your final seed orders or visit a seed rack at a local garden center before some varieties sell out.

Do you have a lonely fruit tree that needs a second variety for pollination in order to set fruit? Contact a friend with a different variety and ask if you can cut a few branches from his or her tree during bloom time to place in small cans of water hung in your tree. The bees will take it from there.

LAWNS

Mowing season is around the corner. Prepare for the coming months of mowing by having your mower, edger, and string trimmer serviced. This includes changing the oil (unless it is a two-cycle engine where gas and oil are mixed), checking the pull cord, changing the spark plug, and checking the blade for damage. If the blade is in good condition, have it sharpened, and if it's not, replace it with a new blade. Consider purchasing a second blade for changing out during the season so you can continue mowing while your other blade is being sharpened.

PERENNIALS & ORNAMENTAL GRASSES

Don't forget to include perennials in your plans. While annuals often offer longer bloom periods, perennials provide a great return on investment, returning year after year to take their place in the spotlight. Choose a variety of different perennial species to extend the bloom time from spring to fall.

Many of the best perennial species are available locally, but some may need to be mail-ordered. So make your orders soon to give you time to get them planted before the heat arrives.

ROSES

There are many exciting new roses available each year. Do some research before choosing a rose for your landscape. In addition to picking one with beautiful blooms, consider disease resistance, plant growth habit, and whether or not it blooms through the year.

SHRUBS & TREES

Shrubs and trees are long-term investments in your landscape. Consider the best-adapted species carefully before making a purchase. Choose plants with the mature size of the shrub or tree in mind. Picture the new plant as being full sized, and select the location accordingly. If power lines or a building are near the planting site choose smaller tree species, such as a small blooming tree. If a shrub is to go beside your home and beneath a window choose a compact species or variety to avoid years of fighting it with pruners. When choosing and planting shrubs along a walkway, look for compact varieties and plant them far enough away from the walk that a few years later your guests won't have to "run the botanical gauntlet" to get to your front door.

VINES & GROUNDCOVERS

Draw out new groundcover beds or use a garden hose to "sketch" them in the landscape. Step back and see if the design and flow is appealing to you. Remember that broad gradual curves are aesthetically pleasing and easier to mow around. Mix a few inches of compost into the planting bed area to improve the soil, unless you are planting plants native to central and west Texas, which are not fond of highly amended soil. These will do fine with just a little compost added and some loosening of the soil in the planting bed prior to planting. Order a landscape bed mix to build up the planting area if the drainage is not great. (See January, Here's How to Estimate How Much Soil or Mulch is Needed.)

■ *Consider choosing a small- to medium-sized tree such as a Chinese fringetree* (Chionanthus retusus) *when space is limited due to buildings or power lines.*

PLANT

ANNUALS

Set out transplants of alyssum, calendula, ageratum, coneflower, pansies, dusty miller, and calendula in zones 8 and 9. Be ready to protect the new plants against a freeze.

Start seeds of warm-season flowers, including pentas, petunias, marigolds, impatiens, zinnias, Madagascar periwinkle, cosmos, and annual salvias indoors to grow as transplants about four weeks prior to the average last frost date in your area. This means early to mid-February for zone 8, mid- to late month for zone 7b, and late month for zones 7a and 6b. Provide a warm location or a seed-starting mat beneath the seeded flats to speed

germination. When seedlings emerge, move them to a bright window or beneath a grow light to prevent them from becoming spindly. Fertilize with a dilute fertilizer solution once the first true leaves appear, and water only enough to maintain moderately moist soil.

EDIBLES

February is our last chance to get in another planting of cool-season vegetables for most of the state. Hot weather will shut down these vegetables so don't delay, especially if you live in zone 9. Plant seeds of root crops such as carrots, radishes, beets, and turnips, as well as leafy greens such as lettuce, spinach, arugula, and mustard. Use transplants for a head start on kale, collards, cabbage, broccoli, and kohlrabi.

HERE'S HOW

TO PLANT A BARE-ROOT PLANT

1. If the soil in the planting area is unimproved sand or clay, spread compost over the entire bed and mix it in thoroughly prior to digging the planting hole. This provides a wide area of evenly amended soil to support the new plant's early growth.

2. Dig a hole only as deep as the root system but a little wider.

3. Set the plant at the same level it was growing previously. Note the change in color on the stem of the plant indicating the previous soil line.

4. Spread the roots out in the planting hole. Don't wrap roots around the hole. Make the hole larger or prune the roots shorter.

5. Use the same soil removed in digging the hole to refill it. It may seem like a good idea to use compost or potting soil to refill the hole, but doing so can create an "underground flower pot" that discourages roots from venturing out into surrounding soil, especially in clay soils.

6. Stop when the hole is half-filled and firm the soil in around the roots. Then use a hose to drench the soil in the planting hole to settle the soil and remove air pockets.

7. Finish filling the hole as you firm the soil around the roots.

8. Form a raised circular berm of soil about 4 inches high and 24 inches in diameter around the plant.

9. Fill the berm with water to settle the soil and wet the root zone thoroughly. This berm will help get your new plant through the first stressful summer season by ensuring that each watering soaks the soil deeply.

Water the soil prior to planting seeds, enough to moisten it several inches deep. Then after planting, mist the seeded areas to wet the seeds without splashing soil and dislodging the seeds. Cover any seeded and transplanted areas with a row-cover fabric to help hold in moisture, moderate temperatures a little, and keep hungry early-season pests from munching on your new seedlings. Suspend the row cover above the soil on wire or PVC hoops so rain doesn't press the fabric against the soil. Weight the edges with a little soil to prevent wind from lifting up the fabric or pests from sneaking in.

The average last frost date arrives in mid- to late February for gardeners in the southern parts of zone 9a and in zone 9b, which means the first of the warm-season vegetables can be planted in those regions. Make an early seeding of squash, cucumbers, green beans, and corn once the danger of frost is past in your area. Gambling gardeners can set out tomato transplants a few weeks before the last frost date beneath a protective cover to get an early start on the season.

Count back about forty-five days from the last average frost date in your area and plant cool-season peas (snap, snow, English). Cool-season peas have a *very narrow* growing window between too cold and too hot in our climate, so don't delay.

February is planting season for potatoes. Time your plantings to be about three weeks before the last spring frost in your area. Purchase "seed potatoes"

■ *Repot tomatoes and other cold-tender vegetable transplants into larger containers to keep them growing until the danger of frost is past and they can be planted outdoors.*

Plant perennial herbs such as thyme, rosemary, oregano, and mint in zones 8 (late February) and 9 (mid- to late February).

Plant bare-root fruit trees as early in the month as possible to allow them some time to push out new roots before the new leaf growth is coaxed out by warming temperatures.

LAWNS

The last average freeze date is passing in much of zone 9b so it is okay to start laying sod to establish or renovate a lawn in these areas. If you have perennial weeds in the area to be sodded it is best to delay sodding for a few weeks while you dig or spray the weeds to eliminate them completely. (See April, Here's How to Establish a Lawn.)

PERENNIALS & ORNAMENTAL GRASSES

Plant perennials in zone 9 to allow time for their roots to extend into the surrounding soil in preparation for the demands of summer. Perennials

■ *Begin planting gladiolus corms every two weeks for an extended bloom season in spring to early summer.*

and cut them into sections with a bud (eye) on each section and place in a cool, well-ventilated place for a few days to allow the cut surfaces to dry. Then plant them 1 foot apart in the bottom of trenches dug 8 to 10 inches deep. As the potatoes grow you will be pulling soil, compost, or decomposing mulches around the stems to fill the trench and provide a place for the potatoes to form.

Repot indoor transplants that have outgrown their container to a larger container to keep them growing until it is time to transplant them outdoors. Take care not to disturb the roots as you transplant them since some plants don't like to have their roots disturbed much in the process.

Wait a few weeks to mulch the soil to allow it to warm up. This promotes faster early-season growth. Any weeds that emerge prior to mulching can be removed with a hoe when still young and easy to destroy.

can be planted in other zones, but they may not grow much until it warms up a bit. Firm the soil around newly set transplants and water them well. Then mulch the area with a 2- to 3-inch layer of leaves, pine needles, or bark mulch.

Begin to plant gladiolus bulbs in zone 9 in early February and zone 8 in mid- to late month. Set the corms 6 inches deep in a well-drained garden bed, spacing them 6 inches apart. Make multiple plantings about two weeks apart to extend the blooming season in the coming months. Although gladiolus is a perennial, the corms should be dug in late summer, stored indoors over winter, and then replanted in spring for dependable blooming. The old-fashioned Byzantine gladiolus or corn flag (*Gladiolus Communis* subsp. *byzantinus*) is especially good at naturalizing in the central to eastern parts of the state. In the southeastern region, including the Houston and Beaumont areas, parrot gladiolus (*Gladiolus natalensis*) is a good option for naturalizing.

ROSES

This is your final chance to establish bare-root roses for the year. Dig a hole and leave a cone of soil in the bottom. Spread the rose roots over and around the cone of soil and then refill the hole as you water to settle the soil around the roots and eliminate any air pockets. (See February, Here's How to Plant a Bare-Root Plant.) Container-grown roses can be planted now also. Dig a hole as deep as the plant's rootball in the container. Set the plant in the hole and refill with soil as you add water to settle the soil.

After planting, form a 4-inch-high raised berm of soil about 24 inches in diameter around each plant. Sprinkle 2 to 4 tablespoons of slow-release fertilizer inside the berm and work it into the surface inch of soil. Then water well to fill the berm for a good final soaking. This berm will help ensure that supplemental watering the first season will be sufficient to soak deeply into the soil.

SHRUBS & TREES

Now is a great time to plant woody ornamental plants such as shrubs, trees, and woody vines. The sooner you plant them, the longer the new plants will have to establish roots into the surrounding soil before the demands of summer heat arrive, so don't delay, especially if you live in the southern part of the state where summer arrives a little sooner. (See November, Here's How to Plant Container-Grown Shrubs and Trees.)

Container-grown trees do not usually need stakes and wires to support them after planting. As wind

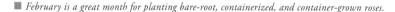

February is a great month for planting bare-root, containerized, and container-grown roses.

moves the trunk the woody tissues grow stronger than if it were held firmly in place by guy wires. If you feel the tree is not well anchored after planting, or if the area is prone to high winds, then three guy wires attached to stakes may be helpful. Use sections of garden hose slipped over the wires where they contact the trunk or limbs to prevent damage (see page 25). Leave a little slack in the wires to allow some movement in the wind. Mark your calendar for six months later to remove the wires as they will have done their job by then.

VINES & GROUNDCOVERS

Prepare soil in areas to be planted with groundcovers by spreading 4 cups of a fertilizer for lawns (but *not* a weed-and-feed product) per 50 square feet and 2 to 3 inches of compost over the area. Rototill or spade the area about 4 to 6 inches deep, if possible, to mix it all in. Begin planting groundcovers and vines after the soil preparation is completed. If you won't be planting for a few weeks mulch the surface with leaves to protect the soil from erosion and deter weeds.

CARE

ANNUALS

Check for young weeds in your annual flower beds. Cool-season weeds are about to take off growing fast and now is the easiest time to remove them by hand or by hoe, while they are still young and shallow rooted. Replenish mulch in annual beds to a depth of 2 to 3 inches.

EDIBLES

This is the season for pruning fruit trees. The goal of training young trees and pruning older trees is to build a strong branch structure and to allow more light to reach the interior of the tree, which increases fruit production in these interior areas. Pruning guides are available from your County Extension Office to provide details on how to prune each type of fruit so your efforts will yield stronger, more productive trees.

While you are pruning make sure to remove any branches that are broken or show signs of disease cankers.

■ *Sprinkle some organic or other slow-release fertilizer around new roses and then water it well to get them off to a good start.*

Prune fruit trees, vines, and bushes this month before the arrival of new spring growth. Prune peaches and plums to create an open bowl or vase shape. Apples are pruned to a central leader with side branches spaced apart along the main leader. Pears are vigorous trees, and they may have multiple central leaders. It is better to prune them less and direct their long, upright branches outward to about a 45-degree angle, which promotes side branching without encouraging excessive vigor. Use branch spacers on branches less than an inch in diameter to push them out to the desired angle. A spacer can be a piece of wood similar in size to a ruler but with a notch in each end to help it hold onto the branch and the trunk.

On larger branches tie a cord to the branch and to a stake in the ground to lean it out to a 45-degree angle. Remove the cord several months later and the branch will remain in that position. Contact your County Extension Office for additional information on how to prune each type of fruit you grow and spend some time learning how to prune before heading outdoors with pruners in hand.

Strawberries are starting to bloom in zone 9. Have some row cover on hand to protect their early

■ *Check with your County Extension Office about the best way to train and prune your fruit trees, vines, or bushes.*

blooms from a frost or freeze. The first blooms to open in a cluster become the largest fruit, so take action to not lose them when cold weather threatens.

Maintain a mulch layer 2 to 3 inches thick in cool-season vegetable beds to protect the soil from erosion or crusting in winter rains and to deter weed seeds from germinating.

LAWNS

If your turf was overseeded with ryegrass in the cool season mow as needed to maintain an attractive lawn and to prevent excessive shading of your warm-season turf. Remove fallen tree leaves and pine needles from a lawn's surface to allow as much light as possible to reach the lawn. This is especially important for St. Augustine lawns growing beneath the shade of a deciduous tree.

PERENNIALS & ORNAMENTAL GRASSES

Remove all aboveground growth on perennials such as lantana, cannas, penstemons, salvias, and gingers that froze to the ground during winter freezes. Cut back to a few inches above the soil line. Complete this task now to avoid damaging the new shoots that will be emerging soon.

Complete the trimming tasks in all zones for any ornamental grasses that still have winter-killed top growth; cut them back to 6 to 10 inches above the soil line before their new spring regrowth begins.

Now is a good time in zones 8 and 9 to divide and reset fall-blooming perennials such as oxblood or schoolhouse lily (*Rhodophiala bifida*), red spider lily (*Lycoris radiata*), 'Autumn Joy' sedum (*Sedum spectabile*), Mexican bush sage (*Salvia leucantha*), mountain sage (*Salvia regla*), Mexican mint marigold (*Tagetes lucida*), fall or autumn aster (*Symphyotrichum oblongifolium*), climbing Carolina aster (*Aster carolinianus*), copper canyon daisy (*Tagetes lemmonii*), garden mums (*Chrysanthemum* spp.), coral vine or Queen's wreath (*Antigonon leptopus*), fall obedient plant or false dragonhead (*Physostegia virginiana*), Maximilian sunflower (*Helianthus maximiliana*), blue mistflower (*Conoclinium coelestinum*), sweet autumn clematis (*Clematis ternifolia*), and cigar plant or candy corn plant (*Cuphea micropetala*).

Summer-blooming perennials such as canna (*Canna* x *generalis*), society garlic (*Tulbaghia violacea*), coneflower (*Echinacea* spp.), shrimp plant (*Justicia brandegeeana*), yarrow (*Achillea millefolium*, *A. filipendulina*), blue plumbago (*Plumbago auriculata*), summer phlox (*Phlox paniculata*), Byzantine gladiolus or corn flag (*Gladiolus byzantinus*), daylily (*Hemerocallis* spp.), and various types of rain lily and copper lily (*Zephyranthes* spp., *Habranthus* spp.) can also be dug, divided, and reset now in zones 8 and 9. It is best to wait until fall to divide spring-blooming perennials, although they can be divided now.

If you aren't sure whether or not to divide a perennial flowering plant, ask the following questions: Is it spreading too vigorously and growing into adjacent plants? Has the interior of the plant become less productive, with most of the blooms around the periphery? Is the plant blooming less than it used to in general? Do you want to make more plants for planting around the landscape or sharing with friends and family?

This is a great time in zones 7 to 9 to divide perennial ornamental grasses, including various types of maiden grass, various muhly species, Mexican feather grass, and fountain grass in the southern half of the state. Dig the clump and use a sharp spade, large sharp knife, or machete to cut it vertically into sections for replanting. Pampas grass starts to die out in the interior as the clump gets larger over time. If you notice that the interior of the clump is dead, prune back the

exterior if you didn't already do so earlier in the winter. Then take a sharp shovel and dig out sections of the exterior for replanting. Finally dig up and discard the dead interior.

In zones 8b and 9 many of the perennial plants that die back to the ground farther north often make it through winter without a killing freeze. Examples include yellow bells (*Esperanza*), sky flower or golden dewdrop (*Duranta repens*), pride-of-Barbados (*Caesalpinia pulcherrima*), and various perennial salvias. Now that winter is ending, go ahead and trim them back to a few inches above the soil, or at least cut them back significantly to prevent them from becoming overgrown, lanky, and unattractive.

Cut ornamental grasses back to 6 to 10 inches high in zones 6 (late month) and 7 (early to mid-month), before the new growth has emerged. Removing the old growth will result in a much more attractive plant when the new growth starts to emerge in spring. Divide and reset perennial ornamental grasses in zones 6 and 7 in late February.

ROSES

Prune roses that repeat bloom through the season. It is best to finish the task prior to the arrival of

■ *Cut a rose stem just above a five-leaflet leaf.*

new spring growth. Keep in mind that any roses that bloom only in the spring should *not* be pruned until after they bloom or you will be pruning away their one big chance in the spotlight. Many climbing roses, such as Lady Banks, are among the "once bloomers" that need to bloom prior to being pruned.

Train climbing roses through the season to encourage more blooms. If you let a climbing rose grow long vertical shoots it won't produce many blooms. A better technique is to weave the shoots back and forth as you move up the trellis, attaching them with twine or plastic plant tape. This way more of the shoot is oriented in a horizontal direction as they climb up a trellis, which results in a bounty of blooms.

Rose pruning can be a daunting task for someone new to roses or if you have more than one type of rose growing in your landscape. Miniatures, floribundas, hybrid teas, grandifloras, and shrub roses are not all pruned the same way. As a general guide, shrub roses need to have only dead, diseased, broken, or rubbing branches removed, and the overall shrub cut back by about one-fourth to one-third. Hybrid teas require the most pruning. Remove the branches (also known as canes) and prune out spindly interior growth, suckers emerging from below the bud union (large swollen area at base of plant), and older branches, which will have a scaly, gray appearance. Make cuts to remove canes by cutting them back to where they emerge from the bud union. Finally, reduce the height of the plant by a third (or about "knee-high"), cutting ⅛ inch above an outward-facing bud. Pull any diseased leaves off the bush, and rake up and remove fallen leaves as they are sources of infection for new growth.

For more specific instructions on pruning each of the various types of roses, check out the many helpful resources available from the American Rose Society website (www.ars.org). Texas has more than a dozen local rose societies in cities across the state where consulting rosarians are available to advise and teach about all things roses. Consider attending a meeting to learn

more, but I should offer a word of warning: Rose growing can be addictive.

SHRUBS

Prune summer-flowering shrubs such as abelia, hydrangea, oleander, rose of Sharon, Virginia sweetspire, smoke tree, gardenia, buddleia, and chastetree (*Vitex agnus-castus*) trained into a shrub form. Avoid the tendency to hedge or shear these plants and instead cut back branches to where they join another branch to maintain a more natural plant form. Minor pruning to remove broken, damaged, and rubbing branches and a few gangly shoots growing out of the overall shrub form is all that is usually needed.

Rejuvenate older multi-stemmed shrubs by removing 20 percent of the oldest stems back to where they emerged from the ground. The plant will respond by sending out new shoots to fill in and create an attractive shrub. If you repeat this process each year you'll avoid having old, unproductive, and unattractive stems that detract from the shrub's appearance. It will also help maintain the shrub at a smaller size.

Overgrown nandinas should not be sheared or "topped." Instead, remove some of the oldest stems back to the soil line each year. This thins the plant, leaving the most attractive stems and promotes new shoot growth from the base.

Prune evergreen shrubs either by selective pruning for summer-flowering shrubs to create a more natural form or by hedging to create a dense wall of foliage. When a hedge is desired, shear the plants every month from late winter to fall. Keep the top of the hedge a little narrower than the base to allow light to reach the lower areas of the shrub. This will help maintain good foliage cover from top to bottom, creating a dense, attractive hedge.

Subshrubs are low-growing shrubs with woody bases and tops that tend to die back in many areas, much like perennials. Examples include autumn sage or cherry sage (*Salvia greggii*), zexmenia (*Wedelia texana*), skeleton-leaf goldeneye (*Viguiera stenoloba*), white mistflower (*Ageratina havanensis*), bluebeard

■ *Late winter is the time to prune summer-blooming shrubs and trees such as chaste tree (*Vitex agnus-castus).

(*Caryopteris* x *clandonensis*), and flame acanthus (*Anisacanthus quadrifidus* var. *wrightii*). Depending on where you live in Texas, some of these subshrubs may freeze back to near the plant's base. Even if they don't freeze back it is best to prune them by about one-half now. They will respond with fresh new growth and a denser, more attractive plant with more blooms in the months to come.

TREES

February is a good time to complete all dormant-season pruning in zones 6 to 8. Make any needed pruning cuts in early February in zone 8b where trees will soon be putting on new spring growth. Follow the instructions for pruning later in this chapter.

Use sharp pruning tools to make clean cuts for fastest healing. (See February, Here's How to Remove a Tree Limb.) Make your cuts outside the natural branch collar so you neither leave a stub nor cut too close to the branch. Stubs tend to die

and then become dead wood, preventing proper wound closure. Cuts made too close to the main branch create larger than necessary wounds, which heal slowly, thus allowing moisture and wood decay organisms a chance to begin to rot the interior wood of the tree.

Pruning procedures change as a tree gets older. Young trees from planting to about 5 years are in their training stage. The goal is to develop a set of strong main branches that are at a wide angle to the trunk, spaced apart adequately to allow growth as the tree ages during the decades to come and which begin at a height that allows necessary access beneath the tree for pedestrian traffic, mowing, or other activities. When a tree is a small "broomstick-sized" new transplant, it will be tempting to leave branches that are too low and too close together. Imagine the tree many years later when those scaffold branches are 10 inches or more in diameter and you will see that what seems far apart now will be squeezed together in time.

Prune summer-blooming trees including chaste tree (*Vitex agnus-castus*), crape myrtle, desert willow, and chitalpa (x *Chitalpa tashkentensis*). These plants are able to set blooms on new growth, so winter pruning is best. Crape myrtles are typically pruned incorrectly and excessively. Only remove broken or rubbing branches and sucker shoots emerging from the base of the trunk. It is okay, although unnecessary, to remove the twiggy outer growth, but don't cut back beyond the point where the branches become "pencil-sized" or larger. During the first few years after planting, you can train the young plants into a desired shape by removing a few smaller branches on the main trunks, leaving those that are best oriented to create a strong, attractive branch structure. The goal is to train them when they are young so that more severe cuts won't be needed later as the plant gets larger.

It is not recommended to paint pruning wounds with one notable exception in Texas. If you live in central Texas or other parts of the state where oak wilt is present, paint pruning wounds *immediately* after cutting. Some tree experts put it this way: "Prune with the saw in one hand and the pruning paint in the other." The tiny beetles that spread oak wilt are active in all but the coldest and hottest months of the year. If you delay painting the wounds even for a few hours the beetles will have time to arrive and transmit the disease.

VINES & GROUNDCOVERS
Mow liriope and mondograss (monkeygrass) to remove the old damaged top growth in zones 7 and 8. New growth will soon emerge and fill in, which will result in a much more attractive groundcover planting. Some vining groundcovers such as English ivy may also benefit from being trimmed back with a mower or string trimmer to remove unattractive older foliage.

Prune old foliage on cast iron plants with hand pruners. Cut the oldest leaf shoots an inch above the soil, leaving the newer, more attractive foliage. The plants will push out more foliage soon, and this renovation will really make an

aesthetic difference in the plants. Fern beds that die back to the ground should have the top growth removed and even evergreen ferns will benefit from a cleaning out of old growth so new fronds can fill in and make for a beautiful, lush new look.

Most woody vines bloom in spring and should not be pruned until after they bloom, or you'll be cutting away potential bloom buds. Some woody vines such as trumpet creeper, sweet autumn clematis, and Cape honeysuckle bloom on new growth in summer or fall. Now is the time to prune them back according to each species' specifications to shape the plant and help direct growth.

WATER

ANNUALS
In the absence of rain, water bluebonnets, sweet peas, larkspur, poppies, and other fall-seeded flowers to keep the plants strong as they prepare to begin their spring growth surge and big bloom show in March and April.

EDIBLES
Maintain moderately moist soil in vegetable and herb gardens to keep cool-season vegetables strong and more able to withstand freezing weather.

LAWNS, VINES & GROUNDCOVERS
Lawns and evergreen groundcovers should not need watering now unless your area is in a drought. If your lawn was overseeded with ryegrass for winter, water as needed to maintain the ryegrass.

PERENNIALS & ORNAMENTAL GRASSES
Cool temperatures and periodic rainfall in most of Texas keeps the soil adequately moist for perennials and ornamental grasses that are dormant now. If your area is in a drought or if you have bulb foliage that is actively growing, however, check the soil and water if it is getting dry.

ROSES, SHRUBS & TREES
Water evergreen shrubs and trees if there's no rainfall to keep the soil adequately moist. In zone 9 roses

may still be holding much of their foliage; they will benefit from watering if the soil begins to get dry. Newly planted roses, shrubs, and trees should be fine if they were watered in well at planting, but in zone 9b they may be leafing out and could benefit from a good soaking as needed to prevent their limited, developing root system from drying out.

FERTILIZE

ANNUALS

Fertilize winter annuals to keep them vigorous and blooming their best. These plants can bloom themselves into a weakened state and in the cool soils of winter a little extra boost is helpful. Sprinkle a cup of complete fertilizer per 25 square feet of planting bed and mix it into the surface inch of soil. Then water it in well.

EDIBLES

Fertilize cool-season vegetables with a complete fertilizer by mixing it into the surface inch or two of soil in the planting beds and then watering it in well. In the absence of a soil test apply 2 cups of fertilizer per 50 square feet of bed space.

■ *The most rapid wound healing occurs in the spring, so late winter is the best time to prune your landscape trees.*

Fertilize fruit trees that are one to three years old with a complete fertilizer in a 3-1-2 or 4-1-2 ratio of nutrients. Apply 2 cups per inch of trunk diameter to the entire area beneath and just beyond the branch spread (drip line), use a hoe or rake to move it into the surface inch or two of soil or mulch, and then water the area well. In sandy east Texas soils, include a cup of potassium magnesium sulfate (K-Mag or Sul-Po-Mag) in the fertilizer application.

LAWNS

If your lawn was overseeded in the fall with a ryegrass mixture you can fertilize now with a turf type product at the rate recommended. (See April, Here's How to Fertilize a Lawn.) Otherwise, don't fertilize or you'll just be wasting money, feeding cool-season weeds, and potentially damaging local rivers and streams when rains wash away the nutrients.

ROSES, SHRUBS & TREES

If you didn't apply compost or well-rotted manure around your woody ornamental plants last month you can still do so now. If the soil around these plants has a covering of mulch, pull it back and apply an inch of compost or manure and then replace the surface mulch. The decomposing organic matter covered in mulch simulates a forest floor environment that will help these plants thrive.

PROBLEM-SOLVE

ALL

To assess whether a hard freeze has damaged a marginally hardy plant's aboveground branches, wait at least a few days after the freeze and scrape the bark back in a small spot on the branch with your thumbnail or a knife blade. The tissues below should be green or a healthy cream color. If you see brown- or tan-colored bark or wood the branch has been freeze damaged. Wait until the weather warms up and new growth begins before pruning the plant back so you will be better able to know how far back to cut.

If you are growing transplants indoors, watch them for signs of "damping off," a disease caused by wet

HERE'S HOW

TO REMOVE A TREE LIMB

1. Make the first cut about a foot away from the trunk or larger limb, cutting upward about halfway through the branch.

2. Make a second cut a few inches outside the first, cutting down until the branch breaks and falls away.

3. Make the third and final cut just outside of the branch collar to remove the short section of branch remaining. If possible, hold the branch as you finish the cut to prevent it from falling and stripping the bark at the point of attachment.

conditions and fungal organisms that rot the seedlings at the soil line. The best solution is to start with fresh, disease-free growing media and avoid keeping it too wet.

ANNUALS

Check for caterpillar damage on the foliage of cool-season flowers in the warmer parts of the state. Most winters are cold enough to keep the pests away but in zone 9b, caterpillars and aphids can appear early. Ignore a little damage here and there but more significant infestations may warrant spraying.

EDIBLES

Watch for caterpillars and aphids in the vegetable garden. If they are found, follow the treatment suggestions mentioned in March.

Treat scale infestations on fruit trees with an application of dormant oil spray. Don't apply dormant oil after the leaves or fruit buds have begun to push out new growth or it will burn the new leaves and blooms. Also avoid applying dormant oil if a freeze is forecast in the next day or two. Shake the sprayer periodically to keep the oil and water from separating. Only those insects and insect eggs that are covered with oil spray will be killed, so it is important to cover all trunks and branches well.

LAWNS

Warm-season weed species such as crabgrass are germinating this month in zones 9 and 8. The best weed control is a dense, healthy turf. Areas of your lawn that are thin due to insect, disease, or past drought damage are an invitation to weed seeds. One way to prevent weeds is with the use of a pre-emergent herbicide. There are both organic and synthetic options for pre-emergent products.

It is critical that you choose a product that is effective against the type of weeds you have, that you apply it prior to weed germination, and that you follow the label instructions. This means applying pre-emergent products to prevent warm-season weeds in early February in zone 9a, mid-month in zone 8, and late in the month for zone 7.

Most products require a light watering to move the herbicide down into the soil surface where it will affect the weed seeds. Contact your County Extension Office for assistance selecting a product and application techniques so your efforts will be successful and to avoid needless damage to the environment. The difficulty in timing and applying these products correctly, and the fact that no one product will prevent all types of weeds, make it best in most cases to focus your efforts on building a dense, healthy turf over time and choking out most weed problems. In the meantime, consider hand pulling and mowing them and collecting the clippings for disposal when the weeds are setting seeds.

Cool-season weeds such as henbit, carpetweed, clover, and chickweed are still fairly small in most of the state. If you are planning to use a post-emergent herbicide product to control them this is the time to do so. The reason is that the weeds are young and more susceptible to the products and the turf is less susceptible to damage when the daytime temperatures are cool. Not all products are equally effective against all types of weeds, so whichever type of product you choose check the label to see if it is labeled for your type of turfgrass and for the weeds you wish to control.

Large patch (or brown patch) begins to reappear in St. Augustine lawns with the arrival of milder temperatures and rainy weather (See October, Lawns.) At this point treatments are not warranted, and the grass in the brown circular areas will green again soon as the weather warms.

■ *Scrape back the bark of shrubs or trees to check for the extent of freeze damage. Healthy, undamaged tissues are cream to green in color. Cold-damaged wood will be brown.*

ROSES

Old foliage has been persisting on roses in the southern parts of the state. It is usually looking diseased or yellowing but will soon be falling with the arrival of warmer weather and new growth. If you just have a few plants with few remaining leaves, remove any leaves that have disease spots or are yellowing, especially on disease-prone varieties. Rake up and discard fallen rose foliage around the plants to reduce the amount of spores that can infect new foliage as it emerges soon.

SHRUBS

Check junipers and cedars for bagworm pouches. They appear as small, elongated sacks of dead plant bark and needles from ½ to 2 inches long. Snip them out of the plant and destroy them and the eggs or larvae inside to reduce the damage these pests can cause.

Check pyracantha, cotoneaster, loquat, and ornamental pear trees for dead blackened shoots, a sign of past fire blight infection. Prune these areas, cutting 4 inches back into healthy branch areas to reduce infection during spring when the disease is most active. Dip pruners in 70 percent isopropyl alcohol or a 10 percent bleach water solution between cuts to sterilize the pruning equipment. If you use a bleach solution, it is important to wipe a coating of oil on the metal surfaces of equipment after pruning to prevent rust. Discard diseased plant material in the trash.

HERE'S HOW

TO IDENTIFY PROBLEMS WITH GERMINATING SEEDS

Problem: Seedlings fall over, wilt, and die.

Cause: This condition is known as "damping off" and is caused by diseases that cause root and stem tissues to decay.

Solution: Use fresh, disease-free growing mixes and avoid excessive moisture to prevent this problem. If you see drops of water forming on the inside of the clear plastic cover over seedlings or if the soil surface appears continually *wet*, not just moist, then remove the cover for a few hours to allow the excess moisture to evaporate away.

Problem: Seeds don't sprout.

Cause: Old seeds, lack of adequate moisture during the germination process, or the growing media is too cold or too hot.

Solution: Check the expiration dates on seed packages. Store seeds in airtight containers in the freezer to extend their viable life. Maintain a constant growing medium moisture. Check the media's temperature and the setting on a seed-starting mat if you are using one. Sometimes seed trays in a windowsill can get hot from too much direct sun or become too cool on a very cold night.

Problem: Seedlings are spindly with weak stems.

Cause: Lack of adequate light, excessive nitrogen, and warm growing conditions.

Solution: Move seedling trays to a bright window. Turn trays daily to prevent seedlings from bending toward the sun. Set up a grow light a few inches above the seedlings. If florescent bulbs in the grow light are more than a year old replace the bulbs for better light quality.

OPTIMUM TEMPERATURE AND TIME NEEDED TO GROW TRANSPLANTS

Vegetables	Optimum Growing Media Temp. (°F)	Days to Germinate	Time (in Weeks) Needed to Grow Transplants*
Cabbage, broccoli, cauliflower, kale	75	4–7	5–7
Lettuce	55	7–14	4–5
Onion	75	4–6	8–10
Tomato	85	6–8	5–6
Pepper	85	7–10	7–8
Eggplant	85	7–10	7–8
Cucumber, squash, muskmelon, watermelon	85	3–5	2–3

*Depends on growing conditions (temperature, light levels, nutrition, and so forth.)

Flowers	Optimum Growing Media Temp. (°F)	Light Requirement**	Days to Germinate	Time (in Weeks) Needed to Grow Transplants*
Ageratum	70°F	L	5 days	6–8
Alyssum	70°F	L	5 days	3–5
Calendula (pot marigold)	70°F	D	10 days	7–8
Carnation (annual)	70°F	DL	20 days	11–12
Celosia	70°F	DL	10 days	8–9
Coleus	65°F	L	10 days	7–10
Cosmos	70°F	DL	5 days	6–8
Dahlia (from seed)	70°F	DL	5 days	6–8
Dianthus (annual pinks)	70°F	DL	5 days	6–7
Dusty miller (Centaurea gymnocarpa)	65°F	D	10 days	7–8
Dusty miller (other species)	75°F	L	10 days	6–7
Gaillardia (annual)	70°F	L	20 days	7–9
Impatiens	70°F	L	15 days	4–6
Lobelia	70°F	DL	20 days	5–6
Marigold (dwarf types)	70°F	DL	5 days	6–7
Marigold (tall types)	70°F	DL	5 days	3–4
Nicotiana	70°F	L	15 days	10–12
Pansy	65°F	D	10 days	10–12
Petunia	70°F	L	10 days	5–7
Phlox, annual (Phlox drummondi)	65°F	D	10 days	5–6
Portulaca (rose moss)	70°F	D	20 days	4–6
Rudbeckia (coneflower)	70°F	DL	10 days	6–7
Salvia splendens	70°F	L	15 days	5–6
Snapdragon	65°F	L	10 days	5–7
Verbena	65°F	D	20 days	5–7
Periwinkle (Vinca rosea)	70°F	D	15 days	7–8
Zinnia	70°F	DL	5 days	3–5

**Light requirement:
   D-Seeds germinate best in darkness; DL-No light requirements; L-Seeds germinate best in light.

*Depends on growing conditions (temperature, light levels, nutrition, and so forth).

March

The cold of winter is giving way to mild temperatures as the last average frost date passes in most areas this month. Warm-season flowers, herbs, and vegetables will be appearing in our landscapes. Gardening gamblers are getting an early start in hopes that there are no more frosts to come. If you're itching to plant a bit early, have some cold-protection covers and perhaps some lights for warmth on hand to fend off frosts and freezes.

March is an exciting time to be gardening. Gardening fever has struck and almost everyone has a desire to plant green things. Thomas Jefferson said, "No occupation is so delightful to me as the culture of the earth, and no culture comparable to that of the garden." Gardening is therapeutic, and I have worked through many issues of life as I worked in my garden.

It makes sense to try to do things right the first time. Before you bring plants home, take time to build your soil with compost or purchase a quality bed mix. Create raised beds where your plants can thrive. Plan before you plant so your gardening dreams will come true. Determine how many plants you need to purchase before you go shopping, and know which ones are best adapted to your soils and climate.

Seventy-five percent of your success has been determined by the time the plants are in the ground. You've already prepared the soil (or not). You've chosen plants that are well adapted to the climate and soil (or not). You've placed them in the sun or shade exposure they need (or not). You've planted them properly (or not). So it makes sense to start off right so you can enjoy beautiful flowers, bountiful gardens, and aesthetically pleasing landscapes.

March was made for gardeners. Each year brings a parade of new plants and new gardening gadgets. Nature likes to throw us a curve, and it seems that no two years are alike. There's no worry about getting bored in the garden.

Here's to your best gardening year ever.

PLAN

ALL

Start your garden journal if you haven't done so already. This journal will be a record of what you planted, how it performed, and any insects, diseases, or other problems that showed up. That makes it useful in planning new plantings and anticipating issues that might arise. Choose a paper journal or an electronic version. (See January, Here's How to Keep Track of Your Gardening Activities.)

When designing and planning a landscape you have many options, including having the same cookie-cutter landscape as most of the neighbors. Consider creating a landscape that has a sense of place instead. This means that it fits the local region you live in. Native plants and adapted non-natives are an important part of this. Dare to try some new and different plants for a uniquely beautiful look to your home place.

ANNUALS

Planting season begins this month for the warm-season garden starting in zones 8 and 9. Draw out your beds on paper prior to planting and develop a

■ Use the "thriller, filler, spiller" technique to create container combinations of annual color that really catch the eye.

HERE'S HOW

TO PLAN COLOR CHANGES FOR ANNUAL BEDS

Any single species of annual flower won't survive and look great all through the year. However, sometimes a budget won't allow four color changes per year to keep the beds blooming their best year-round. Here are three options for color changes for an annual bed in full sun.

Number of Color Changes per Year	Plant in March to Early April for Spring to Summer Color	Plant in May for Summer Color	Plant in Late August for Fall Color	Plant in October for Cool-Season Color
2	Heat-tolerant warm-season flowers, e.g. dwarf zinnias	—	—	Cool-season flowers, e.g. pansies/violas
3	Heat tolerant warm-season flowers, e.g. dwarf zinnias	—	Warm season flowers, e.g. petunias or marigolds	Cool-season flowers e.g. pansies/violas
4	Warm-season flowers, e.g. petunias	Heat-tolerant warm-season flowers, e.g. dwarf zinnias	Warm-season flowers, e.g. petunias or marigolds	Cool-season flowers, e.g. pansies/violas

layout for the species and varieties you want to plant, and where. Copy the schematic outlines of your beds to use later in the season as you change spent plantings with new ones. Species that thrive in spring may wither in summer, and summer species can give way to fall color, followed by winter.

Consider planning a minimum of two annual color changes for the growing season, although if time and budget allow, as many as four color changes can be made to keep the landscape beds at their peak throughout the year. (See March, Here's How to Plan Color Changes for Annual Beds page 52.)

Begin with the colors you would like to include. Color pencils are a great way to help draw and visualize the planting beds. So rather than buy plants and then try to figure out how to use them, begin with a plan and *then* go shopping for the plants that can create the effect you desire.

Don't forget to plan some super color container combinations for the spring and summer seasons. Fill a planter with one species or make a combination planter to add pizzazz to any deck, patio, porch, or walkway. Use the "thriller, filler, spiller" system for easy combinations. Start with a taller focal plant (the thriller), add something to provide the central mass of the planting (the filler), and then include a trailing plant around the sides of the container (the spiller).

EDIBLES

Most of the state is busy planting warm-season vegetables beginning this month and cool-season vegetables are still going strong. It makes sense to plan before you plant. Draw your garden plot noting where various vegetables will be planted. Resist the urge to plant too much at one time unless you'll be freezing or canning the excess. Consider the sun exposure and place taller species such as corn, tomatoes, and trellised crops on the north or west side of shorter species.

Vegetables can be grown in containers too. Many are ornamental and quite attractive either by themselves or mixed in with flowers. Examples include lettuce varieties with burgundy or splotched leaves, bok choy, and 'Bright Lights' Swiss chard.

Herb gardens are also going in this month across the state. If you don't have room for a formal herb garden, consider tucking some herbs into containers or landscape and garden beds. There's no rule that flowers, vegetables, and herbs can't mix, and the combinations can be helpful in attracting beneficial insects when various plants are in bloom. Trailing herbs such as thyme and oregano look great spilling out of a container. You don't need much harvest to keep you supplied in the kitchen, so if space is limited container herbs may be the best option. Choose at least a 2-gallon container (larger is better) so you won't have to water as often.

LAWNS

Consider having your irrigation system evaluated. This can save water and money over our long, hot growing season and ensure a beautiful lawn even during drought conditions. The system should be checked for broken or misaligned spray heads, improper pressure, poor coverage overlap, and even distribution. If you don't have a rain switch, get one; it will pay for itself in water savings over time.

If your lawn has been plagued by large patch (brown patch) this past fall to spring season, make

■ *Vegetables, such as this Swiss chard can be colorful and most do well in containers for dual-purpose plantings.*

HERE'S HOW

TO USE COLOR EFFECTIVELY

Color choices are a matter of personal taste, but there are some principles to keep in mind that help you get the most impact from your color beds. Here are a few tips:

1. When planning beds that will be viewed at a distance, choose large swaths of color for the greatest impact.

2. Mixtures of many colors are interesting when viewed up close, but as you move away from them they tend to blend into one another. A riot of colors around a patio or along a walkway can be very effective.

3. Dark colors such as dark purple or dark red can be less noticeable in a flower bed. They'll be noticed more if you use them in bright sun, combine with lighter colors to set them apart, and use them near sitting areas and walkways where they can be viewed up close.

4. Use light colors in shade where they can brighten the shade and stand out. Remember that white is a color, too, and is very effective in shady spots.

5. Choose colors that complement one another. A good guide is to use colors from opposite sides of the color wheel, such as purple and yellow, blue and orange, or green and red.

6. Combinations of colors that are adjacent on a color wheel can be interesting, such as violet, lavender, fuchsia, and pink.

7. Don't forget foliage when choosing colors. Many plants have colorful foliage that makes a great color feature or that can provide an awesome backdrop to other colors.

a note to back off fertilizing and watering next fall. Promoting lush growth predisposes the turfgrass to this disease. The same is true for chinch bug problems, as excessive spring-to-summer fertilizing and watering encourages lush growth.

PERENNIALS & ORNAMENTAL GRASSES

Make a plan for your perennial flowers that will provide color throughout the season. It is easy to find things that bloom in spring. The palette of summer and fall options are more limited but many great choices are available. Too many landscapes become a "sea of green" in the summer. Plan now for planting perennials that will color your landscape even when blazing summer heat arrives.

Remember that "perennial" is a regional designation. Something that is a dependable perennial in Houston may be a marginal perennial in Austin and an annual in Dallas-Fort Worth. Examples of such regional perennials for summer heat for our southern zones and annuals in the northern zones include lantana, yellow bells or esperanza (*Tecoma stans*), pride of Barbados (*Caesalpinia pulcherrima*), and plumbago (*Plumbago auriculata*).

ROSES

The rose is the queen of the floral landscape. Look around your yard and consider where a blooming rose would be a great addition. The site will need six or more hours of direct sun and good drainage. If an area tends to stand in water after a rain, make plans to build a raised planting bed for better results. Order a blend of soil and compost from a local source in a quantity sufficient to build a raised planting bed 6 inches high in moderately well-drained areas and 12 inches high if the soil drainage is poor. (See January, Here's How to Estimate How Much Soil or Mulch Is Needed.)

SHRUBS & TREES

Spring-blooming shrubs and trees, such as spirea, flowering quince, Texas mountain laurel, silver bells, ornamental pears, fringe trees, and redbuds, are putting on their big show in most areas of Texas. Note which ones you like best and make

■ *Texas mountain laurel is a spring-blooming tree that adds beauty and fragrance to the landscape.*

plans to prepare a spot for adding them to your landscape this spring.

Good site preparation is critical to the success of new trees and shrubs. Do some research to choose species that will thrive in the planting location (sun vs. shade, wet vs. dry, and so forth). Even if you have already purchased plants, if the site is not ready, place the plants off to the side and keep them watered each day while you get their new home ready.

As you are choosing shrub species and varieties also consider their mature size. Too often we plant a shrub under a window that will soon grow to block the window. Then we spend years in an ongoing battle to prune it back. Dwarf species and varieties are available that can better fit the space, whether it's height or width, and would save a lot of work for years to come.

VINES & GROUNDCOVERS

Areas where turf is performing poorly or where you want a groundcover planting can be planned this month. Draw out your landscape area on paper and sketch where you want the groundcover to go. This will allow you to design an attractively shaped planting area. Consider the areas where sun and shade will be throughout the day, as most plants prefer either sun or, at least, part sun. Remember when you're planning the layout of your groundcover bed that the sun will be more directly overhead in summer.

PLANT

ANNUALS

Hanging baskets add another dimension to landscapes. Create your own by planting these great options to add versatility to your landscape color: petunia, angelonia, bacopa, calibrachoa, alyssum, geranium, impatiens, caladium, begonia, verbena, nierembergia, and others. Try some moss-lined wire baskets or coconut coir-lined baskets this season. Not only can you plant the tops, you can also punch holes through the sides to create a full and attractive basket. The larger the basket, the greater the effect and the less often you will need to water.

Gardeners in zones 6 and 7a can still start seeds of warm-season annuals for transplanting outdoors when the danger of frost is past.

The last average frost date is passing in zones 7 to 9, opening the door to move transplants out into the landscape. (See Frost-Freeze Data for Texas Cities on page 214.) Do so gradually over the course of ten to fourteen days. It can still be quite cool at night and a sudden change from the balmy indoors to the windy, chilling landscape beds can shock tender new plants if they are not acclimated. Start by moving them outside during the daytime, then leave them longer into the evening until they are acclimated to the bright sun and chilly nights.

Plant warm-season flower seeds outdoors after the danger of frost has passed in your area. When seedlings come up, thin zinnia, celosia, spider flower, and cosmos to about 6 inches apart. Thin Mexican sunflower (*Tithonia*) and regular sunflower to a foot or more apart.

Set out transplants of warm-season flowers, including nierembergia, wishbone flower (*Torenia*), zinnias, celosia, marigold, tropical sage, Mexican sunflower, cosmos, impatiens, pentas, and lobularia.

Select caladium tubers while there are plenty to choose from in local garden centers. These plants love warm to hot conditions so wait to plant them until the *soil temperature* is at least 70°F. They love a soil enriched with plenty of compost. The strap-leaved types can take more sun than most of the fancy leaf types can tolerate, although

plant breeders are providing new varieties with increased sun resistance.

EDIBLES

March is when vegetable planting season shifts into high gear. The average last frost date is passing in most of the state this month and with it comes the green light to plant frost-sensitive crops, including tomatoes, beans (bush and pole), squash, and cucumber. (See, Spring Planting Guide for Vegetables, page 216, and Frost-Freeze Data for Texas Cities, page 214.) After considering planting schedules and maps it comes down to a little weather predicting and gambling as to when you should plant. Some gardeners plant a little early in a gamble that it won't frost again, and then just replant if it does. You can also count on getting a few degrees of protection with row covers if you want to try your luck at an early planting.

The planting season for cool-season vegetables winds down about two weeks *prior* to the last frost date in your area. A few cool-season crops, including collards, kale, lettuce, radish, and turnips, can still be planted up to the last frost date.

Vegetables grow best in soil that has been amended with compost. Mix 1 or 2 inches of compost into the soil about 6 inches deep to prepare the soil for planting. If you are planting seeds, rake the surface

■ *Be prepared to cover an early planting of tomatoes or other warm-season vegetables if a frost is forecast. A PVC hoop structure provides a support for blankets or plastic sheeting.*

■ *Thin carrots, turnips, radishes, and other root crops, spacing plants out well to ensure they develop good-sized roots.*

well to remove clods and debris and to create a finely textured surface for sowing seeds.

Plant seeds at a depth of about three times their width except for some, such as lettuce, that need light to germinate. The seed packet should specify if seeds are to be barely covered rather than buried. There isn't a rule how to arrange seeds for planting, but most leafy greens, legumes (beans and peas), and root crops are seeded in rows. Squash, melons, and cucumbers are planted in "hills," which are 6- to 12-inch-wide groupings of *seeds*, not raised soil as the term might imply.

Avoid the temptation to plant seeds too thickly. Think about the final spacing and plant just a few more seeds than that as insurance against some seeds not germinating or being destroyed. If you plant seeds too thick the work to thin them later can be overwhelming, and those you leave to grow can be damaged in the process. Space rows according to the mature size of the plant. See the seed packet for row spacing instructions. In general, rows are spaced slightly wider than a plant's mature width.

Once seedlings are up and growing, thin them to their final spacing according to the packet instructions. As a general guide thin root crops to the mature width of the root at harvest. Thin beans and peas to about 2 to 4 inches apart, and thin melons to 3 to 5 per hill.

Some plants, such as tomato, pepper, eggplant, and cole crops (broccoli, cabbage, cauliflower, and kale

are examples) are typically set out as transplants in the spring garden. Transplants give you a head start on the season, which is important here, where summer comes quickly. Unlike gardening in the midsection of the country, here in Texas we have two short mild seasons (spring and fall) with a blazing summer season in between that shuts down most of our spring garden plants. Thus it is important to plant early and to plant varieties that mature quickly, before the heat of summer sets in.

Most other vegetables, except root crops, can be grown as transplants to get a head start on the seasons. Melons, cucumbers, and squash should be started three to four weeks before you will set them out into the garden. Don't leave them much longer in their transplant trays or they will be stunted and will not perform well. Water all transplants with a soluble fertilizer solution at planting.

LAWNS

The weather is now warm enough to lay sod in zones 8 and 9. Prepare the site by removing perennial weeds and debris, filling low spots, and raking the soil smooth to allow good sod-to-soil contact. (See April, Here's How to Establish a Lawn.) If you are planting a lawn from seed wait until next month in all zones except zone 9b to allow the soil time to warm up for better germination of warm-season turfgrass seed.

PERENNIALS & ORNAMENTAL GRASSES

Start seeds of perennials to save money. Seeds are much less expensive than plants and, with some patience, they can be grown to transplant size in two or three months. Start these transplants indoors if your average frost date hasn't passed or outdoors if it has. Keep the seeds moist to help them get a good start. If they dry out before they finish germinating they will not recover.

This is a great month to set out perennial transplants in the landscape. There are a multitude of great perennials for our landscapes, including southern hibiscus (*Hibiscus moscheutos*), coneflower (*Echinacea* spp.), fall aster (*Aster oblongifolius*), Hinkley's columbine (*Aquilegia chrysantha* 'Hinckleyana'), ox-eye daisy (*Chrysanthemum leucanthemum*), cigar plant

■ *Ornamental grasses add fine texture and graceful movement to the landscape. This Gulf muhly also provides color and is especially beautiful with the sun shining through the wispy seedheads.*

(*Cuphea micropetala*), lantana (*Lantana* spp.), yarrow (*Achillea* spp.), gaura (*Gaura lindheimeri*), Mexican mint marigold (*Tagetes lucida*), copper canyon daisy (*Tagetes lemmonii*), perennial phlox (*Phlox paniculata*), plumbago (*Plumbago auriculata*), and many types of salvia. (See June, Super Salvias for Heat-Tolerant Color.)

When planting perennial transplants, prepare the bed by mixing 1 inch of compost into the garden bed soil and then digging the planting hole the same depth as the transplant was growing in its container. Firm the soil around it and water thoroughly with a soluble fertilizer solution to get them off to a fast start.

Transplants of native western and southwestern drought-tolerant perennial plants and subshrubs, including zexmenia (*Wedelia texana*), blackfoot daisy (*Melampodium leucanthum*), gaura (*Gaura lindheimeri*), copper canyon daisy (*Tagetes lemmonii*), four-nerve daisy (*Tetraneuris scaposa*), pink skullcap (*Scutellaria suffrutescens*), and Gregg's sage (*Salvia greggii*), will usually do fine without the added compost, but it still is helpful to loosen the soil with a rototiller or spade to get their roots off to a good start. If drainage is at all questionable for these plants, wait to set them out until you have created a raised planting bed to facilitate good drainage.

Ornamental grasses, both annual and perennial, can be planted outdoors in the landscape this month. Some great options include maiden grass (*Miscanthus* spp.), fountain grass (*Pennisetum setaceum*), ornamental millet (an annual), Gulf muhly (*Muhlenbergia capillaris*), and various other types of muhly, many of which are native to Texas. Set them where the morning or evening sun will shine through the grass in winter for an added attraction. Use them individually as specimen plants or in a row to form a border or backdrop to smaller statured annual and perennial flowers. A good watering with a soluble fertilizer solution will really help get your ornamental grasses established and growing quickly as the temperatures warm up in the coming weeks.

ROSES

Bare-root rose planting season is past except for zone 6, but container-grown roses can be planted anytime. Choose a sunny location for best results with roses; at least six hours of direct sunlight is needed for good bloom production, and even more sun is better. The sooner you establish your roses the greater their chance of surviving and thriving through the hot weather ahead. (See November, Here's How to Plant Container-Grown Shrubs and Trees.)

SHRUBS & TREES

To prepare for planting, mix 3 to 4 inches of compost into the soil in an area as large as the shrub's *mature size*. If space allows, amend soil in an 8- to 10-foot-wide area for trees to give them a good start. Bring in a bed mix to build up a raised planting bed at least 10 inches high if the soil tends to stay soggy for extended periods after a rain. If necessary, do some pruning of nearby trees to allow more light, which most blooming shrubs and trees need, as part of the preplanting preparations. With this planning and preparation your shrubs and trees will be more likely to thrive in their new locations.

Remove the plastic nursery tags at planting to prevent them from strangling young trees and shrubs as they grow. Record the variety names in your gardening journal.

VINES & GROUNDCOVERS

Areas that you prepared for planting can be planted this month in zones 7b to 9. Consider the natural spread of the groundcover, and space the plants accordingly. If you want to economize a bit by purchasing fewer plants, make the spacing about 75 percent of the mature width of the plants. This will mean that it takes longer for the planting to fill in. For faster coverage of an area, plant the groundcovers at 50 percent of their mature width. Finish with a covering of mulch to deter weeds in the bare areas until the plants fill in and block out light from reaching the soil.

CARE

ANNUALS

Deadhead annual flowers that have unsightly spent blooms remaining on the plants. Pinch the tops out of new annuals that were recently planted if they look lanky to encourage branching and more compact growth. Sunflowers are an exception to this advice; most traditional sunflowers have a central stem with a flower on top (as opposed to naturally branching), so pinching would remove this and detract from the plant's potential form and beauty.

EDIBLES

Hill up potatoes by pulling soil up around their stems, leaving just the tops sticking out. Potatoes form on offshoots from the main stem and this will

■ *Deadhead annual flowers, weekly, using your scissors, snips, or hand pruners to snip off dead flowers. Always cut and remove the flower stem at the place where it meets the main plant stem. If you only cut off the flower, you'll have ugly stems hanging around. New growth only sprouts from buds along the main stem.*

■ *Shear back perennial herbs to promote fresh new growth and a tidier form.*

give them some soil in which to form. If you have access to composted leaves or hay you can also use this to hill up the potatoes. That makes digging them later a cleaner, easier process.

Don't mulch new vegetable seedlings and transplants right away as the sun will warm the soil and speed growth of early plantings. You can apply mulch later to smother young weeds. Weeds are also easy to remove with a hoe when they are still very young.

Shear back perennial herbs to remove old growth. That way, new growth will soon fill in to create a more attractive planting, not to mention some tasty new growth for your kitchen cuisine.

Complete fruit trees pruning prior to the spring blooms and emergence of new growth. If you didn't get this done already, and the plants have started to bloom, it is better to go ahead and prune rather

Water Sprouts

Suckers

than leave the trees unpruned. Remove vigorous upright shoots in the interior of the tree (called water sprouts) and vigorous shoots emerging from the lower trunk area (called suckers) by cutting back to the point where they're attached.

If you have a fruit variety that needs a second variety for pollination but you don't have a second variety blooming at the same time, see the February Plan section for a tip on getting by until you can purchase and plant a second variety in your landscape.

Don't harm bees and other pollinating insects with pesticide sprays when the trees are in bloom. You need these pollinating insects to do their work and insecticide sprays can kill them, leaving you with little to no crop of fruit.

After trees have finished blooming and the young fruit start to develop, thin the fruit so they can develop to a good size with high sugar content. Thin plums to 4 inches (apart) and peaches to 6 inches. Thin apples and pears to one fruit per cluster. Citrus and persimmons will drop their excess fruit over time. The earlier you thin between

blooming and the fruit reaching half of its full size, the less it will affect the overall yield and the greater the effect will be on fruit size.

LAWNS

If you have a significant cool-season weed problem or if your lawn was overseeded with a cool-season grass such as rye, mow as needed to keep the weeds short, discourage seed formation, and prevent the weeds or ryegrass from shading the warm-season lawn species as it begins to emerge from winter.

In zone 9b the weather is warm enough to begin mowing warm-season turfgrasses. (See May, Here's How to Select the Best Mowing Height For Your Lawn.)

If your turf has become thin, spread compost over the lawn to about ⅓ to ½ inch deep. Then water the area well and aerate the lawn with a core-type aerator. Follow this with an application of about 1 inch of sprinkler irrigation unless rains arrive to do the job for you. This process should rejuvenate the lawn and prepare it for next month's fertilization as growth really takes off.

■ *Semi-hardy perennials such as* Duranta *that don't fully die back in a mild winter in southern parts of the state can be cut back this month to regrow for an attractive, more compact plant.*

PERENNIALS & ORNAMENTAL GRASSES

Zone 6 gardeners who haven't cut back their ornamental grasses should do so now as new growth is about to emerge with the arrival of some mild weather. Gardeners in zones 6 to 7 can divide summer- and fall-blooming perennial flowering plants and ornamental grasses in early March, preferably before new growth emerges. See February for a list of plants that bloom in summer and in fall, and for instructions on cutting back ornamental grasses.

While it is best to divide perennials in the months opposite their bloom times, it is still okay to divide summer-blooming perennials in zones 8 and 9. Just take care to get them replanted and watered in right away, and they will be fine. (See October, Here's How to Divide Perennials.)

Clean up perennial beds that still have last season's growth. This should be pretty much killed back by cold and can be removed from the plant to leave the fresh new growth to come in, making for a much more attractive planting area. Gardeners in zones 8b to 9 will find that some perennials aren't killed back in some mild winter seasons. It is okay to cut them back anyway and will help keep the planting tidier and the plants more compact if you cut them back to near the ground now. The plants will quickly fill in when warming temperatures coax them into regrowth. Shrimp plant (*Justicia brandegeeana*), yellow bells (*Tecoma stans*), Brazillian skyflower (*Duranta repens*), and firebush (*Hamelia patens*) are

examples of perennials that may not die back in the warmer zones of the state. Cut them back to about a foot high to promote more compact growth.

ROSES

Complete rose pruning in zones 6 to 7a. If you live in zones 7b to 9 and did not prune your roses in the winter, you can still do so now, but don't delay. Across the state, remove any broken, dead, or diseased branches.

SHRUBS

Shear evergreen hedges to promote denser growth. These shrubs tend to grow outward at the top, shading the lower areas of a hedge. The result will be a loss of foliage in the shaded areas. It is difficult to regain lost foliage in these lower areas, so be diligent to keep the tops a little narrower than the base. The result will be an attractive hedge with good density from top to bottom.

Complete any touch-up pruning of your camellias to shape the plants. These plants don't require much pruning so don't feel the need to prune them a lot. Pruning now will allow plenty of time for the plants to regrow and set bloom buds for their upcoming winter and spring bloom season.

Old shrubs that are lacking vigor will benefit from a heavier than normal pruning to reinvigorate the plants. Then use a hand fork to break up the soil about 4 to 6 inches deep in the area beneath their branch spread. You can also use a spading fork to

■ *Keep the tops of hedges a little narrower than the base to allow light to reach all areas of the hedge for optimum foliage cover.*

just crack open the soil to the 4- to 6-inch depth. Scatter an inch of compost on top and water the entire area to soak it deeply. Then top it off with 3 inches of mulch and stand back to watch the shrubs respond with lots of renewed vigor. If the shrubs are in a hedge, be prepared to shear it again in a few weeks to maintain density and to keep the top narrower than the base.

TREES

Complete pruning tasks in zones 6 and 7. Each species' new growth emerges at a different time, but it is best to prune before any new growth begins. Check the guy wires on staked trees planted in the past year to make sure they are not cutting into the trunks and adjust as needed so there is a little slack to allow the trunks to move a bit in the wind.

Clean and oil your pruning tools now that the main pruning season is ending. Sand the handles of wooden tools to smooth them, and then apply some linseed or other oil to repel moisture and keep them in top shape for years of use.

VINES & GROUNDCOVERS

Mulch all newly planted groundcover areas to cover bare soil. Weed seeds germinate and become established wherever sunlight hits the soil, so keep all soil areas around vines and groundcovers that haven't yet filled in covered with a 3-inch layer of mulch.

WATER

ALL

Watering season is coming so now is a good time to get your drip irrigation system ready for summer. Open the end of the lines and run the system to flush out any loose sediment in the lines. Then close the ends and turn the system back on to check for leaks and clogged emitters. Run the system for a while to check for cuts in the drip tubing. Then check emitters to see if they are dripping at a uniform rate. If there are problems, contact your landscape care company to have them fixed or, if you are a do-it-yourself gardener, contact an irrigation supplier to discuss what parts they have for fixing the problems.

■ *Use a mister to water new seedlings to avoid dislodging the seeds with a hard stream of water or coarse droplets.*

■ *Bottom watering occurs by placing water in the tray beneath newly seeded transplants and allowing it to soak up into the growing medium. This is an efficient way to water and avoid splashing the seeds out of the tray with an overhead spray.*

ANNUALS

Water new annual plantings once or twice a week if there's no rain, depending on temperatures in your area this month. Annual plants are slowly sending roots out into the surrounding soil but will have limited root systems; therefore they have limited drought resilience for the first couple of months after planting. New annual seedlings are especially prone to drying out and should be watered twice weekly for the first few weeks.

Water established annuals as needed to keep the roots moist without creating waterlogged soil, which is detrimental to the plants.

EDIBLES

Water new vegetable plantings regularly to keep the soil moist. Established vegetable plants will do with once or twice a week watering unless they are in containers, which require more frequent watering in order to keep the soil (potting mix) moist.

When watering try not to dislodge newly planted seedlings. Use a mist nozzle to water seedlings so you can wet the soil *gently*. Once seedlings are up and growing strong they will be able to withstand gentle watering from a regular spray irrigation wand. Water transplants being grown indoors with either a gentle mist or by bottom watering.

Water established fruit plants if your area is experiencing drought conditions, especially if they are shallow rooted, such as strawberries or blueberries. (See March, Here's How to Irrigate New Shrubs and Trees.)

LAWNS

In the absence of at least ½ inch of rainfall per week, supplement needed moisture by watering lawns in zones 8 and 9. Apply ½- to 1 inch when you water to soak the soil deeply, which encourages deep rooting and a more drought-resilient lawn. (See June, Here's How to Check the Efficiency of Your Lawn Irrigation System.)

PERENNIALS & ORNAMENTAL GRASSES

New perennial transplants will need some supplemental water as was mentioned above for annual flowers.

If your area is experiencing a drought, some supplemental watering of established perennials will be helpful, but since these plants have an established root system, rainfall combined with the low plant water use at this time of the year usually makes watering unnecessary for perennials and ornamental grasses.

ROSES, SHRUBS & TREES

Water established roses and shrubs as needed to maintain a moderately moist soil. Established trees shouldn't require supplemental watering this month. Water newly planted roses, shrubs, and trees with enough water to soak a plant's rootball deeply. (See March, Here's How to Irrigate New Shrubs and Trees.)

Expand the berm you built when the shrub or tree was planted to twice its diameter to better water the plant's expanding root system. Fill the berm around the plant with water once a day for a good soaking.

HERE'S HOW

TO IRRIGATE NEW SHRUBS AND TREES (IN THE ABSENCE OF RAINFALL)

Trunk Diameter	Month the Shrub or Tree was Planted	Amount of Water per Irrigation [1]	Frequency of Irrigation
1 to 2 in.	Nov. to Feb. [2] March to April and Sept. to Oct. May to Aug.	0 to 1 gallon [3] 1 gallon 2 to 3 gallons	Apply daily for two weeks after planting, then every other day for next six weeks, then weekly for the next three months
2 to 4 in.	Nov. to Feb. [2] March to April and Sept. to Oct. May to Aug.	0 to 2 gallons [3] 2 to 3 gallons 5 to 8 gallons	Apply daily for four weeks after planting, then every other day for next two months, then weekly for the next three months
4 to 6 in.	Nov. to Feb. [2] March to April and Sept. to Oct. May to Aug.	0 to 3 gallons [3] 4 to 6 gallons 10 to 15 gallons	Apply daily for six weeks after planting, then every other day for next three months, then weekly for the next three months

1. Irrigation amounts are applied to soak the plant's rootball and just beyond into surrounding soil.
2. Assuming the plant is deciduous. For evergreens, in the absence of rainfall, increase to March–April rate.
3. Check soil moisture a few inches deep in the rootball before watering and skip watering if soil in the rootball is still wet.

(See February, Here's How to Plant Container-Grown Shrubs and Trees.) If these woody ornamental plants were planted last fall, then water them every two or three days if it hasn't rained at least an inch.

If you are doing any late pruning of oaks in areas where oak wilt is present, take care to treat wounds *immediately* after making a cut to prevent the spread of this disease by small bark beetles.

VINES & GROUNDCOVERS

Water established groundcovers only if it hasn't rained for a month or more. New groundcover plantings will benefit from weekly watering in the absence of rain. Avoid excessive watering as soggy wet soil conditions exclude oxygen from roots, which can be detrimental to plants.

FERTILIZE

ANNUALS

Use a soluble fertilizer solution weekly for the first four to six weeks to give new plantings of annual flowers a nutrient boost as they are establishing roots and increasing their foliage, which is needed to produce carbohydrates that support more rapid growth.

Give established annuals a monthly boost by sprinkling a cup of complete fertilizer per 25 square feet of planting bed and mixing it into the surface inch of soil. Then water it well to start to dissolve the product and release the nutrients to the plants' roots.

EDIBLES

Fertilize new transplants by watering them with a soluble plant food at planting and once a week for two or three more applications.

Fertilize established vegetable and herb plants at a moderate rate starting a few weeks after planting. (See April, Here's How to Fertilize Flowers, Ornamental Grasses, and Vegetables.) Use a turf-type fertilizer with a 3-1-2 or 4-1-2 nutrient ratio. Work the fertilizer gently into the surface inch of soil and then water the area well to activate

■ *Water new transplants with a fish-emulsion-and-seaweed solution or a soluble fertilizer to provide a boost to get them off to a fast start.*

taken up by cool-season weeds that are actively growing now.

Gardeners in zone 9 can make their first fertilizer application late this month after the lawn has grown enough to be mowed twice. (See April, Here's How to Fertilize a Lawn.)

PERENNIALS & ORNAMENTAL GRASSES

Fertilize new perennials as described for annuals. Established perennials don't need fertilizer yet as they are still coming out of their winter rest; they have plenty of nutrients stored in the plant as well as in the soil to support their slow early growth.

Fertilize irises, including bearded and Louisiana types, with a light feeding late this month to support their production of spring blooms and overall good vigor.

ROSES

Pull back the mulch and fertilize with a 3-1-2 (or similar) nutrient ratio to support a strong spring growth of roses. Scatter 3 tablespoons throughout a 1-foot-diameter circle around roses planted since last fall. For older, established bushes apply ⅓ cup per bush scattered beneath its branch spread. If you applied decomposed manure or other fertilizer in January or February you can reduce this application by half.

Scratch the surface of the soil 1 inch deep with a hoe or cultivator tool and water the area well. Then pull the mulch back over the soil surface around the roses.

SHRUBS

Young shrubs that haven't reached their mature size and shrubs in hedges will benefit from a fertilizer boost every six to eight weeks during the growing season. Purchase a turf-type fertilizer with a 3-1-2 or similar nutrient ratio. Sprinkle ⅓ cup (synthetic) or ⅔ cup (organic) fertilizer evenly throughout a 6-foot-diameter area. Use a soil rake to "scratch" it into the soil's surface, and water the area well to start to release the nutrients to the plant's root system.

Late-blooming camellias have completed their bloom cycle. Now is the time to give all camellias

the process of releasing nutrients to the growing plants. Don't fertilize beans and peas as they produce ("fix") their own nitrogen on the plant's roots and excessive fertilizing can promote growth at the expense of bean or pea production.

Fertilize established fruit trees using a turf product with a 3-1-2 nutrient ratio. Apply 2 cups per inch of trunk diameter evenly within the branch spread of the tree. Cultivate it into the surface 2 inches of soil or rake it under the mulch layer and then sprinkle the area with ½ inch of water. If you live in eastern Texas, which has acidic sandy soils, add 1 cup of potassium magnesium sulfate per inch of trunk diameter to this fertilization. (See March, Here's How to Fertilize a Young Tree.)

LAWNS

Wait until you have mowed the turf twice (mowing weeds doesn't count) before applying fertilizer. Our southern turf species do not begin active growth until the weather warms up in the spring, which is sometime next month in zones 6, 7, and 8. Your lawn is not able to use the nutrients fully and some fertilizer will be washed away in spring rains or

MARCH

TO FERTILIZE A YOUNG TREE

Fertilize young trees for their first five to ten years to get them off to a fast start.

1. Choose a product with a low phosphorus content (the middle number) such as a 4-1-2, 3-1-2, or 1-0-1.

2. Measure the trunk diameter about waist high or a few inches below the first branch. For a quick, easy way to estimate the trunk diameter, know that your thumb is about an inch wide.

3. Apply 1 to 2 cups of fertilizer per inch of trunk diameter (double this rate if the nitrogen content is below 12 percent).

4. Spread the fertilizer evenly throughout an area one and a half times the tree's branch spread. (If the area is mulched, first pull back the mulch, then fertilize and place the mulch back over the area.)

5. Water the fertilizer well with ½ to 1 inch of water to release nutrients into the root zone.

a fertilizer boost. Choose a product labeled for acid-loving plants. Options include synthetic blends and organic products such as cottonseed meal and blood meal.

Finish this off with a fresh layer of pine needles, leaves, or composted bark on top of the existing mulch to prepare the roots for summer.

TREES

Fertilize young established trees when their new growth begins to emerge in your area. (See March, Here's How to Fertilize a Young Tree, above.)

Established trees more than fifteen years old that have begun to fill in and are growing well don't generally need supplemental fertilizing. The fertilizer applied to lawns around them is usually sufficient to support their growth due to their extensive root system. Mature trees should not be fertilized, as they have reached the size that soil and climate conditions can support, so pushing it to achieve additional growth is not advised.

VINES & GROUNDCOVERS

Sprinkle two cups of fertilizer per 50 square feet of groundcover bed area. Water the area lightly to wash fertilizer off the foliage and begin to dissolve it, which will release the nutrients into the soil.

ANNUALS, PERENNIALS & ORNAMENTAL GRASSES

Check for aphids and caterpillars on annuals. These pests can damage plants before you realize they are present, so some periodic checking for them will help you detect them early when they are young and most easy to control. See Edibles for suggestions to control these pests.

Plants that are wilting even though the soil is moist may have pests feeding on their roots. Dig up a plant that is declining and examine the roots for wireworms or other pests. Also check for root rotting. If the top of the plant is green, but the roots are turning from a healthy creamy color to brown or a water-soaked black to brown color, root rot is the likely cause. These can be controlled with fungicidal drenches, but in most cases they are brought on by excessive water and poor drainage. Fix these problems and the diseases will not usually cause further damage. If you're in doubt, take a sample plant that is still alive but showing the symptoms to your County Extension Office for diagnostic assistance and pest or disease control suggestions.

Clumps of ornamental grasses that are growing on their periphery but appear dead in the center of the

caterpillar damage. Treat with a product containing *Bacillus thuringiensis (B.t.)* promptly while the pests are still young and most easily controlled. Also check for aphids on cool-season vegetables. Spraying insecticidal soap is a less toxic option.

When working the soil watch for grubs and other insects (such as wireworms) that feed on plant roots. Pick them out and destroy them. If you are fortunate enough to have backyard chickens you can make their day by tossing pests into their pen.

Avoid spraying fruit trees when they're in full bloom or you risk killing the bees and other insects that pollinate the blooms. If an insecticide spray is needed for curculio on plums or peaches, wait until more than three-fourths of the tree's petals have fallen to make that first application. If you see patches of scale insects, after the blooms are gone spray these patches with a horticultural oil spray taking care to completely coat all scale infestations with the spray. Oil kills the insects by smothering them rather than poisoning them.

LAWNS

Cool-season weeds, including clover, henbit, and chickweed, are growing rapidly as the weather

■ *The initial damage caused by young caterpillars often appears as a skeletonizing of the leaf or a lace-like appearance. As they get older they will be able to eat away more of the leaf tissues.*

clump may need dividing. Such loss of the interior is not unusual as these clumping grasses get older. It is okay to dig and divide them now. Discard the dead or weak interior section and replant the healthier exterior divisions right away so they don't dry out. Water the newly set divisions after planting.

EDIBLES

Transplants and new seedlings that are cut off above the ground are a sign of cutworms. Wrap a 2-inch strip of newspaper around the stem several times and cover the bottom ½ inch with soil to deter these pests until your plants are large enough to not be damaged.

Check cabbage, kale, broccoli, and other cole crops in zone 9 for holes in their foliage, a sign of

■ *An easy and chemical-free way to protect plants against cut-worm damage is to place cardboard collars around plants when transplanting them to the garden.*

warms. Most are starting to flower and will soon be setting seed. They are less susceptible to post-emergence controls at this stage of their development. The best options for managing them at this point are hand-pulling or mowing with a grass catcher to catch the weeds and seeds and remove them from the lawn areas.

Warm-season weeds are sprouting in zones 6 and 7 this month. See February for more information about choosing and using a pre-emergence weed control product. In zones 8 and 9, where these weeds are actively growing, you can either mow and ignore them as you focus on building turfgrass density to choke out weed problems over time, or treat with an appropriate post-emergence weed control product. Your County Extension Office can help identify weed species and recommend the appropriate products and application timing. Many of these products can stress or damage St. Augustine and other grasses if they're applied when temperatures are above the mid-80s.

Large, brown circular areas in St. Augustine lawns is a symptom of large patch (brown patch) damage. Once you see them it is too late to treat with a fungicide. This disease only rots the grass blades off of the runners; it doesn't kill the grass. As the weather warms the disease ceases to infect the turf. Any brown areas will green again with new grass blades.

ROSES

If your rose variety is prone to disease problems, such as blackspot and powdery mildew, spray the plants every seven to ten days with a fungicide labeled for roses to protect their foliage, which is needed for good bloom production.

■ *Entomosporium leaf spot on Indian hawthorn and red-tip photinia is favored by wet conditions. Preventative sprays can help minimize damage from this disease.*

SHRUBS

Azalea leaf gall appears as distorted leaf and bud growth over the next month or two. Affected parts later become covered with a whitish mold. If your azaleas have had this problem in the past a protective spray with a labeled fungicide, applied just before flower buds open and at ten-day intervals until flowering ceases, can help prevent the disease. Not all varieties are equally susceptible so consider this when choosing an azalea for your landscape.

Fireblight bacteria cause the ends of new shoots of pyracantha, cotoneaster, loquat, and ornamental pear trees to turn brown and black and bend over like a shepherd's crook. High nitrogen levels and cool, wet weather during the time when susceptible plants are putting on new growth favors this disease. Prune infected areas out. (See February, Care, Shrubs.) Varieties often differ in susceptibility to fireblight.

Entomosporium leaf spot attacks Indian hawthorn, red-tip photinia, and a few less common plants. The disease causes a proliferation of gray to reddish purple spots that can result in defoliation of an entire plant. Rake and discard any fallen foliage and pull infected leaves of plants to reduce reinfection. Avoid overhead watering to keep foliage dry. Sprays only are effective if they're applied as a preventative measure, prior to the spots appearing.

TREES

Cool, rainy weather during the time when leaves are emerging on ash and oak trees can result in some fungal diseases. Ash trees are prone to anthracnose, which causes brown to blackened areas followed by a partial leaf drop. Oaks are affected by oak leaf blister, which causes distorted bumps and depressions on the leaves, and later turn brown. Neither disease is cause for concern or a reason to spray. By the time you see the symptoms it is too late to prevent the damage anyway.

Cankerworms begin hatching in several species of shade trees, including oaks and elms, this month in zones 7b to 9, about the time trees are pushing out their first set of leaves. These inchworms are reddish brown with dull yellow stripes down their bodies. Most years they don't do enough damage to warrant spraying, but in some years they can defoliate trees. Sprays of *Bacillus thuringiensis (B.t.)* on the tree's foliage can help prevent severe defoliation if you make the application early in the infestation. Once the pests have eaten most of the leaves it is too late for a spray to be helpful.

Dense silken webs around the crotches of oak, cherry, plum, peach, apple, and a variety of other tree species are the work of tent caterpillars. The larvae venture out to feed on foliage and retreat to the protection of the webs. Sprays containing *Bacillus thuringiensis (B.t.)* are among the least toxic and most targeted toward cankerworms, tent caterpillars, and other caterpillar pests. These sprays can be effective if applied early in the outbreak of the pests.

Old leaves on southern magnolia, gardenia, abelia, live oak, banana shrub (*Michelia figo*), and some other broadleaf evergreen trees and shrubs naturally will turn yellow and drop during the early to mid-spring season. This is no cause for alarm but is simply a natural occurrence as new foliage emerges and the plants cast off older leaves. Stress can increase the amount of leaf drop, but no action is needed other than watering to alleviate drought stress.

VINES & GROUNDCOVERS

Groundcovers that look ragged due to damage from diseases, pests, nutrient deficiencies, drought, or cold damage can be rejuvenated by shearing them back to the ground with a string trimmer or mower set on the lowest setting. This is best done earlier in the year prior to the onset of new growth, but it can still be done if the plants look bad in order to remove old growth. With the warming weather the plants will respond with fresh, new growth to restore an attractive appearance once again.

April

Frosts are now a thing of the past in all but zone 6, and our plants are growing rapidly in the mild temperatures and April showers of mid-spring. Gardeners are busy planting warm-season vegetables and flowers while harvesting the bounty of the garden. Wildflowers paint meadows and roadsides as parents plop their kids down in patches of bluebonnets for the annual photographic ritual.

The weather is mild, making working in the garden such a pleasant activity. Take advantage of the mild temperatures now to reduce work later when things heat up for summer. Mulch your flowers, vegetables, and woody ornamentals to eliminate most of your weeding chores for later and to get longer-lasting benefits from the water you apply during the upcoming months.

If you haven't begun a garden journal and notebook this is a great time to start one. Your journal tracks your activities while your gardening notebook is a collection of pages on various topics for later reference. It could include newspaper and magazine articles about a new plant or gardening practice, notes and handouts from a lecture at the botanical garden, free publications from your County Extension Office, and even photos of plants, pests, and designs taken in your landscape or others that you visited. A well-organized notebook is a wealth of inspiration and gardening knowledge that will grow into a prized gardening resource. (See January, Here's How to Keep Track of Your Gardening Activities.)

Out in the landscape hedges need to be sheared to maintain density while individual shrubs can use a snipping here and there to keep their natural shape. It's time to thin the crop on fruit trees. The flower garden is bursting with color and with some deadheading and fertilizing will continue to look great. Our southern lawns have been awakened from their cool-season slumber and are asking for a little extra nutrition.

April is indeed a busy time in our gardens and landscapes.

PLAN

ALL

Gardens and landscapes are growing rapidly now that the weather has warmed up. Make sure to keep records of what you plant, when you planted it, how it performs, pests and disease problems, and other observations in your garden journal. Take photos with your digital camera or smartphone to record these things also. This will become a valuable resource as you build it over the years. Keep it handy so you'll take it with you on trips out to the garden. A mailbox placed out in the garden is a great place to hold gloves, hand tools, and a paper journal for easy access when you are gardening.

Visit a local botanical garden and participate in some local garden tours. Take your camera and gardening notebook or journal to make notes of some "must have" plants for your home place. Texas has many wonderful botanical gardens and arboreta including Mercer in Houston, Zilker in Austin, the Lady Bird Johnson Wildflower Center in Austin, Mast Arboretum in Nacogdoches, San Antonio Botanical Garden, Fort Worth Botanical Garden, and Dallas Botanical Garden.

Many types of flowers and vegetables are beginning to set seeds, including poppies, some types of petunias, and cool-season vegetables that "bolt," or send up a bloom stalk, in spring. Consider saving some of your own seeds this year. Keep in mind

■ *Save seeds of your favorite nonhybrid flowers and vegetables. Store them in an airtight jar in the refrigerator or freezer for longer viability.*

that hybrid plants will not produce seeds that are of the same type as the parent plant, but open-pollinated species and varieties will. Allow seeds to dry and then package them in envelopes such as the small coin envelopes or ones you make yourself from folded paper. Label the envelopes with the plant species and variety name and the date collected. Place these envelopes in a sealed jar and put it in the refrigerator or freezer for maximum storage life.

ANNUALS

Containers provide versatile color for the landscape. You can move them around to get the right effect and replace plants or entire containers when they start to look less appealing. Read some magazines, books, and websites to find the plants and combinations that appeal to you and plan to purchase both plants and containers soon so you can create your own combos.

In addition to plants for the containers, consider the container too. There are a number of great choices from terra cotta to plastic to stone to glazed pottery. Some plastics now have the look of stone or pottery but at a fraction of the weight or cost. When planning color combinations, consider the color of the container. A blue, glazed, upright container planted with yellow or orange flowers, such as narrow-leaf zinnia (*Zinnia angustifolia*), spilling over the sides is a beautiful thing.

Annual color can be tucked in to many places. Why not expand a shrub bed with a row of colorful annuals to provide a base to the hedge? Step back and look over your landscape for places where a little extra color would be nice. Just make sure you are able to get water to the area or your beautiful flowers won't reach their full potential.

Annuals are the fastest way to get a load of color in the landscape. Just be careful not to plant more than you can take care of and be ready to replace them as the seasons change and a particular species starts to lose its pizzazz. (See March, Here's How to Plan Color Changes for Annual Beds.)

EDIBLES

If you have a drip irrigation system now is the time to evaluate it and make sure it is working well.

Turn it on and check the lines for leaks. Make sure all drippers are flowing at a uniform rate. Make any needed adjustments so that when temperatures really heat up next month your system will be able to keep your vegetable plants well hydrated.

Bare-root planting season is long past, but there is still time to add some container-grown fruit trees, vines, or bushes to your landscape. You don't need to have a backyard orchard to grow fruit; these plants perform well in various landscape settings. Peaches, plums, apples, and pears are among the beautiful spring bloomers. Persimmons are quite ornamental as they hang on the tree after the leaves drop in the fall. The blooms of citrus trees and bushes have a heavenly scent and the plants are evergreens. Satsumas, Meyer lemons, limes, and kumquats also work well in large containers. So make plans to plant some container-grown fruit plants this month to give them some time to establish before the heat of summer arrives.

■ *Use small cans to measure the amount of water your sprinkler provides in a set amount of time.*

■ *Container plantings and groupings of containers can add instant pizzazz to a landscape area. Consider the many attractive container options, including stone, pottery, and lightweight molded plastic that looks like pottery, when planning your landscape.*

LAWNS

Hot weather isn't far away, so now is a great time to evaluate your sprinkler system for efficiency. Place straight-sided cans such as tuna or cat food cans around the lawn and run your sprinklers for 20 minutes. Measure the water in each can to compare the rate of application. Multiply the depth in the cans by three to find out the number of inches per hour your sprinkler system applies. If the amounts vary greatly it would be wise to contact an irrigation company to work on the system to make it more uniform and avoid wasting water.

If the sprinkler system is inefficient, or if you would like to install an automatic sprinkler system and stop dragging hoses all summer, now is a good time to have a professional irrigation company complete the task. The next five months are when Texans do more than three-fourths of our annual lawn watering, so act now to get the most out of a new or newly renovated irrigation system.

PERENNIALS & ORNAMENTAL GRASSES

Perennials have their moment in the sun. Therefore it is important to plan a succession of them in the landscape so as one is exiting stage right, another can take its place in the spotlight. Do your homework and create a landscape with a nonstop display of perennial color from spring to late fall.

The fine texture of ornamental grasses is one of their key features. Some offer variegated or

GREAT ANNUAL AND PERENNIAL FLOWERING VINES

The following annual and perennial vines will get you off to a great start in choosing a vine for your arbor or trellis. The tropical vines listed are grown as annuals in most of the states or they can be placed in large containers and brought into a protected location to overwinter as perennials.

Annual Vines—from seed

Black-eyed Susan vine (*Thunbergia alata*)

Butterfly pea or blue pea vine (*Clitoria ternatea*)

Cardinal climber (*Ipomoea sloteri*; *Ipomoea* x *multifida*)

Cypress vine or hummingbird vine (*Ipomoea quamoclit*)

Hyacinth bean (*Lablab purpureus*)

Moonflower (*Ipomoea alba*)

Morning glory (*Ipomoea pupurea*)

Scarlet runner bean (*Phaseolus coccineus*)

Spanish flag (*Mina lobata*)

Sweet pea (*Lathyrus odoratus*)

Tropical Vines—from transplants

Allamanda or golden trumpet (*Allamanda cathartica*)—twining

Mandevilla (*Mandevilla* spp.)—twining

Perennial Vines—from transplants

Blue sky vine (*Thunbergia grandiflora*); perennial in zones 8 to 9 (also from seed)

Dutchman's pipe (*Aristolochia* spp.); perennial in zones 8 to 9

Queen's wreath, Rosa de Montana, or coral vine (*Antigonon leptopus*)—tendrils; perennial in zones 8 to 9

Mexican flame vine (*Pseudogynoxys chenopodioides*)—twining; perennial in zones 8b to 9

Passionflower (*Passiflora* spp.)—tendrils; perennial in zones 8 to 9

Pink trumpet vine (*Podranea ricasoliana*)—nonclimbing; perennial in zones 8b to 9

Rangoon creeper (*Quisqualis indica*)—perennial in zones 8b to 9

Snail vine or corkscrew vine (*Vigna caracalla*)—tendrils; perennial in zones 8b to 9 (also from seed)

burgundy-colored leaves, adding an attention-grabbing element to a perennial border. Another feature ornamental grasses bring is movement in the landscape. They sway in the breezes, drawing attention to a planting. Most landscapes could use more ornamental grasses and would benefit from the aesthetic uniqueness they offer.

ROSES

Roses are in their peak spring bloom across most of the state this month. This is a great time to "window shop" in area landscapes and botanic gardens. When you see a rose you like, ask for the variety name and make a note for the next time you are out shopping for plants. EarthKind roses are recommended by the Texas AgriLife Extension Service for being "Texas tough" and survive without sprays and only minimal applications of fertilizer and water.

SHRUBS & TREES

Another windowshop opportunity arises as you drive around the area noting which spring-blooming shrubs and trees would be perfect for your landscape. For some ideas to get you started see May, Small- to Medium-Sized Flowering Trees.

VINES & GROUNDCOVERS

Summer heat is not far away so now is a great time to plant vines to shade an outdoor sitting area to make it a more pleasant place to be on a summer day or to shade a western wall to save on cooling costs. Consider a wall of vines on the west side of a patio or deck to provide a break from the late-day sun. An arbor is a great way to create an outdoor roof for shading an area, often offering flowers and fragrance as well as shade. When building an arbor remember that the larger and taller the arbor, the larger the beams and timbers should be to create a proportionate visual effect.

PLANT

ANNUALS

This is the big month for establishing most of the annual warm-season color across the state. The weather has warmed but is still mild. Rainfall is fairly dependable in most areas. Annual flowering plants are ready to hit the ground running. Give them a boost of soluble fertilizer at planting and stand back to watch them grow.

Some great color plants include begonia, petunia, zinnia, verbena, cockscomb, blue daze (*Evolvulus*), bachelor buttons (*Gomphrena*), cleome, tropical sage (*Salvia coccinea*), nicotiana, Mexican sunflower (*Tithonia*), pentas, purslane, portulaca, Madagascar periwinkle, and cosmos.

If you purchase plants that have been in a container for a while their roots may be packed around the sides of the container. Wet the rootball and gently loosen it with your fingers prior to planting to help the plants establish better. Beds that have not thrived in the past may need some

■ *Cut flowers such as these sunflowers are a great way to bring the garden indoors to beautify your home.*

soil amending. Sandy soils need compost to hold moisture and nutrients better. Clay soils need compost to create better internal structure for better drainage.

Have you ever grown flowers for cutting? That can be fun and provide indoor beauty too. This month is a great time to plant many types of flowers for cutting, including zinnias, sunflowers, coneflowers, various salvias, cosmos, and also flowering shrubs such as roses and hydrangeas.

If your soil is not well prepared with an inch or two of compost mixed in, then wait to plant until you have the bed ready. You'll be glad you did. If it will take a while and you already have plants, move them up into larger containers to keep them growing until their bed is ready for planting. Fertilize these plants "on hold" and they will respond with good growth so the delay is not a big setback.

EDIBLES

Warming temperatures mean that gardeners in zones 6 to 7 are into full swing planting seeds and transplants of warm-season crops out in the garden.

Gardeners in zones 8 to 9 need to get tomatoes planted soon if they hope to have a harvest before hot weather causes them to stop setting fruit.

■ *Mix a few inches of compost into the soil prior to planting to improve internal drainage of clay soil and moisture-holding capacity of sandy soil.*

Heat-loving vegetables such as okra, southern peas, and sweet potatoes are finally interested in growing now that the chilly nights of early spring are past. The Spring Vegetable Planting Guide on page 216 will help gardeners in all zones schedule their vegetable planting.

As the temperatures get warm it is time to plant melons of various types, including muskmelons (cantaloupes) and watermelons. If you have not grown these before due to space limitations, consider growing them on a trellis. Choose a sturdy trellis material and train the vines up onto the trellis. When the fruits reach about the size of a tennis ball, use old hosiery, onion sacks, or sections of old t-shirts to make slings to support the fruit. This support will prevent the fruit from pulling the vine off of the trellis or, in the case of muskmelons, from falling from the vine as it gets larger and nears harvest stage. If you are going to trellis watermelons, select small-fruited varieties for easier supporting.

■ *Slip a section of hosiery over the young fruit of muskmelons and cantaloupes and tie it to the trellis support to save garden space.*

You can grow a lot of vining vegetables in a small space using trellises. Even container-grown vegetables can be trellised. Set a container, at least 5 gallons in size, next to a fence or lattice and plant cucumbers in it. The vines will cover the trellis and can easily be removed after harvest for the next planting in the container. Don't let lack of space stop you from growing tasty vegetables.

Plant perennial herbs, including rosemary, thyme, oregano, summer savory, and Mexican mint marigold, into soil with high organic matter content. If you haven't amended the soil in the past 6 months, work an inch or two of compost into the soil prior to planting. Basil, dill, fennel, and other herbs grown as annuals will also grow well in the warmer temperatures of April. Choose more than one kind of basil to add variety to your cuisine. Herbs love sun so make sure to plant them in a location that receives at least 6 hours of sun a day. They also want good drainage, so if the area is low or drains poorly, build up a raised planting bed.

LAWNS

The weather has warmed up nicely and frosts are a thing of the past in all but zone 6 as we move into April. This is a good time to seed or sod a new lawn area or fill in bare areas. Sod is more expensive than seed but establishes faster and results in fewer weed problems during establishment than can occur when starting seeds in a bare soil area. Also, the best varieties of turf in each species are only available by sod.

Before purchasing your turf, look over the Characteristics of Turfgrass Species for Texas Lawns box in May to help you select the turf species that best suits your site conditions and landscape goals. Prepare the site well before planting by eradicating perennial weeds, filling low areas, and removing debris. Water to wet the soil a few days prior to planting. Lay the sod blocks, leaving no bare soil space for weeds to get a foothold, and then water the sodded turf area well. See Here's How to Establish a Lawn this month for photos of the process.

■ *Rather than plant a lawn across your entire property consider limiting turfgrass to areas where you'll get the most benefit from it and where it is easiest to maintain. This can save on mowing and watering chores.*

HERE'S HOW

TO ESTABLISH A LAWN

1. Rake the area to clear away debris. Fill any holes to level the soil somewhat.

2. Lay the sod pieces, staggering alternate rows (in a pattern like a brick wall).

3. Press the sod pieces into contact with the soil.

4. Water the area well to soak the sod and the underlying soil.

5. Water daily for a week, then every other day for another week, then two or three times per week depending on temperature and sun exposure for the remainder of the first month.

6. Fertilize the sod and begin once- to twice-a-week irrigation, depending on sun exposure and air temperatures.

PERENNIALS & ORNAMENTAL GRASSES

As with annuals, most perennial flowers and ornamental grasses do best in a bed with some compost mixed in or in a bed built with a professional bed mix. This is an outstanding time of the year to plant perennials, and the newly established plants will respond with fast growth. Make sure and choose plants that are adapted to the planting site (wet, dry, sun, shade, and so forth) and to your part of the state. Just because it is for sale in your area doesn't mean it will thrive in your area.

Among the many great perennials for our state are several species of penstemon. If you live in the eastern half of the state consider planting Gulf Coast (or Brazos) penstemon (*Penstemon tenuis*) or wild foxglove (*Penstemon cobaea*). If you live in central or western areas try rock penstemon (*Penstemon baccharifolius*), Hill Country penstemon (*Penstemon triflorus*), or Gulf Coast (or Brazos) penstemon if you can amend the soil a bit to make it more at home.

Space plants according to their mature size and consider the size of plants around them. In

■ *Brazos penstemon is one of many outstanding perennial choices that can take the heat and still look great in the garden.*

most of the state, the stress on plants increases and your chances of success decrease as we approach summer.

That is why it's important to build a raised berm of soil around the new plants after planting to aid in providing deep soakings when you water. Wait to fertilize new plants until they have been growing for four to six weeks.

VINES & GROUNDCOVERS

Plant groundcovers and cold-sensitive vines in zones 6 to 9 this month. If you haven't already mixed compost into the soil or if the bed area wasn't built up using a bed mix then mix a few inches of compost into the soil prior to planting, except for drought-tolerant species native to the central to western parts of the state (which don't need highly amended soil).

Water the plants well with a good, deep soaking after planting. Add mulch to finish the planting process. When planting vines to fill a fence or trellis note the plant's mature size and then plant about half of that distance apart so they will quickly fill the area and provide a wall of foliage to screen a view or cover a wall.

Plant annual and perennial vines now that the weather is warming a bit and they can start to grow soon after planting. See the list of Annual and Perennial Vines this month. Most of these species prefer warm temperatures and won't grow if the soil or air temperatures are cool, so zone 6 gardeners may need to wait until next month for best performance.

general a spacing of 75 percent of a plant's mature width is about right. If a species is somewhat prone to fungal diseases it most likely won't appreciate being crowded and will be more susceptible to diseases under such conditions, so give it a little more room.

Set the plants into the bed in their containers and look over the planting. Then adjust the spacing or layout and proceed with planting. This will prevent you from having too many or not enough plants on hand to finish planting a bed area.

ROSES, SHRUBS & TREES

If you want to add any roses, shrubs, trees, or other woody ornamental plants to your landscape, the sooner you can get them planted, the better. The weather is still mild, but summer is coming with its scorching heat. Although you can plant container-grown plants any month of the year in

CARE

ALL

Mid-spring is a great time to propagate plants from cuttings or air layering. Read up on the various techniques of plant propagation and try your hand at this fun activity. For early success, start with easy-to-root plants such as coleus and rosemary. For help learning how to propagate plants, see September, Here's How to Root Cuttings and Here's How to Air Layer a Plant.

■ *Lay newspaper four to six sheets thick, wet with a hose, and cover with mulch to smother weeds and deter weed seeds from establishing for several months.*

Newspaper is an effective way to prevent or even control young weeds in flower, vegetable, herb, and woody ornamental beds. Spread newspaper, four to six sheets thick at a time, and overlap sections by about 2 inches. Wet the paper as you lay it to cause it to stay down. Put some leaves or other mulch on top to hide the paper and to prevent it from blowing away as it dries. This technique will control annual weeds and provide several months of prevention, until the newspaper and mulch start to break down and allow light to reach the soil surface.

ANNUALS

Tidy up your annual planting beds. Remove spent flowers, shear back excessive growth, or pinch back lanky growth. Then apply fertilizer as directed in the following Fertilize section, and water it in well. Replenish mulch in any bed areas where it is getting thin. Hot weather is on the way but it's not here just yet, so this trimming and fertilizing will rejuvenate the plants and extend their flowering life.

EDIBLES

Hill up potatoes one more time early in April to provide space for the tubers to grow. When you harvest broccoli don't pull up the plants because they will continue to produce enough smaller side shoots that they are worth keeping around for

another month. When other crops that don't keep on producing, such as cauliflower and cabbage, have been harvested, pull the plants and put them in the compost bin to "recycle" their nutrients. The old plants can just harbor pests, and it is best to get them out of the garden and put them to good use.

Allow a few cool-season vegetable plants to remain after you harvest the main crop. These plants will eventually bolt (send up bloom stalks), which will attract beneficial insects of various types that can help you manage the pests in your garden. Carrots, spinach, cilantro, and beets are examples of vegetable plants whose blooms attract beneficial insects.

Shear back herbs that are getting lanky to promote compact growth. Trim off discolored leaves from the shearings and then dry them to store in containers for later use or to share with friends.

Check fruit trees for water sprouts and suckers that are just starting to take off and grow rapidly. Remove them promptly so the tree can put energy into its more productive branches. A proliferation of water sprouts can be a sign of excessive pruning and fertilizing.

Thin fruit to 4 inches for plums, 6 inches for peaches, and one fruit per cluster for apples and pears. Citrus and persimmons thin themselves over time. Thinning properly results in large tasty fruit without reducing overall yield.

LAWNS

In most areas of the state this month is the middle of the transition period when overseeded grass gives way to the emerging turfgrass. Keep the lawn mowed at a moderately short height to prevent the overseeded grass or cool-season weeds from competing with your lawn grass. Cool-season weeds are going to seed now so if you have weeds in the turf, bag the clippings from the first two mowings of the season and discard them in a compost pile. The nitrogen in these green materials will help jumpstart your compost pile or bin, causing it to heat up and destroy any viable seeds.

PERENNIALS & ORNAMENTAL GRASSES

Remove spent blooms on spring-blooming perennials to keep the plants looking their best. As Louisiana irises complete their bloom cycle cut their bloom stalks back to where they emerge from the foliage to prevent the plant's energy going into seed production.

Shear back perennial plants that are getting leggy by about a third to encourage more compact growth. Shear chrysanthemums and fall asters back to about 10 inches tall to promote bushiness and more prolific fall blooming. Stake perennials with tall bloom stalks to prevent them from falling over; examples include gladiolus, summer phlox, and various types of iris.

If you have summer- and fall-blooming perennial flowers that don't bloom like they used to, they may benefit from being divided and reset. Get the job done ASAP since with the heat of summer around the corner, this is really the last call for digging, moving, and dividing perennials until the fall. This is a good time to divide chrysanthemums to expand the planting or share with friends.

This is a good time to take cuttings from plants you wish to root to make additional plants. Do some reading on how to root cuttings, noting whether a species is best rooted from tender growth or "semi-hardwood" cuttings. Dip the cuttings into a rooting hormone to aid their root development, and place them in a moist rooting medium and beneath a clear cover to allow light in—but *not* in an area of direct sunlight. (See September, Here's How to Root Cuttings.)

ROSES

Remove spent blooms on repeat-blooming roses to tidy up the plant and encourage more growth and repeat blooms. Cut bloom shoots back to the first leaf with five leaflets. In zone 9 prune roses that only bloom in the spring after their blooms fade. This will allow them plenty of time to regrow and set bloom buds in late summer to early fall for next year's blooms.

SHRUBS

Prune spring-blooming shrubs such as camellias, bridal wreath (*Spirea*), flowering quince, mock orange (*Philadelphus*), Chinese witchhazel (*Loropetalum*), viburnums, and most azaleas after they have completed their blooming season. This allows the plants plenty of time to regrow and set their bloom buds in late summer to early fall for next year's bloom show. Prune back any long, gangly shoots to the point where they attach to another branch. This helps maintain a neat, natural shape.

As shrubs get older or too large some rejuvenating pruning is in order. See the comments in February about rejuvenating older multi-stemmed shrubs by removing 20 percent of the oldest stems back to where they emerge from the ground.

TREES

Spring-blooming trees, including dogwood, redbud, fringe tree, and deciduous magnolias, can be pruned after their bloom show is done. These trees generally don't need much if any pruning, so just remove any broken or damaged branches and any shoots growing out of the general bounds of the desired shape of the plant. When removing branches, cut them back to where they join another branch or the trunk.

VINES & GROUNDCOVERS

Trim the edges of vining groundcover plantings to maintain a tidy shape. Snip back gangly shoots on

■ *Spring-blooming plants such as spirea can be pruned after their bloom season is over to allow them time to regrow and set bloom buds in mid- to late summer for next spring.*

vigorous vines that are growing into walkways or may be about to grow onto other plants to keep them in-bounds.

WATER

ANNUALS

"April showers bring May flowers," or at least that's what they say. In the absence of showers be ready to water your annual flowerbeds with ½ to 1 inch of water per week. The soil should be kept moist to a depth of about 6 to 8 inches to prevent stress on plants. In the eastern half of the state the mild temperatures and periodic rainfall eliminate the need for supplemental watering most of the month.

EDIBLES

Water vegetable gardens once or twice weekly if it doesn't rain at least ½ inch. Vegetables in sandy soil and sun will need watering twice as often as the same plants in a loam or clay soil or those growing in partial shade. Maintain moist soil in herb beds. Herbs grown in containers are prone to drying out, especially in terra cotta containers, which act as a "wick" to draw moisture from the soil. Water them daily if they're located in the sun or every other day if they're in part day shade. In our heat, herbs can be grown in full sun to part sun and shade.

Irrigate new fruit trees, vines, and bushes to help them get off to a good start by filling the berms with water to provide a good soaking of the original rootball and surrounding soil. See March, Here's How to Irrigate New Shrubs and Trees, as a guide to how much water is needed both this month and through the growing season.

LAWNS

Rainfall is usually adequate for sustaining a lawn during April. If there's been no rain for more than two weeks provide ½ to 1 inch of irrigation to sustain the turfgrass in a healthy condition. Newly established lawns will need frequent watering to help them establish roots into the soil and become more drought resilient. See Here's How to Establish a Lawn this month for information on how to water new sod.

PERENNIALS & ORNAMENTAL GRASSES

Continue to water newly planted perennials to help them become established. If it rains at least ½ inch you can forgo watering for a few days to a week. Established perennials shouldn't need supplemental watering unless you live in zone 9 or in the far western part of Texas where rainfall is scarce.

ROSES, SHRUBS & TREES

Provide young woody ornamentals with supplemental irrigation in the absence of rainfall to maintain good vigor. (See March, Here's How to Irrigate New Shrubs and Trees.) This is especially important for maintaining the vigor of summer-blooming plants such as roses, rose of Sharon (*Althea*), vitex, and crape myrtles. Azaleas, camellias, gardenias, hydrangeas, Virginia sweetspire, pieris, and other drought-susceptible species also need enough supplemental irrigation to maintain moderate soil moisture as the weather warms.

VINES & GROUNDCOVERS

Water vines and groundcovers planted since late winter every three to seven days in the absence of rainfall. Established groundcovers may only need watering every seven to ten days. Established woody vines should not need supplemental watering this month except in west Texas where it is usually very dry and in southern areas of the state where temperatures are heating up more. Even so, a seven- to ten-day schedule should suffice if it doesn't rain.

FERTILIZE

ANNUALS

Apply a complete fertilizer product to both new warm-season flowers and established cool-season flower beds at a rate of 2 cups per 50 square feet, or double this rate if it is an organic product as those tend to be lower in nutrient concentration. The fertilizer will boost growth of the new plantings and help reinvigorate the cool-season plantings for one more round of blooms.

If the soil surface is mulched it helps to "scratch" the fertilizer into the mulch using a hand cultivator tool so the fertilizer can reach below the soil surface. Always water after you fertilize to wash any product off foliage where it could burn the plant tissues; this is especially true for most synthetic products. Watering also helps to begin the process of releasing the nutrients to the soil and plant roots.

EDIBLES

Fertilize all vegetables except beans and peas with an application of a complete fertilizer. For guidance on rates to apply see Here's How to Fertilize Flowers, Ornamental Grasses, and Vegetables in this chapter. Most vegetables will do fine at a moderate rate. Sweet corn should be fertilized at the medium to high rate. Fertilize root crops at the low rate to avoid pushing them into top growth (leaves) at the expense of roots. Fertilize beans and peas at the low rate. Mix fertilizer into the surface inch of soil and water it in with a good soaking with a water wand on the end of a hose.

Fertilize herbs lightly and then water the area with ½ inch of irrigation. An alternative is to apply ½ to 1 inch of compost around the plants, cover 1 or 2 inches of shredded leaf mulch, and water it well. This mulch will decompose slowly over the coming months, releasing its nutrients to the growing plants.

A few weeks after *newly planted* fruit trees or pecans start to produce new growth, begin fertilizing them. Apply 1 to 2 cups per inch of trunk diameter evenly beneath and just beyond the branch spread of the tree. If you have *established* fruit trees and didn't fertilize them in March you can do so this month. Cultivate fertilizer applications into the soil surface and water with ½ inch of sprinkler irrigation to start the process of releasing the nutrients to the plant's root system. (See March, Here's How to Fertilize a Young Tree.)

LAWNS

This is the big month for making the spring fertilizer application to lawns in zones 8 (early to mid-April), 7 (mid- to late April), and 6 (late April). Spring weather can be erratic so a better way to know when to make the first application of fertilizer is after you have mowed the lawn twice. If you live in zone 9 and haven't fertilized yet, go ahead

■ *When you have mowed the lawn twice it is time to make the first application of fertilizer. The turf will be actively growing and able to take up and utilize the extra nutrients you provide.*

HERE'S HOW

TO FERTILIZE A LAWN

1. Choose a product with a 3-1-2 or 4-1-2 nutrient ratio. Established lawns that have been fertilized for years and that have the clippings recycled back into the turf may do fine with a 1-0-0 ratio. (The numbers on a fertilizer bag represent the percent of nitrogen, phosphorus, and potassium by weight.)

2. Divide the first number (nitrogen) into 100 to get the pounds of that fertilizer to apply per 1,000 square feet of lawn area.

3. Apply half going in one direction and half going at a 90-degree angle to help ensure an even application.

4. Fertilize in spring after mowing the turf twice, and again in fall about six weeks prior to your location's first frost.

5. Sweep or blow fertilizer off hardscapes such as a driveway following fertilizer application to prevent runoff into creeks, lakes, and aquifers.

6. Water the fertilizer in with ½ inch of irrigation.

HERE'S HOW

TO FERTILIZE FLOWERS, ORNAMENTAL GRASSES, AND VEGETABLES

The following chart is a guide for fertilizing flowers, ornamental grasses, vegetables, and other bedding plants at light, moderate, and heavy rates using products with various nitrogen concentrations. In the absence of a soil test, choose a product with a 3-1-2 or 4-1-2 nutrient ratio. If only nitrogen in needed choose a product with a 1-0-0 ratio of nutrients, such as ammonium sulfate or blood meal.

Fertilizer Numbers*	Amount per 1,000 sq. ft.			Amount per 25 sq. ft.		
	Light Feeding (.5#N/1,000)	Moderate Feeding (1#N/1,000)	Heavy Feeding (2#N/1,000)	Light Rate	Moderate Rate	Heavy Rate
6-x-x	8.3 lb	16.6 lb	33.2 lb	.41 ½ cup	.82 ¾ cup	1.64 1⅔ cup
8-x-x	6.2 lb	12.5 lb	25 lb	.31 ⅓ cup	.62 ⅔ cup	1.24 1¼ cup
9-x-x	5.5 lb	11.1 lb	22.2 lb	.28 ¼ cup	.56 ½ cup	1.12 1 cup
11-x-x	4.5 lb	9.1 lb	18.2 lb	.23 ¼ cup	.46 ½ cup	.92 1 cup
15-x-x	3.3 lb	6.6 lb	13.2 lb	.17 3 tbsp	.34 ⅓ cup	.68 ⅔ cup
20-x-x	2.5 lb	5.0 lb	10 lb	.13 2 tbsp	.26 ¼ cup	.52 ½ cup
21-x-x	2.4 lb	4.8 lb	9.6 lb	.12 2 tbsp	.24 ¼ cup	.48 ½ cup
29-x-x	1.7 lb	3.4 lb	6.8 lb	.09 1½ tbsp	.18 3 tbsp	.36 ⅓ cup

* To determine the amount of phosphorus and potassium, you will need to have your soil tested.

and do so early in the month. See Here's How to Fertilize a Lawn this month for more information.

PERENNIALS & ORNAMENTAL GRASSES

Perennials that were planted this spring will benefit from another fertilizing at the rate described for annuals. Established perennials that are not growing well or that have less than a normal, healthy green color may also benefit from the same fertilizing. Soils differ in their fertility and their ability to hold nutrients. Therefore it is best to learn to "read" your plants and feed them when they begin to lack vigor or when the older leaves start to lose color.

ROSES

Fertilize established repeat-blooming roses again this month following instructions given in March. Good nutrition promotes healthy plants, and is needed for continued bloom cycles. Increase the fertilization rate for roses planted this past fall through winter season to a ¼ cup per plant.

SHRUBS

Azaleas, camellias, and gardenias don't need a lot of added fertilizer, especially if growing in beds with plenty of decomposed organic matter. However, if plants lack vigor some added nutrients may be helpful. Use a product for acid-loving plants following the product label for application rate.

Cottonseed meal makes a good fertilizer also and can be applied by sprinkling ½ to 1 cup evenly beneath the branch spread around each plant and then working it into the surface inch of soil. Avoid disturbing the soil around azaleas too deeply as the plants have very shallow roots.

If your azaleas, gardenias, Chinese witch hazel, or other shrubs are showing signs of yellowing new growth with leaf veins that remain green, it is likely a sign of iron deficiency. This is common in the high pH black clays of the Houston-Beaumont area, parts of the Dallas-Fort Worth area, the Hill Country soils of central Texas, and the high pH soils of west Texas. It is usually not practical to acidify these soils, but a chelated iron product can provide temporary benefits. If symptoms persist rebuild the beds incorporating lots of decomposed bark, peat moss-sand mixes, and decomposed leaves with other acidifying products, such as sulfur. Some soil and compost retailers have special acidic mixes for azaleas, blueberries, and other acid-loving plants.

TREES

Fertilize trees planted since last fall four to six weeks after they have begun to put on new growth. Also fertilize young (one- to ten-year-old) established trees now to promote faster growth. You want to be able to hang a hammock on them soon, right? See March, Here's How to Fertilize a Young Tree, to determine how much to apply to trees of various sizes.

VINES & GROUNDCOVERS

If you didn't fertilize groundcovers earlier in the year do so now at a rate of 2 cups of turf-type fertilizer per 50 square feet of area. Vines that are naturally vigorous, such as trumpet creeper, wisteria, Confederate star jasmine, and queen's wreath, probably won't need any extra fertilizer. Vines lacking good vigor and growth will benefit from a boost at the rate mentioned for groundcovers. Water the area well after you apply the fertilizer.

PROBLEM-SOLVE

ALL

Deer can be a big problem for gardens and landscapes in some parts of the state. While they may be skittish in some areas, in others they are bold and brazen. In parts of northern San Antonio north to Austin and above they may be so bold as to lie in your yard in the middle of the day, no doubt digesting the meal of your landscape plants. The only real solution is a fence 6 feet high or taller around your garden.

Caterpillars can attack many different species of plants and are especially common this month. Sprays of *Bacillus thuringiensis (B.t.)* can be an effective, low-toxicity control option if used when the caterpillars are young and actively feeding. Keep in mind, however, that it also kills the caterpillars that turn into butterflies so take care not to get it on plants such as passion vine and milkweed, which are larval food sources for butterflies.

Sooty mold grows on plants when insects produce a sugary substance called "honeydew" that falls onto plant surfaces. The mold grows rapidly on the honeydew. While minor occurrences can be ignored or washed off with a blast of soapy water, the solution to more serious insect infestations is to treat the insects. Whiteflies, aphids, mealybugs, and scale are among the more likely pests producing the honeydew. The first three can be set back with an insecticidal soap spray if you get complete coverage of all plant surfaces, especially the undersides of leaves. Horticultural oil will control all four, but coverage is also critical with oil sprays. There are other options, including systemic products, if these are not sufficient to shut down the pests.

ANNUALS, PERENNIALS & ORNAMENTAL GRASSES

Yellowing older foliage on annual or perennial flowers may be a sign of a nutrient deficiency, such as nitrogen or magnesium, or a sign of overwatering. Check the soil moisture and if it seems to be adequately moist then try applying a little fertilizer to a few plants to see if they improve over the others. This will help you get to the bottom of the problem.

Leaf spots are promoted by wet foliage conditions and mild to warm temperatures. Powdery mildew is increased by high humidity and mild temperature conditions. Both are better prevented than cured. Therefore, try to minimize leaf wetness, and when

■ *Sooty mold is a sign of certain pests such as these scale insects or also aphids, mealybugs, and whiteflies. Your County Extension Office can assist you with identification and effective control options.*

conditions are favorable to the diseases, consider using a labeled fungicide spray, taking care to follow label instructions carefully. Not all plants are equally susceptible so note which species or varieties have disease problems and make a note in your journal to look for more resistant ones next time you plant.

Madagascar periwinkles that suddenly wilt and rapidly turn brown or black are likely the victims of aerial phytophthora blight. This disease favors cool, wet conditions. The Cora and Nirvana series are resistant to this blight. If you use other varieties it is best to wait to plant them until the weather warms up more in May in zones 6 to 8, or in late April for zone 9.

Watch for slugs and snails on tender new growth. Sections of foliage that have been chomped away may be due to these pests or to insects with chewing mouthparts such as caterpillars and beetles. Some pests prefer to feed in the evening so if you don't see the culprits around the areas where

damage is occurring, check for their telltale slime trails or go outside in the evenings with a flashlight to examine plants for these pests. There are special baits formulated for slugs and snails that can be an effective control and that avoid the need to spray the area. Your County Extension Office can assist you with solving "the case of the missing leaves" and also suggest some low-toxicity options to control of slugs and snails.

EDIBLES

If some of your vegetables, herbs, or fruit plants are not growing well, or their foliage is yellowing, or you spot other signs of nutrient imbalances, have your soil tested. This will determine if the pH and nutrient levels are where they should be for best plant performance and the results will guide fertilizing efforts in the coming months. When the results are in contact your County Extension Office to ask for assistance in interpreting them and to decide what products need to be added and in what amounts.

Check for tomato hornworms feeding on your vegetables. Handpicking and destroying them is usually sufficient since there are seldom that many present on a tomato plant. If you catch them early a spray of *Bacillus thuringiensis (B.t.)* is another effective, low-toxicity control option. Keep an eye on those tasty tomatoes. Our state bird, the mockingbird, is as fond of them as you are, and so are the neighborhood squirrels. Bird netting may be required to protect your prize tomatoes.

Blossom end rot is a condition of tomato fruits in which the blossom ends of the fruits rot due to a lack of calcium. Fluctuations in soil moisture from very wet to very dry can cause this condition. Soil tests can determine if your soil has sufficient calcium levels. If it does, then the problem was brought on by moisture fluctuations. The earliest fruits of the year, when the plant's root system is less extensive, are most often affected. The problem will go away with time and with proper watering. Calcium sprays are available to treat the problem if it is an annual occurrence for you. Just be sure to treat early, before the symptoms appear.

Harlequin bugs often show up about now on cole crops. There are sprays to control these pests, but most gardeners just call it the end of the season and pull the crops to replant with summer crops. Squash vine borers are laying eggs on your squash plants. The eggs hatch into larvae that tunnel in the vine, causing it to wilt and collapse. Look for the orange and black moths that look like wasps, sitting on the plant's leaves, especially in the morning. That is a sign that treatments may be needed. If you catch the problem early you can also use a knife to split open a section of vine lengthwise to kill the larvae inside. This "operation" won't kill the vine; it will usually keep on growing fine.

Watch for fruit rots on squash during warm, rainy weather. Choanephora rot and other fungal diseases thrive in warm, wet conditions. Promptly pick and discard affected fruit and the problem will usually go away on its own, if the weather cooperates.

Check fruit on fruit trees for signs of insect damage such as cuts on the fruit or sap leaking out. Take some damaged fruit to your County Extension Office for identification and control recommendations.

LAWNS

Mow and bag turf clippings if you have cool-season weeds present. These weeds are producing viable seeds that should not be left to sprout next fall and winter. Compost the clippings in a hot compost pile to destroy the seeds.

Stop using post-emergence broadleaf weed control products on St. Augustine lawns since these products can damage and weaken the grass when temperatures rise into and above the mid-80s.

ROSES

Watch for early signs of blackspot and powdery mildew on susceptible rose varieties. Blackspot is most active when temperatures are mild to warm and the foliage is wet for periods of time. Powdery mildew likes mild temperatures and high humidity. The best no-spray remedies are to plant resistant varieties, avoid crowding plants to improve air circulation, and avoid wetting the foliage with sprinkler irrigation. If you have a favorite variety that is susceptible to these diseases, preventative fungicide sprays are the best option for stopping them from seriously damaging the plants. Your County Extension Office or a local certified rosarian can recommend appropriate products.

■ *Black spots and yellowing leaves are a sign of blackspot, a fungal disease that is common when the leaves on roses are damp for an extended time.*

■ *Powdery mildew can affect many plants, including annuals, perennials, shrubs, and trees. This rock rose (*Pavonia*) shows the typical symptoms of deformed growth and a white powdery coating.*

SHRUBS

If the distorted leaf growth of azalea leaf gall is appearing on your azaleas it is a little late to control with preventative sprays. Pick off distorted leaves before they turn white with the powdery spores and discard them to lessen future infection. Do not compost!

Powdery mildew attacks many types of trees and shrubs, including roses, crape myrtles, rock rose (*Pavonia*), Turk's cap, dogwood, euonymus, honeysuckle, and privet. It appears as white to gray powdery spots on leaves and shoots and results in deformed growth of infected tissues. Warm days, cool nights, and high humidity favor the disease, as do shady conditions. Preventative fungicide sprays are effective, but once the white powdery mildew appears, the damage has been done and spraying is less helpful, except for preventing additional infections as new growth appears. Choose resistant varieties when possible, space plants to improve air circulation, and minimize foliage wetting from sprinkler irrigation.

Indian hawthorns that were defoliated by entomosporium leaf spot and are starting to regrow new foliage will benefit from a series of fungicide sprays every ten days to protect the new foliage. Your County Extension Office can recommend a labeled and effective product. Consider replacing them with a shrub species that is not so prone to disease problems.

TREES

In zones 6 to 8 keep on the lookout for cankerworms in elms, oaks, and several other shade tree species. Also continue to check susceptible species for tent caterpillar webbing in the crotches of branches. See March for more information on these pests.

Anthracnose can be a problem on ash trees during cool, wet spring weather when the plants are pushing out new growth. The disease causes browning edges on the leaves and defoliation of young leaves. When you see the problem it is too late to spray. Preventative sprays with a labeled fungicide during bud break can prevent the disease in future years, but these are generally not recommended. This disease, although unsightly, is generally not a significant threat to the health of the trees most of the time.

VINES & GROUNDCOVERS

Powdery mildew can be a problem on some vines, including coral honeysuckle. This disease appears as powdery white spots on the top surface of leaves. It usually doesn't warrant fungicide sprays, but if you decide to spray, do so early because once the disease has affected the foliage it is too late to be beneficial to treat the plants with a protective spray. When new growth begins a spray can protect the growth if the disease continues to be a problem.

On young vine seedlings, watch for signs of pest damage, including that from cutworms, which can sever the vine at the ground, caterpillars feeding on the foliage, and root-feeding insects, which cause the seedlings to wilt and die even when the soil is adequately moist. Damage is usually minimal, but when damage is severe, treatment with a labeled product may be necessary to protect a replanting of seeds.

The weather is getting warmer and although May is a spring month on the calendar, it is more like a summer month in Texas. The roar of lawnmowers and scent of fresh-cut grass will assure you that summer is making its annual debut.

Our warm-season flowers are putting on a gorgeous show and will benefit from some added fertilizer to keep them vigorous and blooming into summer. Many of the species that are willing to bloom in spring and early summer decline when the weather sizzles, so plant some summer-tolerant color plants this month to keep the landscape beautiful all summer long.

In the vegetable garden the harvest season for warm-season crops is underway. Tomatoes are being carted around town for bragging rights among gardeners. Many of these spring crops will cease to be productive in summer, so plant a few heat-tolerant vegetables to keep the produce coming all summer. Fruit trees are starting their production in the southern zones with the arrival of the first juicy peaches of the season.

When you build it, they will come. Pests appreciate the salad bar we have provided, and we need to be diligent to check our plants every few days for signs of an outbreak. If you catch an infestation early your options for control include much less toxic products and cultural practices. Learn to identify pests and beneficial insects so you don't kill the "good guys."

Beneficial insects are attracted to pests and to small flowers with nectar and pollen. Accept that a few pests is a good thing because having a population of beneficials around can help prevent a pest outbreak. Plant flowers that attract beneficials, such as plants with small, daisy-like blooms; flowering herbs; and plants with umbrella-like blooms (umbels), including dill and fennel. (See June, Here's How to Attract Beneficial Insects, for more on how to build a garden that attracts the "good guys.") Make your garden and landscape an inviting place for beneficial insects. If you build it, they too will come.

PLAN

ALL

Take digital photos of plants in bloom or their foliage for your gardening journal. This will help with future planning and is especially helpful for perennials and bulbs, which may have a rather short blooming season. Digital cameras date-stamp photo files, which is very helpful when you are trying to remember when that plant was in bloom last year.

Take advantage of trips to other people's gardens, botanical gardens, or garden tours, and snap photos for reference as you plan your own gardens. Take a notebook along to record plant names, or if the plant is labeled, snap a photo of the label, too, and you'll have it later when you need the name.

The weather is heating up, making it necessary to water more often. Plan to install a drip irrigation system in some garden and landscape beds to get ready for summer. These systems are not difficult to install, and home garden kits are available to make it even easier. See A Simple Drip Irrigation System later in this chapter. Drip irrigation uses water more efficiently than sprinklers and, because it doesn't wet the foliage, can help reduce disease problems when compared to sprinkler irrigation.

ANNUALS

Now that the weather is warming up it is time to create some heat-loving container combinations. Whether you are using a single species or the "thriller, filler, spiller" system mentioned in March, make sure to use large containers. Small containers require much more frequent watering, and in the heat of a Texas summer they are seldom practical options. So plan to choose containers one or two sizes larger than what you may see in photos from more northern areas when designing your container plantings.

Get creative with container plantings. Anything that will hold a few gallons of soil can become a whimsical container. Keep your eye out for such containers at antique and junk shops. A rusty old wheelbarrow looks great with flowers spilling over its sides. For drought-tolerant plants even a gallon of soil may be sufficient, so that old teapot may

■ *Drip irrigation is an efficient way to provide water right where plants need it, at their roots, and helps avoid wetting the foliage, which promotes leaf diseases.*

be a future succulent container for the front steps or for a table on an outside patio.

Don't forget hanging baskets. These add another dimension to a porch or landscape. Many, because they are hanging from your home or a structure, are planted with shade-loving plants. Include plenty of white and light colors when planning your hanging baskets so they show up in the shade. Window planters do not usually hold enough soil to provide adequate water-holding capacity for annuals in our hot climate. There are, however, some large planters made of metal racks lined with coconut coir that are great on a porch railing or along a sunny wall if provided adequate anchorage.

There are some great metal hangers used for hanging baskets in sunny spots. Some are designed to attach to a wall, post, or fence. This can help break up a long privacy fence, adding color to the wall of wood! Also look for "half containers" for decorating a wall. These look like a pot cut in half vertically, and they come with slots to attach them to a wall or fence.

Summer arrives early in Texas so it makes sense to get these and other heat-loving color plants established soon. Take some time to plan your color beds to create aesthetically pleasing designs and color combinations. New gardeners often buy a mix of colors, not thinking about the overall effect when the planting is viewed from a distance. See March, Here's How to Plan Color

Changes for Annual Beds, for tips on planning your color combinations.

EDIBLES
Summer is arriving in the southern part of the state, and it will soon be hot in all the zones. Our spring gardens look good, but many of the crops will be declining in the weeks to come. Plan your next edible gardens for hot weather now. Make a note in your journal of what will be pulled out and what will replace it so you can purchase seeds, start some transplants, and do any soil prep work if the beds are currently open.

Herbs aren't just for the herb garden. Include them in other parts of the landscape. Purple basil with burgundy leaves or Thai basil with burgundy-tinged leaves and blooms are quite attractive. Thyme and oregano make excellent groundcovers. Trailing rosemary is beautiful cascading over a rock wall or out of a large container. If you want to expand your perennial herbs to other parts of the garden or landscape, plan out the new bed designs so you can make the plantings or divisions sometime this month. Consider the height of an herb and its tendency to spread. Mint is a wonderful herb, but it has a mind to take over the world. Mints may be better suited to a container

where they can be, well, contained, or planted with an underground wall to contain them. See the Care section for more on this.

Warm-season vegetable harvest is underway in zones 7b to 9. Many types of fruit are beginning their harvest season in zone 9 and nearing harvest in other zones. If you plan to freeze, can, dry, or make jams and jellies, prepare now by gathering supplies and reading the how-tos of food preservation. It's a great way to get more from your garden, especially when production outpaces what you can use in the kitchen.

LAWNS
It is heating up outside. Check your irrigation controller to make sure it is running long enough to apply ½ to 1 inch per week in the absence of rain. See April for tips on how to check the uniformity of your sprinklers. Have any needed adjustments and repairs made soon since this is the start of the main irrigation season for lawns.

PERENNIALS & ORNAMENTAL GRASSES
Summer heat shuts down many perennials that looked great in spring. This is where planning can really pay off. Do some researching to find some

■ *When planning your landscape include various foliage textures and consider the height of the various plants so that taller plants can show off behind shorter ones.*

SMALL- TO MEDIUM-SIZED FLOWERING TREES

Depending on where you live in Texas there are some small- to medium-sized blooming trees that will do well in your area. Here are a few examples to get you off to a good start in selecting trees for your landscape. Check on hardiness and suitability to acidic or alkaline soil conditions.

Name (Genus & Species)	Bloom Season
Dogwood (*Cornus florida*)	Spring
Deciduous magnolias (*Magnolia stellata*, M. × *soulangeana*)	Spring
Native fringe tree (*Chionanthus virginicus*)	Spring
Chinese fringe tree (*Chionanthus retusus*)	Spring
Eastern redbud (*Cercis canadensis*)	Spring
Texas redbud (*Cercis canadensis* var. *texensis*)	Spring
Mexican plum (*Prunus mexicana*)	Spring
Ornamental pears (*Pyrus calleryana*)	Spring
Ornamental peach (*Prunus persica*), such as 'Red Baron' or 'Peppermint'	Spring
Texas mountain laurel (*Sophora secundiflora*)	Spring
Two-winged silverbell (*Halesia diptera*)	Spring
Hawthorn (*Crataegus* spp.)	Spring
Rusty blackhaw viburnum (*Viburnum rufidulum*)	Spring
Huisache or sweet acacia (*Acacia farnesiana*)	Spring
Wright or catclaw acacia (*Acacia greggii* var. *wrightii*)	Spring
Eve's necklace (*Styphnolobium affine*)	Spring
Anacacho orchid tree (*Bauhinia lunarioides*)	Spring (sporadic in summer)
Japanese snowbell tree (*Styrax japonicus*)	Late spring-early summer
Crape myrtle (*Lagerstroemia* spp.)	Summer
Mexican olive or anacahuita (*Cordia boissieri*)	Spring-summer-fall-winter (mild areas)
Retama, Jerusalem thorn, or palo verde (*Parkinsonia aculeate*)	Late spring-summer
Desert willow (*Chilopsis linearis*)	Late spring-early fall
Vitex or chastetree (*Vitex agnus-castus*)	Late spring-early summer (sporadically to early fall)
Golden leadball (*Leucaena retusa*)	Summer-fall
Chinese flame tree (*Koelreuteria bipinnata*)	Fall

great perennials that can provide summer blooms in your zone. Yellow bells (*Tecoma stans*) can take the heat but is hardy only in zones 8 to 9, while *Salvia* 'Mystic Spires' can take the winter across most of the state and return for blue blooms that don't flinch in our heat.

When planting perennials, consider the mature height of the plant. Some plants trail, while others mound, and still others lift their blooms well above the foliage. Garden phlox (*Phlox paniculata*), for example, sends its blooms 3 feet tall in the summer, putting on quite a show. It is worth mention that when planning your beds or containers make sure to put taller plants behind shorter ones so all can be seen and enjoyed.

A great planning resource for choosing great perennials and other plants that can take our summer heat is the list of Texas Superstar plants by the Texas AgriLife Extension Service at texassuperstar.com.

ROSES

If your rose bushes are prone to disease problems, learn about varieties that are naturally resistant to blackspot and powdery mildew, and make a note to replace those this coming fall.

VINES & GROUNDCOVERS

Hot summer weather is starting to arrive. To make your air conditioner unit operate more efficiently consider planting a vine on a trellis or other structure to provide shade from the hot noon-to-afternoon sun. Choose one of many decorative metal structures or build your own and turn an eyesore into something attractive.

PLANT

ALL

Keep your planting records or garden journal up to date as you plant. Plant tags have a way of "disappearing" and you'll later be glad you recorded the variety to help you learn which ones perform best in your landscape. Note when you planted each variety and make notes about how various plants are performing in the garden.

ANNUALS

Continue planting container color to decorate your landscape. Some examples of container color plants that can take the hot weather and sun include coleus, portulaca, purslane, celosia, tropical sage (*Salvia coccinea*), marigolds, dwarf zinnias, lobularia, narrow-leaf zinnia (*Zinnia angustifolia*), and Madagascar periwinkle (choose the Nirvana or Cora series for disease resistance). In shade, plant impatiens, wishbone flower (part shade), pentas (part shade), and caladiums (shade to part sun).

■ *Zinnias come in many colors and sizes and are a great choice for bringing heat-tolerant color to the summer landscape.*

Make sure to use a container with drainage holes and a quality potting soil that holds water but also allows excess water to drain away. Successful container combinations are a combination of tough plants, a large enough container, and a mix that can hold moisture. As container size decreases and the potting mix choice becomes coarser and more porous, the need for frequent watering will increase. You probably don't have time to water containers twice a day, so make sure to plant in a good-sized container with a good-quality potting mix.

The plants mentioned above do well in garden beds also. By now the cool-season flowers you've been coaxing along through spring are turning to toast. It is time for a summer change, if you haven't already done so. Work an inch of screened (fine-textured) compost into the soil along with 2 cups of a balanced fertilizer per every 50 square feet. Then set out your transplants and water them with a soluble fertilizer solution. They will grow well in the well-prepared soil with good nutrient content.

Plants we consider houseplants are also good annuals in the landscape. Pothos makes a great hanging basket plant for deep shade or a groundcover around trees that cast a deep shade, such as southern magnolia and live oak. A dracaena with white- or burgundy-streaked foliage is an excellent choice for the thriller in a thriller-spiller-filler combination for shady areas (see more about this in March). So pick up some young houseplants at a local garden center this month to include in your color plantings for shady areas.

Succulents make great container plants. They are very forgiving if you forget to water them. Some succulents and related drought-hardy species include echeverias, sedums, and sempervivums. Include dwarf agaves, dwarf yuccas, and dyckias in large containers.

EDIBLES

Now that things have really warmed up, it is time to plant okra, winter squash (including pumpkins), Malabar spinach and amaranth greens, and muskmelons (cantaloupe) and watermelons. Plant okra individually or in rows, spacing plants 3 feet apart to allow them room to

■ *Some types of okra offer burgundy pods that, along with the yellow blossoms, can make an attractive ornamental as well as a vegetable garden edible.*

branch. Some types have burgundy foliage and pods, which, along with the yellow blooms, make them a great plant to include in the landscape with annual and perennial ornamentals.

Plant squash, pumpkins, and melons in "hills" (small groups of seed), spacing them according to packet instructions. Sun and wind can dry out the soil surface and tender seedlings fast, so water daily to keep the soil moist during the critical germination stage. Place a lightweight row-cover fabric over plants to keep out the pests that can destroy the tender seedlings. Once they have several true leaves they are not as susceptible to serious, overnight damage as they are at the seedling stage.

If space is limited, start the heat-tolerant vegetables as transplants outdoors. This gives you a little more time to harvest your cool-season and heat-sensitive warm-season vegetables. When the transplants are about three to four weeks old, you can pull the garden plants and set out these heat-tolerant vegetables. Transplants give you a head start on the season and help you get more out of limited garden space. Start transplants in a location with some morning sun. Protect them from hungry pests with some lightweight row-cover fabric. Keep them moist as they will dry out fast in the sun and warm temperatures.

Did you get all the herbs you want planted yet? You can still plant perennial herbs and heat-tolerant annual herbs such as basil. Do so as soon

as possible to give them as much time as possible to establish roots before the stressful, hot, dry summer weather arrives. Firm the soil around their roots, water the plants with a soluble fertilizer solution, and then mulch around the plants to deter weeds and help hold in moisture around the new plants.

There is still time to plant container-grown fruit trees, but don't delay. For guidance on how to plant see November, Here's How to Plant Container-Grown Shrubs and Trees. You'll need to be a little more attentive to watering them regularly to help them become established in the heat.

LAWNS
The weather is heating up, but it is still a good time to establish a new lawn or to fill in bare spots in an existing area of turfgrass. Take special care to

■ Succulents work well in the ground or in containers. They need little water, so if you neglect them they will still be fine.

keep the new sod or seedlings moist but not soggy during the critical transition as they establish roots into the soil and become better able to withstand drought periods.

PERENNIALS & ORNAMENTAL GRASSES

Plant perennials that won't flinch in summer heat now. Garden centers are still well stocked and perennial plants can be a great investment that returns annual dividends on your gardening dollars. Be extra diligent about watering these new plants to help them transition as their roots venture out from the container media into the surrounding soil. Even drought-tolerant perennials need a little extra TLC until their roots establish, and they can become quite resilient.

Now that the soil is warming up it is time to plant ginger into beds prepared with several inches of organic matter. Most gingers prefer a shady spot, although the butterfly gingers can take some sun. Gingers are a versatile way to provide color for shady areas of the landscape. They come in many species from the low-growing peacock ginger (*Kaempferia*), to the knee-high arching blooms of dancing lady (*Globba winitii*), or the upright stalks of butterfly ginger (*Hedychium* spp.), hidden ginger (*Curcuma* spp.), pinecone ginger (*Zingiber* spp.), and shell ginger (*Alpinia* spp.).

These add some tropical elegance to the garden and the blooms of white butterfly ginger will intoxicate garden visitors on a late summer's evening. The yellow-streaked foliage of variegated shell ginger (*Alpinia zerumbet 'variegata'*) is a great way to draw attention to a shady area. Place gingers in bright shade in a spot where you can provide dependable soil moisture. They are great for beds beneath the eaves of the north side of a home or beneath the shade of a live oak tree.

ROSES, SHRUBS & TREES

Continue to plant container-grown woody ornamental plants in the landscape. Maintain moist but not oversaturated soil moisture in the original rootball and surrounding soil for several months after planting. This will avoid stress to the plants as the rising temperatures increase their demands for a steady supply of soil moisture.

VINES & GROUNDCOVERS

Continue planting container-grown vines and groundcovers. If there are plants that died or are not thriving from winter or spring plantings, replace them with new healthy plants. Water the new plants with a soluble fertilizer solution to get them off to a fast start.

Established groundcovers can be used to obtain new plants by digging and dividing some plants out of the planting. Note where some vines are rooted into the ground. Cut the vines back to 6 to 8 inches and dig out a 6-inch rootball to plant elsewhere to expand the planting or to pot up and share with friends.

CARE

ANNUALS

Many types of annuals tend to leave their spent blooms hanging around looking ugly. Zinnias are a good example. Snip these spent blooms off, a process called deadheading, to tidy up the planting and improve its appearance. Cut back to the first set of leaves when removing blooms. Doing this promptly as blooms start to fade away allows the plant to put its energy into more blooms rather than into seed production.

■ *Maintain a blanket of mulch around all of your garden and landscape plants to moderate soil temperature, conserve moisture, and deter weeds. Leaves and pine needles make excellent mulching materials.*

■ *Snip off the spent blooms of flowers that don't naturally drop them to tidy up the planting and make it more attractive.*

fertilizer, mulch around the plants, and they will become established in time to face the summer heat that is on the way.

Installing a border of metal or stone can help set boundaries to guide you when trimming the edge of the sprawling herb plants and it looks nice too. Mint is notorious for spreading both above- and belowground in its plans for world domination. One technique to keep it in-bounds is to sink a container of mint in the ground so the container stops underground spreading. Another is to create an underground wall by installing metal flashing

■ *Pinch the growing tips off of blackberry shoots about "chest high" to encourage branching and a tidier, more productive row of plants.*

Some plants take care of their spent blooms by dropping the blooms or having them shrivel to be unnoticeable. Examples include impatiens, narrow-leaf zinnias, pentas, and wax-leaf begonias.

Some annuals such as petunias will tend to bloom themselves into a weakened state and will succumb to the heat of summer soon if they're not rejuvenated. Cut them back by about one-third and follow with fertilizer and water to promote fresh new growth and more blooms. Don't wait until they decline to do the shearing and rejuvenating, and be ready to repeat the process a month later if they are still around.

Geraniums have been happy to sit in the full sun during our mild late-winter-to-spring season. However, with the mercury rising they will benefit from a move to a bright semi-shade or mid- to late-day shady spot. When daytime temperatures rise into the 90s look for a place where they can get a break from the summer sun to keep them in good condition.

EDIBLES

If your herbs are getting out of the boundaries you set for them, this is a good time to cut them back. Use the trimmings in cooking, dry them for use later, or root a few to make more plants for sharing. This month is also a great time to divide and reset herbs. Water them well with some soluble

vertically underground around the area where mint is allowed to grow.

Pinch the suckers out of tomato plants; see Care in April for more on this. Basil tends to stop growing nice large leaves when the blooms appear. Shear the blooms off basil plants, cutting back to the first set of larger leaves below the bloom. Then fertilize and water them to promote fresh new foliage growth for harvesting.

Pinch the tips of new, vigorous, upright blackberry canes when they reach about chest high. This pruning encourages side branching and increases productivity when those canes bear fruit next spring.

Replenish mulch to maintain a 3-inch depth around fruit trees, vines and bushes, vegetables, and larger herbs. Leaves, pine needles, compost, hay, and dried grass clippings all make great mulching materials. If you use hay or grass clippings, make sure they are

from fields and lawns that were not treated with broadleaf weed-control products. There is often enough residual herbicide on the mulch to damage plants, especially sensitive species such as tomatoes, beans, and grapes. Mulch is critical in helping the plants get through summer heat and drought, while keeping down weed competition.

LAWNS

The warming weather has turf growing rapidly. If you set the mower blade low in spring to remove weeds and dead or discolored turf blades, begin to raise the mowing height to allow longer leaf blades and to promote deeper rooted grass. Mow at the optimum height for optimum density, which helps shade the soil surface and minimize weed seed germination. See Here's How to Select the Mowing Height for Your Lawn on the next page. Mow when the grass is about 50 percent above this height so you cut off one-third of the leaf blade with each mowing. For example, if you mow St. Augustine

CHARACTERISTICS OF TURFGRASS SPECIES FOR TEXAS LAWNS

Characteristic	St. Augustine	Bermuda	Buffalo	Zoysia japonica*	Zoysia matrella*
Leaf texture	Coarse	Fine	Fine	Medium	Fine
Mowing frequency	5–7 days	3–7 days	7–14 days**	7–10 days	5–7 days
Mowing height	2.5–4 inches	1–2 inches	2.5–4 inches	1–2.5 inches	1–2 inches
Shade tolerance	High	Very low	Low–medium	Medium–high	Medium–high
Water requirement***	Medium	Low–medium	Very low	Medium	Medium
Drought tolerance	Good	Very good	Excellent	Very good	Very good
Traffic tolerance	Low	High	Low	High	Medium
Cold tolerance	Low	Medium	High	High	Medium
Disease potential	High	Low–medium	Low	Low–medium	Low–medium
Fertility requirement	Medium	High	Low	Low–medium	Medium

* There are two species of zoysiagrass available to homeowners, *Zoysia japonica* (a medium-leaf grass well adapted for home lawns) and *Zoysia matrella* (a fine-leaf grass that produces a dense, beautiful turf but may require more maintenance).

** Buffalo may also be grown as a "mini-meadow" by mowing it once or twice a year.

*** To maintain attractive appearance.

HERE'S HOW

TO SELECT THE MOWING HEIGHT FOR YOUR LAWN

Mow low for the first mowing in the spring to remove weed growth and old discolored turf blades. Then gradually raise the mowing height to the upper range noted in the chart below. Maintaining grass at a taller height results in a deeper and more extensive root system for a more drought-resilient lawn. The higher you cut the turf the less often you will need to mow to remove one-third of the blade. The more often you mow, the denser your turf will become.

Turfgrass	Mowing Height Range	Optimal Mowing Height	Mowing Frequency
St. Augustinegrass	2.5–4 inches	2.5 inches	5–7 days
Common Bermudagrass	1–3 inches	1.5 inches	5 days
Hybrid Bermudagrass	0.75–2 inches	1 inch	3–5 days
Buffalograss*	3–4 inches	2.5 inches	7 days*
Zoysia japonica (coarse-bladed zoysia)	1–2.5 inches	1.5 inches	5–7 days
Zoysia matrella (fine-bladed zoysia)	0.75–2.5 inches	1 inch	3–5 days

* Buffalo can also be maintained as a drought-tolerant "mini-meadow" by mowing it twice a year in the spring and late summer. Follow each mowing with an inch of irrigation.

at 3 inches, don't let it get above 4½ inches before mowing to minimize stress on the grass and maximize turf density.

PERENNIALS & ORNAMENTAL GRASSES

Perennials with tall bloom spikes, such as echinaceas, gladiolus, and parrot gladiolus, usually need to be staked to prevent the blooms from falling over in a wind- or rainstorm. Individual bamboo stakes are one option. Another is one of the wire-support products that allow the blooms to grow through them.

Like annuals, many perennials need to be deadheaded to remove unsightly spent blooms and direct the plant's energy into more blooms. Some species, such as most perennial salvias, continue to bloom on the ends of their terminal stalks. It may be difficult to bring yourself to cut off these blooms, but at some point they will be less of an aesthetic asset, and the plant will lack vigor to produce fresh new blooms.

Shear the plants back by one-third to remove these blooms and the terminal parts of the shoots. Give a boost of fertilizer and water, and the plant will send out more shoots for a new flush of blooms and a more compact appearance. Subshrubs and other perennials such as Gregg's sage (*Salvia greggii*), zexmenia (*Wedelia texana*), and Texas betony (*Stachys coccinea*) will benefit from this shearing anytime the plant's blooms start to dwindle.

Bulbs that bloomed in late winter and spring need some time to replenish their stored reserves before their foliage is removed. Don't cut them back until the foliage turns yellow or brown. By that time the bulbs are replenished and you can remove the unsightly top growth. If you need to rework the beds, this is also a good time to dig the bulbs and set them aside while you renovate the soil in the beds. Then reset the bulbs at their proper depth for the species.

ROSES

Prune roses that only bloom once, now that their spring blooming period is over in most areas of the state. Remove dead and damaged branches, and cut out the oldest one-fifth of the canes back to where they originate at the base of the plant. This with some fertilizing and watering will invigorate new growth for next year's spring bloom show.

Shear shrub roses back by one-fourth to promote regrowth and more blooms. Remove spent blooms on other repeat-blooming roses back to the first leaf with five leaflets to promote more blooms.

SHRUBS

Prune gangly shoots growing out-of-bounds on shrubs to maintain a desirable shape. Shear hedges, making sure to keep the top a little narrower than the base to maintain good foliage density from top to bottom.

Shear subshrubs such as skeleton-leaf goldeneye (*Viguiera stenoloba*) back by one-third, fertilize, and water well to promote fresh new growth and more blooms.

TREES

Check guy wires on any new trees to make sure they are a little slack. Movement in the wind helps a tree's trunk grow stronger. Check mulch around the tree and replenish as needed to maintain a depth of 3 inches to help deter weeds and hold in soil moisture.

■ *Provide a support for tall blooming plants such as these coneflowers (*Echinacea purpurea*) to prevent them from being blown over in a wind or rainstorm.*

■ *Shear back subshrubs such as* Salvia greggii *and other perennials when bloom production is decreasing. Then provide a boost of fertilizer and water to spur new growth and more blooms.*

VINES & GROUNDCOVERS

Attach vines that don't have tendrils, aerial roots, or holdfasts to their trellis support as they grow. Wind them through openings in the structure or use jute twine or garden tie tape to hold them in place. Trim away vines growing in undesired directions or redirect them in a desirable direction by tying them to the support.

WATER

ANNUALS

Water sufficiently to prevent the soil from drying out to the point that plants are wilting. This may mean watering once or twice a week depending on how warm it has become in your area. When possible, use drip irrigation as it puts the water on the *soil* rather than on the foliage. This is more efficient and may reduce some foliage diseases that are promoted by wet leaf conditions.

EDIBLES

Water vegetable and herb gardens based on the soil and sun exposure. In general your garden should need watering twice a week this month. Shady areas and heavy clay soils need watering less frequently than sunny areas and sandy soils. The best way to get to know your garden's watering schedule needs is to dig down a few inches and feel the soil. Water when it is no longer moist to the touch. This is much more accurate than a set watering schedule.

Water blueberries and blackberries with ½ inch of irrigation once a week or enough to wet the soil to a depth of about 8 to 10 inches. Fruit trees and grapevines can get by with a thorough soaking once per week this month. New plants are the exceptions to all this. They need watering every other day in May. (See March, Here's How to Irrigate New Shrubs and Trees.)

A SIMPLE DRIP IRRIGATION SYSTEM

Drip irrigation is an efficient way to water a garden or landscape bed. You can hire someone to install a system for you or you can purchase a kit or individual components to do it yourself. This photo shows the basic parts of a drip system that connect to a garden faucet.

Most companies that sell drip irrigation equipment will provide some basic designs or complete ready-to-assemble kits for gardeners, making it easy to install your own drip irrigation system.

Backflow
Preventer

Screen
Filter

Pressure
Reducer

LAWNS

The weather is warm enough now that your lawn is using about ½ inch of water per week in most of the state. In the eastern half of the state it usually rains enough to meet most of the water needs this month, but in the absence of rain irrigate with ½ inch of water every seven to ten days.

PERENNIALS & ORNAMENTAL GRASSES

Most perennials and ornamental grasses do best with a good soaking to wet the soil at least 6 to 8 inches deep followed by a dry period from a few days to a week to allow the soil to dry out a little and oxygen to move into the root zone. When the soil is barely moist to the touch a few inches deep, water again. A schedule like this is better than keeping the soil soggy or giving shallow, daily waterings that promote shallow rooting. A deeply rooted plant is much more drought resilient.

Some perennials, such as Louisiana iris (*Iris* spp.), spider lilies, bog sage (*Salvia uliginosa*), and cannas, are very tolerant and even fond of wet conditions.

■ *A rain switch is a simple, inexpensive water-saving device that will prevent your irrigation system from running during or a few days after a rain. Water is too precious to waste.*

HERE'S HOW

TO DETERMINE HOW LONG TO WATER

Different sprinklers and drip systems put out water at different rates, making it difficult to know how long they should be run to provide an adequate irrigation. Determine how deep you wish to wet the soil and use one of the following techniques to determine how long to water.

Technique	Directions
Catch Can Test	Set out several rain gauges or straight-sided catch cans in the area and irrigate until you've caught ½ to 1 inch of water in the cans. Set watering times based on soil type* and depth of wetting desired for the plant species. If runoff occurs before ½ to 1 inch is applied, use a "cycle-and-soak" method to apply at least ½ inch without runoff. Water until just prior to runoff, wait an hour, and water again. Repeat until at least ½ inch of water has been applied.
Screwdriver Test	Push a long-handled flathead screwdriver into the soil. The screwdriver will push through wet soil easily but less easily when it reaches dry soil. Grab the screwdriver at the soil surface, remove it, and note how deep the soil was wet.**
Digging Test	Run your irrigation for a specified time, wait 30 minutes, and then dig a hole to see how deep the soil is wet. Note the length of time and depth to guide you in setting future watering durations.

*Approximate amounts of irrigation to wet various soils to 12 inches deep:
  Sand—1 inch
  Loam—1.5–2 inches
  Clay—2.5 inches

**This technique works best in loam and clay-type soils.

ROSES, SHRUBS & TREES

Newly planted shrubs and trees need moderately moist soil and should not be allowed to go into drought stress. (See March, Here's How to Irrigate New Shrubs and Trees.) This means watering twice a week now that the temperature is getting hot. Adequate watering is the key to their survival during their first growing season. While a good soaking is important, frequency is more important than quantity according to research trials in the South. See July for how to water these plants.

VINES & GROUNDCOVERS

If there's no rain, provide a good soaking to groundcover areas by running sprinklers until you've caught 1 inch of water in a catch can or rain gauge. If you use drip irrigation, water long enough to wet the soil about 6 to 8 inches deep.

FERTILIZE

ANNUALS

Fertilize annual flowering plants and foliage plants with a moderate application of fertilizer every four to six weeks. Monitor how the plants are growing and adjust fertilizing accordingly. They should have good green color and be blooming well. If plants lack nutrition their foliage may lose the green and the plants won't have the energy to keep up strong bloom production. See April, Here's How to Fertilize Flowers, Ornamental Grasses, and Vegetables, for help with how much fertilizer to apply.

EDIBLES

Cool-season plantings are nearing their end and don't need additional fertilizing at this point. Give warm-season vegetables, with the exception of beans and peas, one moderate fertilizer application or two light applications (two weeks apart) this month. Take a look at how your plants are doing. If they lack good color or vigor they probably need more nutrition. If they are growing rapidly it is best to hold off to avoid overdoing it.

Fertilize fruit trees, vines, and bushes less than a year old with a turf-type fertilizer once this month using the application tips in March, Here's How to Fertilize a Young Tree.

LAWNS

If you didn't fertilize your lawn this spring, do so now to provide a boost to support strong growth and

■ *Fertilize bearded and Louisiana iris plants with a light to moderate application of fertilizer to help them replenish their stored reserves.*

density. (See April, Here's How to Fertilize a Lawn.) Lawns that were fertilized earlier in the year won't need additional fertilizer until fall, especially if you return the clippings to the lawn when you mow.

PERENNIALS & ORNAMENTAL GRASSES

When you shear back perennials that are declining in bloom production, give them a moderate dose of fertilizer. Pull back the mulch and sprinkle the fertilizer evenly throughout the bed and then use a hoe or hand cultivator to work it into the surface inch of soil. Then water the area and replace the mulch. If it is not practical to remove the mulch, spread fertilizer over the mulch and stir the mulch with a rake to settle the fertilizer down to the soil surface. Water the area well to wet through the mulch and down into the soil.

Fertilize bearded and Louisiana irises early this month to provide good nutrition as they prepare for their summer rest period and next year's bloom season, or in the case of some reblooming bearded irises, more blooms in the fall.

ROSES

Feed all roses that have been planted for at least two months, including those that bloom only in spring, with ¼ cup of fertilizer for small plants (less than 2 feet in height or width) and ⅓ cup of fertilizer for larger plants. Scatter the fertilizer on the soil beneath the branch spread of the plant, work it into the surface inch of soil, and water it in well. Use a product with approximately a 3-1-2 nutrient ratio.

SHRUBS

Fertilize young shrubs with a turf-type fertilizer to promote good vigor. See March for information on fertilizing shrubs.

TREES

Fertilize young trees according to instructions provided in March, Here's How to Fertilize a Young Tree, which will guide you in how much to apply to trees of various sizes. Repeat every six to eight weeks during spring and summer to promote maximum growth.

VINES & GROUNDCOVERS

Fertilize newly established groundcover and vines by applying 2 cups of turf-type fertilizer per 50 square feet of bed area, followed by ½ inch of irrigation. Repeat monthly during the growing season until the plants have filled in the open spaces.

PROBLEM-SOLVE

ALL

Carry a smartphone or digital camera with you when you are out in the garden. Be ready to snap photos of pests, diseases, and other problems to get assistance from your County Extension Office and to include in your garden journal or planner for future reference. Many pests and diseases show up about the same time each year so these photos will help you be ready the next time around to detect and, if needed, treat the plants early, before serious damage occurs.

Diseases can proliferate in warm conditions following rainy weather. Leaf spots caused by fungi and bacteria are unsightly but often not damaging enough to warrant spraying. Not all products work against the various leaf spot and leaf blight diseases, so an accurate diagnosis by your County Extension Office is a good place to start.

Root rots are caused by fungi and bacteria; however, they are usually brought on by soggy wet, poorly aerated soil conditions. You can't control rainfall, but you *can* make sure your plants are in well-drained raised beds if drainage is a problem. By fixing soggy soil conditions, most root rots will not be a problem and thus no spraying or drenching will be needed.

Small, roundish tan spots on the foliage of herbs, flowers, and some types of vegetables may be the work of the four-lined plant bug. These pests are small with yellow-and-black stripes going down

■ *Control nutsedge regularly and diligently to prevent a minor infestation from turning into a major invasion.*

their backs. They can do significant damage to plants by creating a multitude of tiny feeding spots in the foliage. If you catch them early insecticidal soap or horticultural oil spray can be effective against them at the young nymph stage. If you wait until they grow into adults stronger products are required for control.

Nutsedge plants form side tubers so one plant will soon become a half dozen, greatly increasing your job in controlling it. Wet the soil a couple of days in advance and dig up the nutsedge plants, taking care to get all of the tubers or "nuts" that you can. Stay with this process every few weeks to get the remaining tubers and prevent their proliferation. It is much easier to keep it in control early than to try and control it after these weeds have proliferated.

ANNUALS

Check your annual foliage and flowering plants for signs of pest damage. If leaves have holes or sections missing it could be caterpillars, beetles, snails, or slugs. Check under the foliage and on the soil surface around the plant for these pests. Look for the telltale slug and snail trails on plants. If you can't find the culprits, then play Sherlock Holmes by going out at night with a flashlight, as some of

■ *Leaf-footed bugs and other stink bugs can ruin a tomato, southern pea, or okra crop if not controlled early when they are still young and easier to control.*

blights, insects on the plants, or discolored foliage, take a sample of the plant or pests and place them in a zip-top bag. Write your name, phone number, and email on the bag and take it to your County Extension Office for a free evaluation. They can help identify what is causing the problem and recommend the steps you may need to take to remedy it.

Early blight is a foliage disease of tomatoes that can destroy the majority of a tomato's leaf area. Take early action by removing spotted leaves and spraying the plant with a solution for fungal diseases that is labeled for use on tomatoes. *Read and follow the label carefully.* If much of the plant is already affected it is too late for a spray to be of any benefit.

these pests are nocturnal. When you know what the pest is your County Extension Office can help prescribe an appropriate course of action.

EDIBLES

Warm weather brings out pests, including caterpillars, stink bugs, beetles, aphids, and perhaps an early outbreak of spider mites. Take time to look over your plants. If you see signs of damage, leaf spots or

Stink bugs and their cousins, the leaf-footed bugs, are a major pest of tomatoes and can also affect peaches and other vegetables and fruits. Their feeding can deform developing fruit and leave yellow and white spots on tomato fruit. They are difficult to control with sprays, but if you use a spray it is best to do so when the pests are young. Learn to identify these pests when they hatch out and lack wings to fly away. You can easily suck

■ *If your lawn is thinning due to too much shade from trees, a little thinning of the tree canopy can brighten the shade enough to allow the grass to develop better density.*

Before

After

them up with a hand vacuum at this stage if you repeat the process every two or three days until you aren't seeing more of these pests. If you just have a few plants, vacuuming young stink bugs may be a practical option, although your neighbors may think you're crazy when they see you vacuuming your tomato plants.

Peaches and plums that fall from the tree early may have plum curculio larva inside. Cut into a fruit and examine it for larvae. If you find some, make a note next spring to pick up a fruit tree spray handout from your County Extension Office. Always pick up and discard fallen fruit promptly to remove any pest or disease spores that may be present in the fruit. Peaches and plums rotting on the tree are a sign of brown rot disease. Remove these from the tree to minimize infection of more fruit. The same goes for apples and bunches of grapes that start to rot on the plant. The Extension spray handout can provide options for managing these diseases also.

LAWNS

St. Augustine grass is the most shade-tolerant warm-season turf species. If your turfgrass is getting thin in shady areas, try to increase light by hiring an arborist to do some minor tree pruning to brighten the shade. Minimize foot traffic in those areas and set the mower at a higher setting. If all this is not enough consider replacing the turf with a shade-loving groundcover.

PERENNIALS & ORNAMENTAL GRASSES

Perennials are damaged by the same pests as annuals. Check them periodically to catch problems early on before significant damage has been done. Early detection can provide the benefit of less toxic options as some of the least toxic products are most effective when pests are very young.

Are you seeing brown tips on ornamental grasses? If ornamental grasses dry out they will lose vigor and may start to brown on the leaf tips. Maintaining soil moisture is the way to prevent this. When damage is severe, you can cut the grass clump back to a foot high and then water the area well to rejuvenate the clump and bring on fresh new foliage.

ROSES

Blackspot and powdery mildew are the most common diseases of roses. Preventative sprays on a seven- to fourteen-day schedule can fend off these diseases. Unless you *really* love a particular variety, consider changing to a disease-resistant variety to save the time, money, and hassle of spraying.

SHRUBS & TREES

Azalea foliage that is losing its green color because of a yellowish or brown stippled or specked pattern is usually a sign of lace bug damage. These pests are found on the undersides of the leaves and appear as ⅛ inch or smaller, black and clear insects. Texas sage (*Cenizo*) can also be attacked by a different lace bug species. Neem, insecticidal soap, and spinosad sprays have proven to be effective but need to be applied two or three times at two-week intervals.

If you notice the ends of shoots on your juniper, cedar, arborvitae, or cypress plants turning brown, the cause is likely a twig blight fungus such as phomopsis. Prune diseased areas, cutting 4 inches back into healthy branch tissues. Discard all prunings to reduce reinfection and minimize overhead watering, as wet foliage favors these diseases. Follow with a fungicide spray labeled for the disease and the plant species, carefully observing label instructions.

Watch for early signs of the white powdery substance on mildew-susceptible species (see April, Problem-Solve) and take early action to prevent damage to the plant's foliage.

VINES & GROUNDCOVERS

Vines that are not thriving may have something restricting the stem at or below the ground level. Dig down a few inches to check for a plant label, circling root, or anything that may be strangling the stem and remove it.

Browning areas of groundcovers may be due to a disease either killing roots or rotting leaf and stem tissues. Take a sample to your local Extension Office along with a photo of the overall planting for assistance diagnosing the problem. Proper diagnosis is essential for proper management.

June

Summer sun brings an end to the cool-season flowers that were hanging on and to warm-season flowers that thrive in spring but can't take the heat. Truly heat-tolerant annual and perennial plants, including the all-important foliage plants, now take over the task of keeping our landscapes colorful until fall brings a break in the weather.

Sunshine is a wonderful thing but can pose a danger to gardeners in its effect on our skin and the danger of heat exhaustion. The effects of skin damage are cumulative so be wise and wear loose, long-sleeved cotton shirts with a wide brimmed hat. Cover exposed skin with a sunscreen. Our plants need extra water in the heat and so do we. Drink plenty of water as you work and try to get most of your work done early and late in the day when it is cooler. Heat exhaustion and sunstroke can sneak up on you, so don't take chances by overdoing it.

Pests and diseases can spoil the show in our gardens and landscapes. Indiscriminate spraying has negative consequences for beneficial insects, the environment, and our health. Integrated Pest Management (IPM) is a better approach. It avoids the need to spray whenever possible by starting with resistant plants, following good cultural practices, supporting beneficial insect populations, and learning to identify pests and beneficials in their various life stages. When spraying becomes necessary, use low-toxicity sprays that affect pests without wiping out beneficial insects. Remember that a pest-free landscape or garden is neither good nor possible, so accept a little pest or disease damage here or there as no cause for alarm.

The more you learn about good horticultural practices and the pests and beneficials in your garden, the less you will find you need to spray. Become a proactive rather than a reactive gardener. When the heat drives you indoors in search of air conditioning, take advantage of this time to learn more about the best gardening practices and the cast of six- and eight-legged characters that are part of the balance of nature.

JUNE

PLAN

ALL

Consider installing a timer for your drip irrigation systems. It makes it easier to water since most types of timers can be set to water on specific days of the week and for set lengths of time. There are even hose-end timers that attach to a faucet and will control an attached drip irrigation system.

Notice what is blooming around town as the weather heats up. Depending on where you live some shrubs that can carry blooms on into the hot weather include crape myrtle, hydrangeas, thryallis (*Galphimia glauca*), oleander (*Nerium oleander*), althea or rose of Sharon (*Hibiscus syriacus*),

■ *A hose-end timer can be set to turn your sprinkler on and off, even when you are away. It is a great water-saving device.*

HERE'S HOW

TO HAVE SUMMER COLOR WITHOUT FLOWERS

Summer heat shuts down many great blooming plants. But we can continue to paint our landscapes with color by using plants with colorful foliage.

Artemisia (*Artemisia* 'Powis Castle')

Banana (*Musa* spp.)

Blood banana (*Musa zebrina* 'Rojo')

Beefsteak plant or chicken gizzard (*Iresine herbstii*)

Brazilian snow bush (*Alternanthera* spp.)

Caladium (*Caladium* spp.)

Canna (*Canna* spp. 'Phasion', 'Blueberry Sparkler', 'Bengal Tiger', 'Australia' , 'Minerva')

Coleus (*Solenostemon scutellarioides*)

Copper plant (*Acalypha wilkesiana*)

Duranta 'Gold Mound' (*Duranta repens*)

Dusty miller (*Artemisia caucasica*)

Elephant's ear (*Colocasia* spp. and *Alocasia* spp.)

Hibiscus 'Fire and Ice' (*Hibiscus rosa-sinensis*)

Hibiscus 'Mahogany Splendor' (*Hibiscus acetosella*)

Joseph's coat (*Alternanthera* spp.)

Magilla perilla 'Magilla' (*Perilla frutescens*)

Ornamental millet 'Purple Majesty' (*Pennisetum glaucum*)

Sweet potato vine (*Ipomoea batatas*)

Persian shield (*Strobilanthes dyeranus*)

Polka dot plant (*Hypoestes phyllostachya*)

Purple heart (*Setcreasea pallida*)

Purple shamrock (*Oxalis regnellii atropurpurea*)

Tricolor hibiscus or variegated sea hibiscus 'Albo-variegatus' (*Talipariti tiliaceum*)

Triostar stromanthe 'Tricolor' (*Stromanthe sanguinea*)

Variegated shell ginger 'Variegata' (*Alpinia zerumbet*)

Variegated tapioca 'Variegata' (*Manihot esculenta*)

Wax begonia 'Big™ Red with Bronze Leaf' (*Begonia semperflorens*)

SUPER SALVIAS FOR HEAT-TOLERANT COLOR

Few genera offer the Texas tough resilience and beauty of salvias. There are salvias for every landscape across the state. Here are a few outstanding options:

Tropical sage (*Salvia coccinea*), annual (perennial in zones 8b to 9)

Mexican bush sage (*Salvia leucantha*)

Gregg's sage (*Salvia greggii*)

Salvia 'Mystic Spires' and 'Indigo Spires' (*Salvia* x spp.) (perennial in zones 6 to 9)

Mealycup sage (*Salvia farinacea*)

Blue anise sage (*Salvia guaranitica*)

Pineapple sage (*Salvia elegans*)

Salvia 'Wendy's Wish' (*Salvia hybrid*) (perennial in zones 8b to 9)

Bicolor sage (*Salvia sinaloensis*)

Make vacation plans for your plants. Arrange to have someone stop by to water when you are gone for an extended time. Automatic drip irrigation systems can help reduce the workload. Group container plants for faster hand watering. In a pinch, a plastic wading pool can keep several containers watered for a couple of weeks or more. Place the containers in the pool and add a few inches of water. The containers will "wick" up the water over time as they need it. Place a mosquito dunk, or another product containing the natural mosquito larvae control ingredient *Bacillus thuringiensis israelensis* strain, in the pool to prevent it from becoming a breeding ground for mosquitoes. If you move plants to a less sunny location their water needs will greatly decrease, making them less susceptible to drought injury in such a short time versus if they were in full sun.

ANNUALS

Summer can take its toll on our annual flower and foliage plants. Take a look at these to see how they are performing. It may be time to plan another color change or to at least change out a species that is not performing well and appears to be on the decline.

EDIBLES

Summer is a time when there aren't as many vegetables in the garden and some areas can lie fallow. Use this time to "build" the soil for fall planting. Mixing compost into the soil is a big part of soil building. If you don't have compost on hand order a large supply of bulk compost or pick up a few bags (if your garden area is small), so you'll be ready to amend the soil when spring crops are done and pulled out. By building soil now you will be ready to plant when fall gardening time rolls around and your fall garden will be more productive. There is something beneficial about giving the soil time to settle in for a few weeks or more after adding organic matter.

butterfly bush (*Buddleia davidii*), cenizo or Texas sage (*Leucophyllum frutescens*), repeat-blooming roses, as well as vitex (*Vitex agnus-castus*) and desert willow (*Chilopsis linearis*), which are actually trees. You can plant year-round, so you can go shopping now for these plants or make a note on your calendar or garden journal to include some of them when the fall planting season arrives so you'll have more blooms next summer.

Make note in your garden journal of pests and other insects you are seeing in your landscape and garden. Take a digital photo of them for future reference. Here's a tip: If the pests won't hold still for the photos, place them in a jar or bag in the refrigerator for a few minutes. Then when you take them out you'll have a minute or so to get your photo before they become active again. Take the photos of some insects that you've captured to your County Extension Office for help identifying them. That way you'll learn to tell friends from foes for future gardening success.

ROSES

Repeat-blooming roses can provide waves of blooms throughout the season. If your roses are succumbing to blackspot or powdery mildew their lack of foliage will decrease their blooming potential. Consider replacing them this fall with more disease-resistant and dependable reblooming varieties. Do some research now to pick the ones with bloom color and plant form that appeal to you most.

VINES & GROUNDCOVERS

If you have a sunny spot that you'd like to make shady fast consider a fast-growing vine on an arbor. Perhaps a tree or major limb was lost in a storm, leaving a shady spot blazing hot. Check out the list of woody vines in January or the list of annual and perennial vines in April for some great ideas. Include a vigorous annual vine (morning glory or hyacinth bean) or perennial vine (blue sky vine or Queen's wreath) for faster coverage while a woody vine is becoming established. You can always move the perennial vine in a year or two to another location.

PLANT

ANNUALS

If you are able to water an area daily for a couple of weeks to help plants become established, you can still plant heat-tolerant annual flowers and foliage this month. See comments on foliage in the perennials section that also apply to annual foliage.

It is easier to wet soil that is moist than it is to wet soil that is dry. A couple of days prior to planting annuals water the beds thoroughly to provide deep moisture and to make the soil easier to work. If the soil is very dry this may take two or three waterings with an hour to soak between each one to soak the soil deeply. When you set out your new transplants it will be easier to give the new plants a good soaking and the moisture from deep in the soil will wick upward to supply the annuals' expanding root systems.

This pre-plant watering is especially important if you are planting seeds; it's even more important than watering *after* you plant seeds. The moist soil below will help germinating seeds establish their newly forming roots quickly. Water again after

■ *Coleus is a great way to add a lot of color fast during the summer months despite the heat and humidity. Snip off the blooms of coleus as they appear to encourage the plant to continue producing new foliage.*

planting with a misting attachment to your hose to avoid dislodging the seeds with a strong spray of water.

It often helps to provide a little sun protection after seeding a garden bed. Row-cover fabrics suspended over the planted area or a very light scattering of pine needles can help lessen the effects of the blazing sun, slow drying of the soil, and moderate the soil temperatures a bit. Once seedlings are up and have developed true leaves you can remove the row cover.

EDIBLES

You can continue to plant heat-tolerant vegetables, including okra, southern peas, Malabar and amaranth greens, and sweet potatoes, this month. It is important to do a pre-plant irrigation to supply water to deeper parts of your soil. Soak the area two days before planting. This may mean watering until it starts to run off, waiting an hour, and watering again two or three times since water tends to not want to move readily into dry soil. This deep wetting will provide a bank account of water that will wick upward to help keep seeds moist despite surface drying and will also be available for new transplants as they develop roots.

On planting day, rake the surface. Plant seeds at a depth of about three times their width and firm in the soil gently over the seeds to create good seed-to-soil contact for more successful germination. Also firm in soil around transplants and make a small berm of soil about 8 inches in diameter to hold water and ensure a good soaking at the plant's roots. A piece of shade cloth or row-cover fabric suspended over the row to deflect the brunt of the summer sun for a couple of weeks is also helpful in getting seeds and transplants off to a good start when the weather has turned very hot.

Container-grown herbs and fruit plants can still be planted if you are able to keep their roots moist without overwatering. Soggy soil for extended periods of time can kill vegetables, herbs, and fruit plants fast in the heat of summer.

LAWNS

Turfgrass can be sodded or seeded this month. Since it is very hot, water about ½ to 1 inch per

■ *Malabar greens will thrive despite the brutal heat of a Texas summer and can be planted now if provided moist soil to support good growth.*

week to help the new sod or tender seedlings develop a root system that will ensure resiliency and summer survival. Keep the mower blade sharp, especially with tougher-to-mow species of grass such as zoysia.

PERENNIALS & ORNAMENTAL GRASSES

When the mercury climbs into the upper 90s or triple digits for days on end, and even nighttime temperatures can be sultry, flowers that are called "heat-tolerant" in milder climates often either die or stop blooming. While there are some perennial flowers that can take the heat (see the list of hot weather perennials in July), we need to shift strategies and look to plants with colorful foliage to paint our landscapes with color. There are many annual and perennial plants that can make a dramatic impact with their foliage. See Here's How to Have Summer Color Without Flowers earlier in this chapter.

One key player for summer foliage is elephant ears (*Colocasia* spp. and *Alocasia* spp.). These plants offer giant foliage to 3 feet long in a variety of colors, including chartreuse, burgundy/purple, splotches of burgundy in chartreuse, and almost black. They *love* heat, tolerate poor drainage, and command attention. So include some in your summer plantings. Elephant ears are perennial in most areas of the state, although they should be dug and brought indoors for winter in zones 6 and the colder parts of zone 7.

Provide foliage plants with well-amended soil by adding 2 inches of compost prior to planting. Feed them moderately to keep them growing well (see April, Here's How to Fertilize Flowers, Ornamental Grasses, and Vegetables) and *don't let them dry out.* The burgundy to purple colors of foliage plants often fade more to green in deep shade, so give them some sun exposure for best color; even a few hours can help maintain their deeper color.

Ornamental grasses will perform well even in hot weather if provided adequate moisture. Continue to plant them this month but be sure to do the pre-plant watering mentioned previously and then maintain soil moisture with frequent watering after planting.

ROSES, SHRUBS, & TREES
You can still plant container-grown woody ornamental plants this month, but you'll need to be extra diligent to keep the soil moist without overwatering. When the soil stays oversaturated for extended periods the roots can't get oxygen and will die. Dig down a few inches in the area of the rootball and feel the soil to determine if it is soggy, moist, or dry, and water accordingly.

VINES & GROUNDCOVERS
Plant vines to shade a western wall. See Woody Vines for Landscapes in January for a listing of vines that maintain aboveground plant parts from year to year. Note which ones need trellising and which can attach to walls. Some are able to attach to a wall by aerial roots or holdfast discs. Think twice before planting these types to climb up a wall with wood siding or they can damage the paint or wood and trap moisture, which can promote decay. They work best on brick or stone masonry walls.

Annual and perennial vines can still be planted in the landscape. They are a fast way to fill in a trellis or arbor to block a view or provide some shade, and many offer blooms in summer and fall. See April for a list of annual and perennial vines.

■ *Planting an annual, perennial, or woody vine such as this evergreen wisteria, can provide shade for an arbor, or to a western wall of your home from the hot, late-day sun.*

CARE

ANNUALS
Annual flowers either are tidy plants that drop the spent blooms or they remain on the plant, detracting from its appearance. Snip these spent blooms back to the first set of leaves below the bloom to keep the "messy" plantings looking their best.

Coleus is grown for its beautiful foliage. When it starts to bloom any new foliage is smaller and less impressive. Snip out the bloom stalks of coleus as they first appear, cutting back to just above a set of larger leaves. The plants will regrow and be fuller and more compact.

EDIBLES
Remove crops that have stopped producing or that are being plagued by pests. If you don't wish to plant

heat-tolerant vegetables in their spots, prepare these areas to lay fallow over summer. Mix an inch or two of compost into the soil and water the area to moisten the soil. If you have extra leaves or grass clippings on hand you can also mix them into the soil where they will rapidly decompose in the warm, moist conditions. This is called "sheet composting."

Mix in a few inches of leaves or grass clippings at a time to make the job easier. Shred the leaves first to make it easier to mix them into the soil. Soil microbes will go to work decomposing the organic matter, including the mulch where it's in contact with the soil. Then cover the ground with a thick blanket of leaves, pine needles, hay, or dried grass clippings. By fall planting time you'll just need to pull back the surface mulch and plant. That's good news when planting in the heat of August.

Remove suckers and water sprouts from fruit trees, cutting them out close to where they attach to the tree to remove the latent buds at their base. When the harvest is over do some minor pruning to open up the interior tree a little so light can filter in, which will help the lower branches set bloom buds in midsummer to early fall for next year's crop. Remove any weeds beneath a tree's canopy and mulch this area 3 to 4 inches deep; that will deter weeds that rob water from the fruit plants. Remove any diseased fruit on the tree or fallen fruit as a sanitary measure.

LAWNS

Mow at least weekly to build optimum density in your lawn. Dense lawns choke out weeds and frequent mowing at the proper height is the most important way to increase density (see May, Here's How to Select the Best Mowing Height for Your Lawn).

PERENNIALS & ORNAMENTAL GRASSES

Perennial plants that are starting to get lanky can be pinched back to control their height and keep

■ *Shear back fall aster and other fall-blooming perennials by a third to promote more bushy, compact growth for a more attractive plant during their fall flower show.*

them more compact. Don't be afraid to snip back perennials often as this really helps promote new growth and compactness. This is especially important for perennials that bloom at the ends of the new shoots, such as chrysanthemums and salvias. More new shoots equal more blooms.

Prune the spent blooms out of garden phlox and other summer-blooming perennials when the blooms fade. Stake the stems of gladiolus, Philippine lily, and any other tall perennial flowers that are blooming this month or next to prevent them from falling over in rainstorms or wind.

Fall-blooming perennials, including chrysanthemums, fall aster, and copper canyon daisy, should be pruned back by one-third to encourage more bushiness and more new shoots in preparation for a great fall bloom show.

■ *Weave the canes of climbing roses back and forth horizontally across their trellis as they grow to help them produce more blooms next spring.*

ROSES

Weave shoots (or canes) of climbing roses back and forth as you move up a trellis. Attach them with twine or plastic plant tape. Orienting them horizontally will result in more blooms than if they are allowed to grow vertically.

Shear shrub roses, if you haven't done so in the past four to six weeks, to promote more blooms.

SHRUBS

Shear shrubs in hedges every few weeks to maintain dense growth. Shrubs with a natural form don't need regular pruning, just an occasional snip to maintain a balanced look that is appealing to you.

This month is the time to complete any needed pruning to spring-flowering shrubs, trees, and woody vines. The plants need time to regrow and set bloom buds on the growth from midsummer to early fall, so pruning during the coming months will reduce their bloom next spring.

TREES

Remove storm-damaged branches cutting back to where they joined another branch. See February, Here's How to Remove a Tree Limb, for guidance on how to make a proper cut when removing a branch. Remove dead wood in the interior of the tree, but leave living branches. Stripping out the center of a tree is *not* recommended.

VINES & GROUNDCOVERS

Newly planted vines that twine need some tending during the first months after they begin to grow to help them get started wrapping around the support. Vines that don't twine or that lack aerial roots must be attached to or woven in the support structures to help them fill the trellis. Once they have been trained to a trellis they will only need some minor pruning to shorten long shoots and direct growth so that it continues to fill the trellis, arbor, or other support structure.

Prune vigorous vines such as star jasmine (*Trachelospermum jasminoides*) by shearing them back

HERE'S HOW

TO ATTRACT BENEFICIAL INSECTS

1. Don't kill them. Broad-spectrum pesticides upset the balance of nature and can result in pest outbreaks.

2. Provide a source of water. Birdbaths, water features, and irrigation all can provide beneficial insects water that they need. Some, such as dragonflies, are especially attracted to water.

3. Provide pests for them to eat. Most beneficial insect larvae and some of the adults feed on pests. They lay eggs when pest are present so their young will have a food source. A few pests is usually a good thing.

4. Provide pollen and nectar for nutrition and energy. Many beneficial insects don't eat pests but rather need pollen and nectar for food. Include some plants with daisy-like blooms (coreopsis, black-eyed Susan, feverfew, chamomile, zinnia, copper canyon daisy, fall aster), plants with umbrella-like blooms (yarrow, dill, anise, fennel, coriander/cilantro), and blooming herbs (thyme, chives, oregano, bee balm, basil, trailing rosemary, mint, and rue).

to maintain density and to keep them inbounds. This is especially important if they are growing to form a living wall on a fence or alongside a building.

Trim the edges of vining groundcovers to maintain the desired shape for their bed and prevent them from sprawling into other plantings or the lawn. Trim vines and groundcovers growing up a tree trunk to prevent them from going where you don't want them. Some regular trimming is needed to maintain these wandering plants where we want them to be.

■ *Plants in containers have confined root systems and can dry out quickly. Choose larger containers to lessen how often you need to water them.*

WATER

ALL

Deep, infrequent soaking is the best way to build an extensive healthy root system and drought-resilient plants. Avoid drought stress from underwatering or anaerobic (lack of oxygen) conditions in the soil, which is caused by keeping it soggy wet for several days or more.

ANNUALS, PERENNIALS & ORNAMENTAL GRASSES

Foliage plants need plenty of water to stay hydrated in this heat. If they're allowed to dry out they will wilt and often start to drop older leaves. Water as often as needed, which may be every two or three days, depending on the soil conditions and sun exposure.

Container annuals need regular watering to avoid drought stress. It is not unusual for a container to need water *every day* if it is in the sun. If a plant is a bit large for its container, or the container potting mix is very coarse, it may require watering twice a day.

Hanging baskets that dry out can be difficult to water as the water runs off the surface and around the sides of the container because the soil and rootball have shrunk away from the sides of the container. Like a dry sponge, dry growing media can actually *resist* wetting. Water gradually in small amounts, giving it time to soak until you have wet the soil thoroughly throughout the container.

A good way to water hanging baskets is to fill a tub or kids' wading pool with water and set them in it to soak for a while. Then lift them out and return them to their locations to drain the excess water. This is an especially effective technique for ferns in hanging baskets.

EDIBLES

Water enough to keep the soil in vegetable and herb gardens moist. The best watering gauge is your hand, so dig down a few inches and feel the soil to determine if it is moist or not. If it's not, apply ½ inch of sprinkler irrigation on sandy soil and 1 inch on loam or clay soil. If you have drip irrigation, then water long enough to wet the soil to a depth of at least 8 inches.

Water fruit trees, vines, and bushes enough to wet sandy soil a foot deep and clay or loam soils at least 8 to 10 inches deep. Established trees will need only one (clay/loam soil) or two (sandy soil) irrigations per week this month. For new trees planted this year, see March, Here's How to Irrigate New Shrubs and Trees, for watering instructions.

LAWNS

Now that the weather is getting really hot turfgrass will need about 1 inch of water per week either as rainfall or supplemental irrigation. It is better to water more when you irrigate but to irrigate less often than it is to water a small amount every day or two. If you've been irrigating three or more times per week, gradually wean your lawn back to one or two waterings (at most) per week, over the course of a few weeks.

ROSES, SHRUBS & TREES

Now that the weather is getting really hot it is very important to keep less than one-year-old shrubs, trees, and roses adequately watered to help them survive in the heat. Water recently planted woody ornamentals according to instructions provided in March, Here's How to Irrigate New Shrubs and Trees.

VINES & GROUNDCOVERS

Provide supplemental irrigation in the absence of rainfall, but take care not to overwater the drought-tolerant groundcovers such as silver ponyfoot, woolly stemodia, trailing rosemary, lamb's ear, and santolina. Soggy wet soil conditions combined with the heat of a Texas summer are a sure recipe for rot diseases and a rapid death.

■ *Wean your lawn to once- or twice-a-week watering to save water and help develop a deep, resilient root system.*

HERE'S HOW

TO CHECK THE EFFICIENCY OF YOUR LAWN IRRIGATION SYSTEM

1. Set out rain gauges or tuna cans.

2. Turn on the system and collect the cans after 15 minutes.

3. Note the differences in the amounts collected to assess uniformity of application (if the amount of water in the can with the least is less than two-thirds of the amount in the can with the most, consider hiring an irrigation company to renovate the system).

4. Multiply the average depth in collection cans by four to determine the inches per hour that your irrigation system applies.

FERTILIZE

ALL

Don't just sprinkle fertilizer on the surface and leave it there. After applying fertilizer, use a cultivator to "scratch" it in about 1 inch deep around annuals and perennials and a couple of inches deep around woody ornamentals and fruit plants to avoid damaging the plants' shallow roots. Then water the area with ½ inch of irrigation to start the process of dissolving the fertilizer and releasing the nutrients to the plant's roots.

ANNUALS, PERENNIALS & ORNAMENTAL GRASSES

Fertilize annual and perennial flowers and foliage with a light to moderate feeding once this month. See April, Here's How to Fertilize Flowers, Ornamental Grasses, and Vegetables, for rates to apply per amount of flowerbed area. If you mixed compost into your flowerbed and the flowers are already growing well you can forgo this month's fertilizer application. In warm, moist soil conditions organic matter decomposes rapidly, releasing its nutrients to the growing plants.

Fertilize ornamental grasses with a moderate application of a lawn fertilizer with a 3-1-2 or 4-1-2 ratio of nutrients to carry them into summer with good vigor.

■ *Avoid overwatering drought-resilient groundcovers such as woody stemodia. It thrives in full sun and well-drained soil.*

Tropical flowering plants, including mandevilla, allamanda, tibouchina, and tropical hibiscus, are growing rapidly in the rising temperatures. Keep them vigorous and strong with a moderate application of fertilizer. You can use a slow-release synthetic or natural product to feed them gradually over time. If you use a fast-release synthetic product, apply it in two or three small doses spaced a few weeks apart.

EDIBLES

Make a light application of fertilizer to summer vegetables once or twice this month. Check out April, Here's How to Fertilize Flowers, Ornamental Grasses, and Vegetables, for a helpful guide on how much fertilizer to apply. Summer peas don't need feeding; in fact, excess nitrogen can result in vine growth at the expense of production. Herbs in soil with good organic matter also can forego fertilizer applications this month.

Fertilize new vegetable and herb transplants at planting by watering them in with a soluble fertilizer product. Repeat this for new vegetable transplants twice more about five days apart. Vegetable seedlings can be fertilized with a light application of dry fertilizer when they have been growing for about three weeks.

Fertilize fruit trees, vines, and bushes less than a year old with a turf-type fertilizer once in June.

Here's How to Fertilize a Young Tree in March will provide help on which fertilizer ratio to use, how much to apply, and where to apply the product.

LAWNS

Return clippings to the turf with each mowing to feed the lawn. Clippings contain the perfect blend of nutrients for turf and decompose rapidly in the warm, moist conditions of an irrigated lawn to release their nutrients. If you recycle clippings into the turf, over the course of a mowing season your lawn mower will apply more "fertilizer" than your fertilizer spreader does in two or three applications.

ROSES

Continue to feed established, repeat-blooming roses with ⅓ cup per bush every four to six weeks. Start fertilizing newly planted roses after they have been in the ground for four to six weeks by sprinkling 2 tablespoons beneath the mulch around each bush and working it into the soil surface.

SHRUBS

If your azaleas or gardenias are showing signs of yellowing on new growth, fertilize them with a product for acid-loving plants that contains some iron and sulfur. This will green them up again and better prepare them to set next year's bloom buds in late summer and early fall.

Fertilize young, single shrubs and hedges according to instructions in March to promote good vigor.

■ *Don't throw away grass clippings. Return them to the lawn as you mow to gradually feed the turfgrass as they decompose slowly over time.*

TREES

Feed young trees every six to eight weeks to promote fast growth so they reach a desirable size sooner rather than later.

VINES & GROUNDCOVERS

Fertilize only the young groundcovers and vines that you want to fill in faster. See the fertilization rates mentioned in May.

PROBLEM-SOLVE

ALL

Missing plants or large areas of foliage are a sign of deer damage. Deer get hungry as the native habitat they depend on dries up in summer. This makes our landscapes pretty appealing. Desperate deer will munch on plants, often doing significant damage. They have their plant preferences, but when they're hungry they will expand their palates to include most of our garden and landscape plants. (See July, Here's How to Protect Landscapes from Deer.)

Continue to check periodically for chewing pest damage that will show up as holes or other eaten-away areas of a leaf. Some pests have piercing-sucking mouthparts and leave discolored spots on foliage or cause leaf growth to be malformed. These pests come and go, so don't treat with a pest-control product if you don't actually see the pests. Often by the time we notice the damage, the pests may have already moved on.

Spider mites *love* hot weather and dry, dusty conditions. They hide under plant leaves and suck the juices out of the leaves, causing a loss of color in tiny specks. In severe infestations they leave a fine webbing under the leaves. Junipers, roses, tomatoes, beans, morning glories, butterfly bushes (*Buddleia*), and marigolds are among the plants they often target. Check for spider mites by placing a white piece of paper under some affected plant leaves and thump the leaves with your fingers. Then watch the paper for tiny reddish brown specks the size of the period at the end of this sentence. They will be moving around slowly. If you see any then measures are needed to prevent or deter an outbreak.

Three options are to blast the mites off with a strong spray of water directed upward from beneath the foliage (repeated weekly for three weeks), or sprays either of insecticidal soap or horticultural oil, also directed upward to contact all of the lower leaf surfaces. These sprays should be repeated again a week later.

ANNUALS, PERENNIALS & ORNAMENTAL GRASSES

It is normal for the foliage of Louisiana and bearded irises to turn yellow and brown this time of the year as they begin a sort of "summer dormancy," especially if they are *not* growing in wet conditions. Trim back the unsightly foliage to make the planting more attractive.

■ *Cut back the foliage on an overgrown perennial by about one-half to reduce water loss in the transplanting process.*

Brown tips and edges of foliage are often due to drought damage or fertilizer burn. Salt-based synthetic fertilizers are prone to burning tender plant roots when applied in excess, especially when water is also in short supply. The remedy is to drench the bed with an inch or more of irrigation to move the salts down and away from the plant roots. Then hold off on the water and allow the soil to dry to a moist stage before watering again.

EDIBLES

Grasshoppers often join the parade of pests interested in your garden this month. You can kill them with an insecticide, but then more fly in to take their place. A better solution is to cover plants with row-cover fabric or just take the losses and replant when necessary. Stink bugs and leaf-footed bugs are significant pests of tomatoes and okra in the summer. They are not easy to control with sprays. So if your efforts to control them early were not enough, they are best treated early in the morning (see May, Problem-Solve).

Tomatoes that wilt and don't recover may be attacked by nematodes (look for swollen areas on the root) or a soil-borne wilt disease. Your County Extension Office can help diagnose these problems, but call the service first to find out what type of sample you need to bring. Both nematodes and fungal wilts are best avoided by planting varieties with the letters VFN (or more letters) after their names, indicating natural resistance to various tomato woes.

It is not unusual for the older leaves of tomatoes to curl upward and roll in somewhat from the outside edges at this time of the season. This is a response to the rapidly warming temperatures and no action is needed. Some varieties are more prone to leaf curling than others. If you see tomatoes with twisted, malformed new growth, that is either a virus or damage from an herbicide (drifting from nearby or from using treated grass or hay or manure as a mulch). There is nothing you can do to fix the problem, and affected plants should be pulled up and thrown away.

If you see patches of scale when harvesting fruit or removing water sprouts, spray these patches with summer or horticultural oil, making sure to coat all the scale insects for best control results.

Fruit trees that suddenly die or whose entire limbs die at a time may have succumbed to root rots. Cotton root rot is common throughout the state except in the Panhandle of north Texas and the acidic soils of east Texas. Oak root rot is common in more acidic soils. These diseases tend to move from one tree to another when they are in close proximity to one another, and there is not an effective control option.

It is not uncommon for citrus, persimmon, and pecan trees to drop fruit or nuts at various times of the season. This is their way of casting off a crop load that is more than they can handle. Container-grown fruit are especially prone to drought conditions since their roots are confined to the container. Make sure they are not lacking soil moisture; if moisture level is okay, then don't worry about the dropped fruit. They usually will still produce a full crop on the trees.

LAWNS

Areas of a St. Augustine and zoysiagrass lawns that die with springs of living turf interspersed may be suffering from take-all root rot. Before treating with a fungicide, take a sample to your County Extension Office for diagnosis and recommendations for managing the disease. (See July, Here's How to Take a Turf Sample.)

ROSES

If you see stunted and somewhat malformed new growth on your roses, chili thrips may be the cause. These, along with western flower thrips, which primarily damage the blooms, can be managed with sprays applied periodically according to label instructions. Contact your County Extension Office or a local rosarian for suggested spray options.

Spider mite populations can become *huge* with the arrival of hot weather. Sprays of insecticidal soap directed upward from beneath the foliage will greatly reduce their numbers. Strong blasts of water upward from beneath the foliage to dislodge the mites can also be helpful if done weekly and if *all* foliage is blasted.

SHRUBS & TREES

Yellowing and dropping of older leaves on new shrubs or trees that have been in the ground less

Yellowing of new growth is a sign of iron deficiency or poorly drained soil conditions. Supplement affected plants with an acidifying fertilizer containing iron.

than six months are often due to the soil drying out temporarily. Newly planted shrubs and trees still have a root system largely confined to the original rootball. Make sure to wet the original rootball when you water. Dig down a few inches into the rootball to feel the soil; when it is no longer moist it needs to be watered again.

Yellowing of new growth or green veins with yellow in between the veins is a sign of iron deficiency, especially on acid-loving plants like azaleas, Chinese witchhazel (*Loropetalum*), gardenias, camellias, hydrangeas, and blueberries. Treat with a chelated iron product or mix ½ cup of iron sulfate (also called copperas) into 5 gallons of compost; use as a mulch around the plants or mix into the surface of the soil. Then cover with more mulch and water well. Iron sprays can provide temporary regreening while you are waiting on the chelate or iron sulfate to take effect.

Browning leaf tips and edges can be due to fertilizer in the planting hole (not recommended) or drought. Excess fertilizer salts can be leached away with a significant drenching of the soil to dissolve and move them past plant roots.

Hawthorn lace bugs attack pyracantha foliage, causing white to yellowish brown speckles. If you find them damaging your plants, control them this month or by mid-July before they cause considerable damage, which will persist for months to come on the evergreen foliage. (See May for information on controlling lace bugs.)

If you have had problems in the past with bagworms on juniper, cedar, arborvitae, cypress, or other shrubs and trees, check the plants for the small caterpillars that are feeding and growing larger now. Treat early this month with an approved product while the pests are still small and before significant damage has occurred. Two sprays of *Bacillus thuringiensis (B.t.)* 10 days apart can be effective if the larvae are still very small.

Webworms usually have their spring generation about this time of the year. The current generation will then give rise to the late summer to fall population, which will be much larger. Take steps to control this generation to reduce the one to follow. Use a pole to break up their webs, and wasps will soon start hauling away the caterpillars. Repeat the web-breaking process for several days as the caterpillars will rebuild their protective webs fairly quickly.

Fungal blights are common on junipers if they are wet frequently with irrigation sprays or rainfall. Spider mites are also a problem when the weather heats up and when conditions are dry and dusty. See the comments in Vines & Groundcovers regarding blights and spider mites on juniper trees and shrubs.

VINES & GROUNDCOVERS
Brown areas on prostrate or trailing junipers may be due either to spider mites or fungal diseases. Place a white piece of paper beneath a branch that is starting to lose its green color. Thump the branch sharply and examine the paper for tiny (pepper-sized) brown or red specks moving around; that's a sign of spider mites. Strong blasts of water and insecticidal soap sprays can help reduce spider mite populations if complete coverage is achieved (meaning all plant surfaces are treated—top and bottom).

Fungal blights cause shoot tips to turn brown quickly. Prune out dead shoots a few inches back into healthy green branch areas, dipping pruners in rubbing alcohol between cuts to prevent the spread of disease. Discard prunings in the trash to remove some of the source for reinfection. Minimize overhead watering to minimize incidence of these blight diseases of junipers.

July

July arrives like a blast furnace, earning summer its reputation as the "second dormant season." The big stories this month are water and heat. This is not a time for wimpy plants. Many of the plants that looked great in spring are turning to toast, but there are many truly heat-tolerant options, so triple-digit temperatures are no reason to give up on color. Our landscapes can still be beautiful in summer if we choose plants that can take the heat.

The palette of plants that flower in blazing heat is more limited, but we have many great foliage plants that can step in and paint our landscapes with bold colors. Take advantage of the heat-tolerant flowers and foliage options to keep your landscape looking great.

Water use is high due to the hot weather and, in many areas, reduced rainfall. This means higher water bills. Our state is facing a future of limited water resources, so if we are going to spray drinking water on lawns and landscapes it makes sense to be as efficient as possible.

One way to be water smart is to use evapotranspiration or "ET" as a guide for watering our lawns. ET is a measure of the amount of water that evaporates and moves out of plant leaves based on weather measurements of things such as temperature, solar radiation, wind speed, humidity, and so forth. Anyone can go online to texaset.tamu.edu and find a weather station nearby or with similar weather to determine how much water your lawn has used in the past few days to a week or more. Use this information along with your local rainfall to help determine how often you need to water your lawn, garden, and landscape during any month of the year.

Another way to save water is to install drip and microsprinkler irrigation. These methods apply water to the soil rather than spraying it all over plants, where it evaporates and where it may increase the chance of disease development. You can hire someone to install a drip system or purchase a do-it-yourself kit for individual garden areas. So don't let the heat keep you from having a productive garden or beautiful landscape. Give your plants a moderately moist soil so they can keep on going—despite the summer heat.

PLAN

ALL

If your landscape is looking rather dismal in the summer heat, consider making plans to replace some of the plants this fall with Texas Superstar plants (texassuperstar.com). These plants have proven to have superior performances by Texas AgriLife Research and Extension Service, and they are excellent choices not only for surviving but thriving. Make your list of favorite Superstars and plan where they will go in your landscape.

HOT WEATHER FLOWERING ANNUALS

When the weather is blazing hot most annuals melt away, even many touted as "heat-tolerant." There *are* some, however, that can keep on blooming in the heat and can even be planted during the hotter months of the year.

Portulaca or purslane (*Portulaca* spp.)

Fan flower (*Scaevola aemula*)

Madagascar periwinkle or vinca (*Catharantus roseus*)

'Baby's Breath' euphorbia (*Euphorbia hypericifolia*)

Alyssum Princess series (*Lobularia* hybrid)

Bat face cuphea (*Cuphea llavea*)

Globe amaranth or bachelor's buttons (*Gomphrena globosa*)

Angelonia Serena series (*Angelonia* spp.)

Mexican heather (*Cuphea hyssopifolia*)

Sunflower (*Helianthus* spp.)

Mexican sunflower (*Tithonia rotundifolia*)

Tropical milkweed (*Asclepias curassavica*)

Wishbone flower (*Torenia* spp.)

Tropical sage (*Salvia coccinea*)

'Wendy's Wish' salvia (perennial in southern half of state)

Ornamental peppers (*Capsicum* spp.)

ANNUALS, PERENNIALS & ORNAMENTAL GRASSES

Fall is still far away, but fall planting season for color plants begins in late August to early September (depending on your zone) with the warm-season flowers that will bloom up until the first frost. So now is a great time to take advantage of some air-conditioned time indoors to plan your late summer to fall annual, perennial, and ornamental grass plantings.

Check out your landscape and decide if you'd like more blooming color during these hot summer months. Make plans for next year's garden to include flowers that can take the heat, especially in a few key spots that are the focal points in your landscape. See Hot Weather Flowering Annuals, left, or Here's How to Have Summer Color Without Flowers in June for some great color plants for the summer season.

EDIBLES

Fall gardening begins this month for gardeners in zones 6 and 7; by late month zone 8 gardeners will be setting out tomatoes and peppers. That makes planning now an important part of a successful garden. Sketch your garden space on paper and draw in your initial plantings. What fallow spaces are open now? What crops will be finished late this month or next, opening up space this month or next? Consider sun exposure and the height of the plants so taller ones don't shade shorter ones, unless you want to use some temporary shade from a crop about to be harvested to provide a cooler start for some other species. Plan the initial plantings of warm-season vegetables that will go in from July through September, depending on your zone.

LAWNS

Look over the landscape to see where turf is not thriving. Areas with deep shade may be due a makeover with a shade-loving groundcover. Hot, sunny areas that are difficult to keep watered can be redesigned into a planting of a prostrate shrub or groundcover that is suited to such conditions. See Great Groundcover Alternatives to Turf, next page, for ideas. Draw a design, choose plants, and prepare the soil for planting in late winter to spring.

SHRUBS

Some shrubs may be struggling in too much sun because of the loss of a tree or being planted in the wrong spot. Hydrangeas, azaleas, cleyera (*Ternstroemia gymnanthera*), Japanese aralia (*Fatsia japonica*), and gold dust plant (*Aucuba japonica*) are examples of shrubs that may struggle if placed in an all-day exposure to the broiling hot sun. Make a note to move them to a better location in mid- to late fall when the weather is more favorable for such a move.

Summer-blooming shrubs and trees can add beauty to our landscapes when the weather is blazing hot. Notice what is in bloom as you drive around town or visit a local arboretum.

Walk around your landscape and decide where a summer-blooming shrub would be a nice addition and make a note of the species and varieties that you like so you can ask your favorite local garden centers if they will carry them during the upcoming fall planting season.

TREES

Notice areas beneath the canopy of landscape trees where the shade is too dense for grass and other plants to perform well. Make a note to have some minor pruning done to brighten the shade. Seek the advice and services of a certified arborist because misinformed tree service providers who prune incorrectly and excessively do much harm to trees.

GREAT GROUNDCOVER ALTERNATIVES TO TURF

Groundcovers provide an alternative option for areas not well suited to turfgrass, such as deep shade or sunny spots where you are not able to water consistently. They can also add foliage color and blooms to create a beautiful landscape feature that may also be low maintenance.

Ajuga or bugle weed (*Ajuga reptans*)—shade; moderate moisture

Algerian ivy (*Hedera canariensis*)—part sun or shade; moderate moisture

Asian jasmine (*Trachelospermum asiaticum*)—part sun; moderate moisture

Aztec grass (*Ophiopogon intermedius*)—part sun or shade; moderate moisture

Bicolor sage (*Salvia sinaloensis*)—sun or part sun; moderate moisture

Blue shade ruellia (*Ruellia squarrosa*)—sun or part sun; moderate moisture

Dutchman's pipevine (*Aristolochia fimbriata*)—sun or part sun; moderate moisture

English ivy (*Hedera helix*)—part sun or shade; moderate moisture

Ferns (various types)—part sun or shade; moist

Frogfruit (*Phyla nodiflora*)—sun or part shade; drought tolerant

Germander, wall (*Teucrium chamaedrys*)—sun; drought tolerant

Gregg dalea (*Dalea greggii*)—sun or part shade; drought tolerant

Horseherb (*Calyptocarpus vialis*)—sun or part shade; drought tolerant

Ice plant, heartleaf (*Aptenia cordifolia*)—sun; drought tolerant

Ice plant, trailing (*Delosperma cooperi*)—sun; drought tolerant

Juniper, prostrate (*Juniperus* spp.)—sun; drought tolerant

Lamb's ear (*Stachys byzantina*)—sun; drought tolerant

Lantana, trailing (*Lantana montevidensis*)—sun; drought tolerant

VINES & GROUNDCOVERS

Now that the brunt of summer has arrived you may have some groundcovers that are struggling due to excessive direct sun or excessive shade. You may need to relocate or redesign their planting beds to move them into more favorable light conditions. Make plans to do so when the fall planting season arrives, noting where the new lines for the beds need to be drawn. Some areas may need to have one species pulled and a better-adapted species planted in that location.

PLANT

ANNUALS

Although it is very hot you can still plant summer color plants this month. See comments in June regarding setting out new transplants and starting seeds in these hot summer months. See Hot Weather Flowering Annuals this month for a list of great options.

Even plants that can survive summer often bloom much less when the thermometer climbs into the triple digits and the nighttime temperatures are also warm. Take advantage of the heat and plant colorful tropical foliage and flowers. These plants are perennials in the tropics, but where winter freezes occur they are treated as annuals. Most grow rapidly if provided plenty of water so they never have to face summer thirsty. Prepare the planting area with a little extra compost and water the plants in well. Fertilize lightly at planting to get them off to a fast start. It is especially important to maintain moisture in the rootball and the soil around it while these

■ *Madagascar periwinkle is one of the best annual flowers for summer color. It can take the heat of a Texas summer and look good all season long.*

■ *A bright shady spot outdoors is a great place to start new transplants in the blazing heat of summer for later transplanting out into the garden.*

plants are getting roots established. Until that happens, the plants can quickly dry out on a warm day and go into drought stress.

EDIBLES

July weather is no reason to stop planting. Heat-loving vegetables can still be planted if you give them plenty of water to keep the plants hydrated. It is important in the hot summer months to water *prior* to planting. See the June Plant section for comments on pre-plant irrigation. This trick is a veteran gardener's secret to success with summer seeding and transplanting too.

Heat-tolerant crops that take a long time to reach harvest include sweet potatoes, winter squash (such as kabocha, spaghetti, and butternut), and pumpkins, which may take 75 to 100 days from seed to harvest. Therefore this month is a key planting season for all but zone 9 if you want to harvest them in the fall. Mix a moderate amount of fertilizer into the soil before planting the seeds to supply nutrition to the plants as they begin to grow.

Give newly planted seeds a little shade to keep the soil cooler and aid in a successful germination. Stick a small branch from an evergreen shrub or tree in the ground on the south or southwest side of a group of seeds to provide some shade from the hot noonday to afternoon hours. Once seedlings have a few true leaves they won't need the shade any longer.

Another strategy for dealing with hot weather planting is to start these plants as transplants in a bright shady spot where you can control the amount of sun they receive and thus the temperature of the soil around the seed. When they are up, gradually move into more sun over a couple of weeks. Transplant them when they are three to four weeks old and have several true leaves. If you've acclimated them to full sun while they were growing in the transplant trays, no shading will be needed.

Herbs and container-grown fruit plants *can* be planted this month, but unless there are circumstances that make it necessary, it is best to wait until early to mid-fall, which is a much better time for the plants to become established because of the break in the heat.

LAWNS

Lawns can be sodded or seeded this month, but it will require much more attention to watering during the critical establishment period of the first four to six weeks.

PERENNIALS & ORNAMENTAL GRASSES

We have many perennial plants that can survive the heat of summer, but when it comes to *blooming* in the heat, the list gets much shorter. Some perennials (depending on your zone) that can provide colorful midsummer blooms include square-bud primrose (*Calyophus berlandieri*), firecracker flower (*Cuphea ignea*), Skyflower (*Duranta erecta*), yellow bells (*Tecoma stans*), firecracker fern (*Russelia equisetiformis, R. coccinea*), rose mallow (*Hibiscus moscheutos*), Texas star hibiscus (*H. coccineus*), hummingbird plant (*Dicliptera suberecta*), ice plant (*Delosperma cooperi*), lantana, Mexican honeysuckle (*Justicia spicigera*), garden phlox (*Phlox paniculata* 'John Fanick'), plumbago (*Plumbago auriculata*), pride of Barbados (*Caesalpinia pulcherrima*), rock penstemon (*Penstemon baccharifolius*), Mexican petunia (*Ruellia brittoniana*), and several salvias including Gregg's sage (*Salvia greggii*), blue anise sage or majestic sage (*Salvia guaranitica*), *Salvia* 'Mystic Spires', and *Salvia* 'Wendy's Wish' (tender perennial).

These perennials can also be planted this month if you take extra care to keep the rootball and surrounding soil evenly moist without overwatering for the first month or more while their roots establish and temperatures are still quite hot.

SHRUBS & TREES

Palms do very well when planted in the summer months. So if you have plans to add some to your landscape this is a great time to do so. There are some species with good cold hardiness for almost any area of the state. Consult your local nursery or Extension Service for instructions on planting and after-planting care. The key is not to plant them too deep but to leave the topmost roots that emerge from the base of the trunk just a few inches above the soil line.

VINES & GROUNDCOVERS

It is still okay to plant vines and groundcovers in the landscape, although you will need to be extra diligent to water enough to keep the roots moist but not so much as to keep them soggy wet, which forces out oxygen in the soil, resulting in root death.

CARE

ANNUALS

Deadhead spent blooms on zinnias, Mexican sunflowers, and other annuals that don't naturally drop their blooms. Shear back annuals that have bloomed into a weakened state and are losing their vigor. Then give them a boost of fertilizer and water to promote new shoots and foliage. Without new growth there can't be more blooms, so this is an important part of keeping them going in summer.

EDIBLES

Summer is a bit of a down time in the vegetable garden. Take advantage of this time to replenish your soil by leaving sections fallow. See the comments on preparing the soil for a fallow period in the June Care section. If you prepare the soil properly now, when fall planting season arrives you'll be ready to grow.

If you have tomatoes that are worse for the wear and want to carry them into the fall gardening season, take some cuttings in early July to root and make new plants before ripping out the old pest-infested or diseased plants. Cut off the terminal (end) 6 inches of a shoot. Submerge it in water and slosh it around to dislodge any mites and aphids. Then stick it in a 4-inch or 1-gallon pot filled with potting mix and place the container in a bright area but out of full sun. Water the potting media well and keep it moist. The cutting will wilt, but it will start to recover in a few days. After it has begun to grow, move it gradually into full sun over a few days, taking care to water it regularly. Then plant it by mid- to late July for fall production.

There is still time to sheet compost some leaves and grass clippings or other organic materials into the soil to decompose prior to fall planting. As long as you have at least two to three weeks before planting an area (more time is better) you can start this process now. See the comments on sheet composting in the Care section in June.

Continue to clean up fruit plants as harvest time comes to an end by removing shriveled fruit on the trees, picking up fallen fruit, pruning out water sprouts and suckers, and mulching the soil deeply to deter weeds. Remove blackberry canes that produced fruit this year as they won't fruit again. Cut them off at the ground. Snip out the tops of new canes about "chest high" to encourage side branching, which increases productivity.

LAWNS

Don't bag your grass clippings when you mow, but recycle them with a mulching mower. Clippings don't create thatch because they decompose rapidly. Thatch is caused by excessive applications of fertilizer and water, which promotes excessive growth. If your lawn has a lot of warm-season weeds that are producing seeds, go ahead and bag the clippings to remove the seeds from the lawn area. Put the clippings in a hot compost pile or mix them into soil in fallow garden beds where they can decompose.

Mow often enough so that you are removing one-third of the leaf blade each time you mow. (See May, Here's How to Select the Mowing Height for Your Lawn.) If you live in the Panhandle or western third of the state where buffalo grass is better adapted, one option is to leave it unmowed over the summer. Buffalo grass tends to go dormant in the heat and drought and leaving it unmowed will help to maintain a good cover over the soil. When fall rains return it will resume growth and can be mowed regularly, or only once or twice per year to allow it to form a "mini-meadow" look.

PERENNIALS & ORNAMENTAL GRASSES

Pinch back mums and asters this month to promote compact growth with more branching for more fall blooms. Make the final shearing or pinching about mid- to late July to allow the plants a chance to set bloom buds for their fall bloom show.

Stake tall blooming perennials, including Philippine lily and butterfly gingers, in areas where wind or storms may blow them over. About the time they bloom they get extra topheavy and it is a shame to come out and see them blown over.

■ *Stake tall bloom stalks such as these Philippine lilies to prevent them from blowing over in summer storms.*

When canna shoots have finished blooming cut them back to the soil line to open up the clump and make it look better. Summer-blooming salvias such as Gregg's sage, 'Indigo Spires', and 'Mystic Spires' continue to extend their terminal spikes with more flowers but become less vigorous and less attractive in time. Cut the bloom stalks off—yes, it's going to be okay—back to the first or second set of leaves, then fertilize and water to spur on new growth. More growing shoots mean more blooms and they'll be looking great again soon.

Garden phlox and any other perennials that have spent blooms benefit from having the bloom stalks pruned out to clean up the planting and in some cases to prevent their energy from going into seed formation.

ROSES

Continue to weave shoots (or canes) of climbing roses horizontally on a trellis or other growing support. These plants will be setting next spring's bloom buds in late summer to early fall and training or tying them to be horizontal promotes heavier bloom production.

■ *Climbing roses are often grown as vines but they are not true vines. These plants have long canes, or stems, that must be tied and trained into place to encourage them to grow upward. Use twine or twist ties if stems are light; insulated wire or rubber strips if they are woody.*

Remove spent blooms on repeat-blooming roses back to the first leaf with five leaflets to promote more blooms.

SHRUBS

Shear hedges to maintain dense foliage from top to bottom. Wherever sun reaches the plant leaves will be sustained so it is important not to allow the top of a hedge to get too wide or it will shade the lower areas resulting in loss of foliage and a plant that is more like an umbrella than a wall.

Some shrubs are especially vigorous and need regular pruning to keep them in-bounds; examples include pyracantha, ligustrum, eleagnus, and photinia. If these shrubs are planted beside your home they may soon be large enough to cover windows and rub the eaves. Consider cutting them back and then moving them to a location where they can spread out. Then replace them with a more compact species and variety of shrub. (See November, Here's How to Move a Woody Ornamental Plant.)

Give butterfly bushes (*Buddleia davidii*) a tune-up to keep them looking and blooming well. Shear the bushes back by a third. Then blast the foliage with water from underneath to dislodge any mites hiding under the leaves. Repeat the water blasts three more times about three to four days apart.

Crape myrtles will benefit from some summer care also. Snip off spent blooms before they set seed to direct energy into more blooms rather than seed production.

VINES & GROUNDCOVERS

Shear back groundcovers that are looking ragged or that have diseased foliage. Rake out any diseased foliage if possible, and then water the area well to encourage fresh new growth. Groundcovers are resilient and can take a mowing back if needed; they will respond with more vigor, providing a more attractive groundcover.

Use hand pruners to cut out stalks of cast iron plants and ferns, such as holly fern, that are yellowing or showing brown edges to improve the appearance of the planting. Don't worry if you have to remove most of the growth as the plants will regrow to replenish the area with more foliage.

Stop pruning woody vines that flower in spring such as wisteria, crossvine, and Carolina jessamine by the end of July in zones 6 to 7 to allow them plenty of time for slow growth and to set bloom buds in late summer and fall for next year's bloom show.

WATER

ALL

Drip irrigation is the best way to water all plant areas except for lawns. Sprinklers wet the foliage, which promotes development of plant diseases, so if you use a sprinkler try to water less often. A good soaking as *infrequently* as soil, sun, and plant type factors will allow is the best way to water your gardens and landscapes. Alternating a good soaking

HERE'S HOW

TO PROTECT LANDSCAPES FROM DEER

Deer can often be scared away from our landscape plants with a variety of methods. Fencing them away from our plants is another option; however, keep in mind that when deer are starving they are not easily kept away with scare techniques, and they will often eat plants that they otherwise would avoid. Here are some options for keeping Bambi away from your garden and landscape plants.

Scare them away

- Scents (wild animal urine, human hair)

- Sounds

- Dogs

- Scarecrow motion-activated sprinkler (right)

Fence them out

- Tall plastic mesh such as bird netting (They can't see it well and tend to avoid it.)

- Baited electric fence (Place a folded piece of aluminum foil over the fence wire and smear it with peanut butter to give them a shock when they nose up to it.)

- Electric fence with offset wire (Two wires at 14 inches and 36 inches are set up around the garden. Then 30 inches outside of this fence a wire is placed 30 to 32 inches off of the ground. Hook all up to electric fence charger.)

- Small confined area (Deer won't jump into a fairly small area since they want room to land and also to jump back out. A 10- to 12-foot area with a 6-foot fence around it is usually an effective deterrent.)

- Wire mesh fencing in a cylinder around shrubs and trees and over smaller perennials (Wire mesh protects plants from deer feeding and rubbing of antlers. The perennial plants can grow up through the mesh and will only be eaten back to the wire, preventing loss of the entire plant.)

■ *When the ravages of a hot summer leave a cast iron plant looking worse for wear, prune out the unsightly foliage stems to create a beautiful planting. New foliage will soon emerge to make it even better.*

with a drying out period wets the entire root zone but then allows air to move deeper into the soil as the soil begins to dry out a little. This wet-dry cycle is better than allowing the plants to go into water stress or keeping them soggy.

ANNUALS

Keep the water flowing to annual beds. Even summer-tough annuals need water to survive, so don't let them dry out. Apply an inch of water a week in two applications or use the "digging test" to determine when to water. (See May, Here's How to Determine How Long to Water.) If your soil is a heavy clay it may not drain well and will become waterlogged if you water too much too often. Waterlogged soil is a quick killer for plants struggling in the heat as it prevents the roots from getting oxygen, leading to a fast decline and death.

Water container plants, including hanging baskets, daily to avoid stressing the plants in this hot weather. If the container is a little too small for the plant or if the growing media is loose and does not hold water, you may need to water twice a day, in early to mid-morning and late afternoon, especially if the plant is in full sun.

EDIBLES

Water vegetable gardens twice a week to maintain moist soil. Summer vegetables can take the heat but not heat plus drought. Herb gardens will need watering regularly also, although many of our best herbs for Texas are of Mediterranean origin. They can take heat but don't like soggy soil conditions in summer or winter. So take care not to overdo a good thing, and water only as needed to keep the soil moist.

Water new fruit trees according to the schedule provided in March, Here's How to Irrigate New

■ *Drip irrigation is an efficient way to water and can help save on your summer watering bills while maintaining healthy, vigorous plants through the summer heat.*

■ *Apply at least ½ inch of irrigation when you water the lawn to soak the soil deeply and promote a deep, resilient root system.*

Shrubs and Trees. Established trees should receive 1 inch of sprinkler irrigation per week or, if they're on drip irrigation, enough to wet the soil to a depth of 12 inches. If it has been a year since you added drip emitters, the tree or bush likely needs more emitters to wet a larger volume of soil. Add more drip line with emitters to try and wet as much of the soil beneath the tree's branch spread as possible. Microjet sprays are efficient and wet a larger area than regular drip emitters. Consider switching to them once your plant is four years or older.

Pecans are still growing on the trees, so adequate soil moisture is needed to help them grow larger nuts and prevent nut drop. Persimmons will also drop fruit in drought stress conditions. Provide a good soaking to the entire area beneath the branch spread of these trees every week or two when it hasn't rained at least ½ inch. Citrus trees carrying a crop of fruit also need to be kept moist to help them through the summer heat.

LAWNS

If it doesn't rain at least ½ inch, apply 1 inch of irrigation per week. When you water, apply enough to soak the soil to a depth of at least 6 inches, then allow it to dry out for four to seven days before watering again. This develops a deep-rooted, resilient turfgrass. Bermudagrass and zoysiagrass can tolerate a period of drought, but they will start to look brown. If you want to conserve water you can cut back; then, when you begin to water again or when rains return, it will resume growth but may be thinner and more susceptible to weed invasion. Buffalo grass, although only adapted to the driest parts of the state, can be allowed to go completely dormant in summer and will return with the arrival of fall rains.

PERENNIALS & ORNAMENTAL GRASSES

A good soaking once or twice a week is sufficient to keep perennials happy. The growing conditions dictate the watering frequency from often (sun, sandy soil, and hot temperatures) to less often (shade, clay and loam soil, and cool temperatures). So use May's Here's How to Determine How Long to Water to determine when to water your plants, whatever the season.

Perennial grasses need to be watered weekly with enough irrigation to soak the soil 8 to 10 inches deep. They use a lot of water in the heat and will start to develop dead tips and leaves if allowed to face drought stress. Remember that it is not how often you water but how thoroughly you wet the soil when you water. The goal is to support a deep, extensive root system that makes the plant more drought resilient.

ROSES, SHRUBS & TREES

Give woody ornamentals that are less than a year old a good soaking by filling the berm around the base of the plant or by setting a hose, running at just a trickle, a foot or two out from the base of the trunk. Move the hose as each area becomes saturated to soak the entire area around the plant. (See March, Here's How to Irrigate New Shrubs and Trees, for details.)

If there is not a berm around the plant place a hose beneath the branch spread and allow it to run at a trickle, moving it around periodically to allow it to soak the entire area beneath the branch spread of the shrub or tree. Another option is to run a sprinkler covering the area beneath the branch spread until water starts to run off. Then wait an hour and repeat until you have wet the soil a foot deep.

Water hollies, pyracantha, beautyberry, and other berry-producing plants to prevent drought stress. These plants are carrying a load of fruit and some species will drop fruit if subjected to droughty conditions. Provide moist soil now to ensure a full crop of beautiful berries in the fall to winter season.

VINES & GROUNDCOVERS

Established vines and groundcovers should do fine with a weekly watering in the absence of at least ½ inch of rainfall, provided you soak the soil deeply when you water. Newly established vines and groundcovers will need to be watered two or three times a week (or more often if in the sun) to keep their rootballs moist until they are able to establish roots out into the surrounding soil. Drip irrigation is the most efficient way to water. If you are using a sprinkler to water you may need to water until the soil starts to runoff and then let it soak for a half hour and then water again until you've wet the soil deeply. (See May, Here's How to Determine How Long to Water.)

FERTILIZE

ANNUALS

Fertilize annuals that are actively blooming with a moderate dose of a complete fertilizer. Check out Here's How to Fertilize Flowers, Ornamental Grasses, and Vegetables in April for guidance as to how much of various types of fertilizer to apply. If the plants appear to already be vigorous you can skip this month's application. Always water fertilizer in immediately to remove it from foliage and so it can release the nutrients to the soil and plant roots.

EDIBLES

Hold off on fertilizing herbs this month if you have been fertilizing them in spring or early summer. The rapidly decaying organic matter from compost in the soil and a decomposing layer of mulch, as well as residual nutrients in the soil, are sufficient to keep them going strong if the soil stays moist.

Look at this year's terminal growth (where leaves are on the branches) on *established* fruit trees. If there is on average at least 18 inches of growth on the branches, then no more fertilizing is needed. Trees less than a year old can be fertilized again this month at a moderate rate since the goal is to grow a large tree fast for when it begins to bear in year three or four.

PERENNIALS & ORNAMENTAL GRASSES

Perennial grasses as well as blooming and foliage plants will benefit from a light to moderate dose of fertilizer this month to maintain some vigor and a healthy, attractive appearance.

ROSES

Fertilize roses according to instructions provided in June. Check roses that bloom only in the spring, which includes most climbing types, for good green color and vigor. If they're lacking either, feed as you would the other roses.

SHRUBS & TREES

Fertilize young shrubs and trees if you haven't done so in the past six to eight weeks with a turf-type fertilizer. Apply ½ to 1 cup per inch of trunk diameter and spread it evenly beneath and just beyond the plants branch spread.

Fertilize butterfly bushes (*Buddleia davidii*) that were sheared back this month with a cup of turf-type fertilizer worked into the surface inch of soil and then water them well. They will respond with new growth and blooms on all of their shoot terminals.

Crape myrtles will benefit from an application of 1 cup of fertilizer per inch of trunk diameter spread evenly beneath the branch spread of the plant, worked into the soil surface and watered in well to start to dissolve the nutrients or enhance microbial breakdown of organic products.

VINES & GROUNDCOVERS

Fertilize groundcovers planted this year at the rate described in May to encourage them to fill in faster. Established groundcovers or vines that have already filled in do not need additional fertilizing in summer. Fertilize young vines so they'll fill in faster, but once they are close to covering their arbor or trellis, no fertilizing is needed. In fact, too much promotes excessive growth leading to more pruning work from *you* to keep them in-bounds.

PROBLEM-SOLVE

ALL

This is a good point in the season to flush the filter on your drip irrigation lines. If you are not

■ *Fertilize repeat blooming roses, like this 'Nacogdoches' the "Yellow Rose of Texas," and then water them well to promote new growth and more bloom cycles.*

familiar with this process contact your supplier and they can assist you. Drip irrigation system emitters can become clogged over time due to lime and iron deposits or algae. Turn on your drip system and let it run for a few minutes. Then walk the lines checking for cuts in the lines and also check the emitters to make sure water is dripping out at a uniform rate. Depending on the type of drip irrigation you have, if you find clogged emitters you may be able to pop in another emitter near the clogged one, or remove a cap to clean out an emitter. Your irrigation supplier may have other ideas to offer to get your emitters working properly again.

If the drip system is watering shrubs or small fruit or flowering trees that have grown considerably since they were installed you may need to add lines and emitters to wet a larger area. Another option is to install microjet or microspray emitters. These put out water low to the ground in a circular area, like a mini-sprinkler. Wetting a larger area means more moist soil for roots to supply the small tree or shrub's increasing needs as they grow larger.

Young garden and landscape plants that are uprooted, established annuals and perennials chomped off at the ground, and large areas of missing foliage on trees and shrubs are all signs of possible deer damage. Deer can get very hungry this time of the year, especially if drought conditions are limiting the amount of natural browse they have in the wild. Our landscapes look pretty tasty as we water and tend our plants to keep them lush and vigorous. Deer can destroy valuable plants in a short time. The hungrier they get, the bolder they become, making many of the common scare tactics much less effective. Protecting your landscape from their feeding damage is no simple task. See Here's How to Protect Landscapes from Deer in this chapter for more information and some ideas to help reduce the damage these animals can cause.

There is another culprit that can defoliate several entire bushes or small trees in one evening: the Texas leaf cutter ant. These pests are most common in eastern areas of the state where the soil is deep, well-drained sand or loam. They forage at night in the summer and during the day when temperatures are 50 to 80°F, cutting off foliage to take back to their large colonies of underground chambers. If you see trails of ants hauling foliage back to a nest, sometimes up to several hundred feet away, contact your County Extension Office and inquire as to options for controlling these pests.

■ *Microjet irrigation is similar to drip, applying water low to the ground but over a larger area to supply moisture to more of the plant's root system.*

Grasshoppers become numerous in many areas of the state this month as they reach their adult stage and have wings to fly into our landscapes, often from neighboring grassy areas. Plants can be protected somewhat with row-cover fabrics, and there are several insecticides that will kill the insects. However, if you have large numbers on your property these measures will not provide much protection and damage to your plants is inevitable. Most plants can

■ *Grasshoppers, beetles, caterpillars, and other pests think our landscapes and gardens are their salad bar. Contact your County Extension Office for control options, but start early for best results.*

survive and recover, although some annuals can be set back enough to require replanting.

Fire ants can be a problem in gardens and landscapes. The most effective way to control them is with baits applied late in the day when the ants are actively foraging. A good way to tell if ants are active is to toss some potato chips or tuna can lids (not washed) into the landscape or garden. Check back in 15 minutes and if ants are active they will have found the oily food source and be feeding on it.

ANNUALS, PERENNIALS & ORNAMENTAL GRASSES

Wilting may be a sign of a lack of water, but strangely enough it can also be a sign of too much water. When roots can't get oxygen they shut down and plants wilt. When trying to keep your flowers

and foliage plants well-watered take care not to keep the soil soggy or the plants will become stressed and root rots may gain entry. In summer heat this can result in a fast decline and death, so dig down and feel the soil before you water if there is any question about the soil's moisture content.

If you have container plants that are wilting every day and it seems you can't keep them adequately watered, here are a few solutions. They may be in too much sun. A move to a location with some mid- to late-day shade may be sufficient. There may be a lot of reflected heat around the plants from stone or masonry walls, concrete drives, and especially an asphalt driveway. Move them to a location where they are surrounded by turf, groundcovers, or a mulched surface. Finally, the container may be too small for the plant. If the plant is more than

JULY

HERE'S HOW

TO TAKE A TURF SAMPLE

1. Find the area between healthy and dead turf, where the grass is still alive but declining.

2. Cut a 4x4-inch or 4x6-inch sample of turf with an inch or two of soil.

3. Slide it into a gallon zip-top bag and zip it shut.

4. Place your name and contact information on or inside the bag.

5. Take it to your County Extension Office, along with a photo that shows the overall affected area, for diagnostic assistance.

twice the size of the container, consider moving it up into a larger container.

Hot, dry conditions take their toll on plants out in nature making our irrigated gardens a lush, tempting salad bowl for grasshoppers, caterpillars, beetles, snails, slugs, and other pests. Take some morning strolls through the garden and landscape to see if any pest problems are emerging. Look for holes in foliage, missing parts of leaves, slime trails, or the pests themselves. Take early action when your options are greatest and the least toxic controls, such as hand-picking or use of insecticidal soaps and oils, are most likely to be effective.

EDIBLES

Continue to watch for hungry caterpillars and other insects on vegetables. Spider mites love a dry, dusty leaf surface so this is their kind of weather. See comments on checking for spider mites and controlling them in the June Problem-Solve section.

If you see globs of sap or sawdust on your fruit tree branches or trunk (especially the lower foot of trunk), the cause may be borers. Take a knife and scrape back the sap to see if there is a tunnel going into the tree branch or trunk. Contact your County Extension Office for helpful advice in managing these pests. The sooner you address the problem the more likely you'll be able to save your trees.

LAWNS

If some areas of the lawn are turning brown it could be due to poor coverage by your sprinkler system. Turn on the system and check to make sure all areas are being adequately watered. If not, consider hiring an irrigation company to renovate the system. (See June, Here's How to Check the Efficiency of Your Lawn Irrigation System.)

ROSES

Continue to check for thrips and spider mites. See the Problem-Solve section in June for control options. It is important to keep the foliage on your roses healthy as they will soon be gearing up for their big fall bloom cycle. When diseases kill or damage leaves the plant's ability to produce carbohydrates, which are essential for vigor and bloom production, is compromised. If you have varieties that are prone to blackspot spray them with an approved product following label instructions carefully to prevent an outbreak of this fungus.

SHRUBS & TREES

Young shrubs or trees that are not thriving may be suffering from constriction of the lower trunk. Dig down about 4 to 6 inches and look for anything strangling the trunk, including plastic nursery tags or circling roots that have grown larger as the trunk grew larger and which are now embedded into the base of the trunk. Cut and remove anything strangling the trunk. If the damage was not too severe the plant may recover.

Black sooty mold or clear sticky substances on the foliage of shrubs, trees, and other plants growing beneath them are signs of insects feeding above those leaves. Scale insects, mealybugs, aphids, and whiteflies all secrete this "honeydew" that falls onto plant foliage and other surfaces, and which supports growth of sooty mold. Check with your County Extension Office for help in identifying the pests involved and in selecting an appropriate control option.

Continue to check for bagworms on needled evergreen shrubs and trees, including arborvitae, cedar, juniper, and cypress. See June for comments on controlling these pests early, before they become less susceptible to the least toxic control options and before they do irreparable damage to these plants.

VINES & GROUNDCOVERS

Browning edges of foliage indicate a lack of water. Soil can dry out fast in the heat of a Texas summer so when in doubt, dig down a few inches and feel the soil. Water if it is no longer moist to the touch.

August

Plants need plenty of water to keep going in the August heat. This can mean watering twice a week for many areas of the lawn and landscape. Consider installing a rainwater catchment system on your home and other buildings. Rainwater is free and the best water your plants can have. Consider that for every inch of water that falls on 1,000 square feet of your home or garage, more than 600 gallons of rainwater can be captured. Do the math and you'll find that rainfall capture can save tens of thousands of gallons per year. Plus, it makes your landscape a little more resilient when water restrictions are put into effect during droughts.

Rainwater harvesting can range from a simple rain barrel to an elaborate system with tanks that hold thousands of gallons. Check out rainwaterharvesting.tamu.edu for a wealth of free information on how to create your own rainwater harvesting system.

Although it is really hot outside, veteran gardeners know that fall gardening starts this month. Our mild spring and fall seasons are relatively short and so we need to get a jumpstart on fall in the heat of mid- to late August.

Many vegetables are their best when they ripen in the cooler days of fall, green beans being a prime example. Consider starting a small vegetable patch this month if you haven't in the past. You don't need much space to grow vegetables. Even a 4x8-foot space can be productive. Look for places around the landscape where you can tuck in some vegetable plants. Containers make great vegetable gardens too. When harvest time rolls around you'll be glad you have a garden, and you'll have the best-tasting vegetables of the year.

Fall flowers get their start this month. Those flowers that did great in spring, but couldn't last through summer, will do wonderfully in fall if they're planted toward the end of this month. When the heat breaks they will be ready to bloom with the most vibrant colors they have had all year.

Take advantage of some mild morning and early evening hours to get your gardens and landscapes off to a great start on the fall season this month.

PLAN

ALL

Take photos of flowers and foliage plants you see around town or at a local public garden that survived the summer heat and drought for your gardening journal or notebook. These are obviously heat-tolerant survivors that will come in handy for future garden planning.

Record the names of each one to help you find them when you go shopping or search mail order sources.

ANNUALS

Warm-season plants such as marigolds, petunias, zinnias, and pentas look great in the fall as the days are getting cooler. The large pom-pom type African marigolds are plagued with spider mites in the summer, but in late summer to fall these pests are on the decline and the marigolds will steal the show, even away from those beautiful fall mums.

Mid-August (zones 6 to 7a) to late August (zones 7b to 9) is the time to make a color change for fall blooms. Check out Here's How to Plan Color Changes for Annual Beds in March for information on timing color changes, and draw up a list of warm-season annuals for planting later this month.

■ *Marigolds are blazing beauties in the fall when spider mites are no longer a threat and their colors become especially vibrant in the milder temperatures.*

■ *A rainwater-capture system like this simple barrel system can collect rainwater, which is the best water for irrigating your plants.*

Order compost for preparing beds for fall planting. To help determine how much is needed see January's Here's How to Estimate How Much Soil or Mulch Is Needed. You can save money by ordering compost and mulch for bulk delivery. However, much of the cost is in hauling it by truck to your house, making it unfeasible to purchase just a cubic yard or two. Some places will let you bring a trailer or sturdy pickup to pick it up yourself. Another option is to get with some neighbors to make a joint purchase so that delivery is more economical for everyone. Most compost and mulch businesses are willing to dump part of the load at one driveway and part in a neighbor's driveway.

EDIBLES

Fall is a great time to plant herbs. If you plan to install a formal garden, draw out a pleasing design and plan when to order compost, when to prepare the soil, and where you'll get your plants so that in

HERE'S HOW

TO ESTIMATE THE NUMBER OF PLANTS NEEDED TO FILL AN AREA

Layout	Inches between Plants in a Row	Inches between Rows	Approximate Number of Plants per 100 sq. ft.
Square			
	4	4	900
	6	6	400
	8	8	225
	10	10	144
	12	12	100
Offset			
	4	3.46	1,039
	6	5.20	462
	8	6.93	260
	10	8.66	166
	12	10.39	115

September and October you can make it all happen. Many herb gardens are created in a geometric design such as concentric circles. If you prefer a more natural look consider a winding pathway of herbs or, if cottage gardening is your thing, scatter herbs all about the landscape and gardens. Just make sure in your planning that the herbs have adequate sun exposure and good soil drainage. Include more prostrate herbs such as thyme, oregano, and pennyroyal among pathway stones so foot traffic will release some of their aroma into the air.

The cool season vegetable garden starts late this month in zones 6 to 7a and next month in zones 7b to 9. Plan the transition, as things can get crowded in the garden with heat-tolerant vegetables still producing, other warm-season vegetables on their way to production, and cool-season vegetables looking for a place of their own. In your transition plan consider starting cool-season crops in the shade of taller crops such as okra, which can be removed a few weeks after the weather cools in mid-fall. Pencil in or sketch your planned succession plantings in your garden journal with a list of the number of plants that will be needed. There is still time to start cool-season crops from seed to plant as transplants, if you wish.

Fall is the best time to plant strawberries but they are not usually available at local garden centers in the fall. Find out if your local nursery will be carrying strawberries; if not, find a mail order source. Fall is a good time to plant fruit trees, but availability is always good. You may need to search around this month to find the species and varieties you want. If fruit trees are not available make a note in your garden journal to look for them again in late winter, either in local garden centers or by mail order.

LAWNS

Turf areas that died from summer drought, disease, or insect attacks, or that were worn by foot traffic, can be replanted in early fall and still have plenty of time to establish before winter. Take measurements of how much sod you need and order sod for planting in early to mid-September in zones 6 to 7. If you are in zones 8 to 9 the planting time can extend into early October.

PERENNIALS & ORNAMENTAL GRASSES

Fall is the best planting season of the year and it's just around the corner. Do some investigating to learn about the perennials that are the best for your area. When planning your fall perennial plantings consider when the plant blooms. Spring is an easy time to have flowers, fall is a little more challenging, and summer is a *really* challenging

time for flowering perennials. But there *are* plants that perform well in all these seasons.

Don't forget the ornamental grasses. They add a fine, linear texture to the landscape, look great all summer, and can even be a winter asset as their seedheads and straw-colored stems and foliage add interest, especially on a frosty morning. Ornamental grasses are available in foliage that is green, variegated white or cream, or burgundy and purple. Look over your landscape and determine where some ornamental grasses would be a great fall addition.

ROSES & SHRUBS

Fall planting season is just around the corner. Sketch out some new rose or shrub beds, determine any needed bed mix to order, and begin the process of preparing the soil. The beds will be able to settle in, and if the weather is rainy when the time comes to plant, your beds will already be prepped and ready to go.

■ *Heat tolerant impatiens, fall blooming Mexican bush sage, and the bold foliage of copper plant make this landscape beautiful even at the end of summer and early days of fall when the weather is still hot.*

PLANT

ANNUALS

Warm-season annuals that may not be tough enough for lasting through the summer can be outstanding choices for fall. Fall is our "second spring" and offers months of milder temperatures and usually some nice rainfall too in most of the state. This makes for excellent growing conditions for warm-season plants.

Some good choices for color up until frost include marigolds, pentas, petunias, impatiens, zinnias, Madagascar periwinkle, cosmos, tropical sage (*Salvia coccinea*), 'Baby's Breath' euphorbia (*Euphorbia hypericifolia*), Lobularia Princess Series (*Lobularia* hybrid), *Angelonia* Serena Series (*Angelonia* spp.), wishbone flower (*Torenia* spp.), and ornamental peppers. These can be planted in mid-August in zones 6 to 7 and late August in zones 8 to 9. Less heat-tolerant annuals can be added in early September in zones 8b to 9.

Prepare your beds for planting in early to mid-August. Start by watering the planting bed thoroughly a couple of days prior to beginning bed prep work. After the water has soaked in and it is no longer soggy on top, remove the fried remains of your spring flowers along with any weeds that may have snuck in. This will be much easier if the soil is moist. If you have perennial weeds such as nutsedge or bermudagrass either dig them out, making sure to get all of their underground tubers or rhizomes, or use a broad-spectrum weed control product that will be taken up by the plant to kill the entire weed. Give it a week to move into the weeds and kill them before continuing on with the bed prep.

Next spread an inch or two of compost and work it into the bed, down 4 to 6 inches of soil. Then smooth the soil surface and break up any clods. Set your annuals out on top of the bed in their containers, spacing them at about 50 to 75 percent of their mature size. For help knowing how many plants to purchase for your annual beds, check out Here's How to Estimate the Number of Plants Needed to Fill an Area earlier in this chapter.

If you are planting multiple colors and if the plants have blooms, pause to note where the various

■ *Space your bedding plants about 50 to 75 percent of their mature size apart so they will fill in quickly and create an attractive floral display.*

colors are set. When you are happy with the layout go ahead and plant them, setting the plants at the same depth they were growing in the container. If they'd look more aesthetically pleasing in a different layout, then move them around a bit to get them spaced just right, until you're satisfied, and then plant.

Water the new plants with a soluble fertilizer solution at the full (not "constant feed") labeled rate. Finish with a 2-inch layer of mulch to cover the soil surface and deter weeds.

EDIBLES

A final planting of heat-tolerant summer vegetables that will reach harvest in less than sixty-five days (see seed packet labels for days-to-harvest) is still possible in zone 9. In zones 8 to 9 gardeners are planting other warm-season crops such as summer squash, bush and pole beans, and cucumbers in early to mid-month (zone 8) or mid- to late month (zone 9). Zones 8 to 9a gardeners can still get in a late planting of pepper and eggplant transplants. Water transplants with a soluble fertilizer solution. When planting, just pull back the mulch to set transplants and then replace it to keep the roots cool and weed seeds from sprouting. If planting seeds, pull back the mulch to expose only a narrow band of bare soil. Leaving mulch over most of the bed will minimize weed problems and maintain moderate soil temperature in the planting bed.

■ *Start transplants of cool-season vegetables such as kale, broccoli, mustard and chard this month for planting out in the garden next month when the weather cools off just a bit.*

There is a narrow window for planting potatoes for fall in early August (zones 6 to 7), mid-August (zones 8 to 9a), and late August (zone 9b). The goal is to get them in the ground early enough so that a crop of tubers can mature before the first frost knocks them out. If possible, use small whole potatoes for "seed" rather than cut pieces of potatoes, as the latter tend to rot in the warm soil. Place the seed potatoes in a trench so you can fill in soil and mulch around them as they grow. You can also plant them in a large container half-filled with growing media, which is then filled the rest of the way as you cover the growing potato stems.

If you'd like to grow a pumpkin for this fall, early this month is still time to plant the seed out in the garden in zones 8 and 9. Most take seventy or more days from seed to harvest. Plant them where you have space for the vines to sprawl.

Start seeds of cole crops (such as broccoli, cabbage, kale, and cauliflower) as transplants in early August, either indoors or in a cooler, shady spot outdoors for transplanting out into the garden next month. When seedlings emerge and produce their first true leaves,

start to fertilize them with a soluble plant food at the lower "constant-feeding" rate. Move seedlings gradually into more sunlight over the course of two weeks so they spend their last week or more in full sun prior to being planted out in the garden.

LAWNS

Turf can be established by seed or sod this month. (See April, Here's How to Establish a Lawn.) Fill in

■ *Keep plugs well-watered until they are obviously established.*

bare areas where drought, disease, or insects have killed the turf by planting 4x4-inch plugs 10 to 12 inches apart. Water them well and continue to water the plugged areas daily for a week, then every other day for another week. If only a few small areas are being plugged you can give them a boost so they will fill in by the end of the growing season by fertilizing them once every seven to fourteen days with a soluble plant food applied with a watering can.

PERENNIALS & ORNAMENTAL GRASSES

Perennial flowers and foliage plants can be planted this month, but it is generally better to wait until fall to plant them, when temperatures have cooled off a little. An exception is if you want to plant a *fall-blooming* perennial. While it would still be a small plant and not as showy as it will be next fall, it is worth having the color even if it is on a much smaller scale.

Your perennials will be spending a long time in the site where you plant them so make sure the light is right and the drainage is good, unless it is a plant that tolerates poor drainage, such as canna, elephant ear, or Louisiana iris.

Amend the soil with an inch of compost prior to planting. If the plants spent a long time in their container the roots may be a tangled mass. Soak the rootball and then loosen the roots so you can spread them out in the planting hole. Don't worry if much of the growing medium falls off. They will be fine if you get them planted before they dry out. Water the new plants with a good soaking after planting. Hold off on fertilizing for now and give them time to become better established.

ROSES, SHRUBS & TREES

Woody ornamentals can be planted this month, but since fall, the best planting season of the year, is just around the corner, wait a few months longer to increase their chances of surviving and thriving.

VINES & GROUNDCOVERS

Container-grown vines and groundcovers can be established now, but it is difficult for them to become established in summer heat. With fall

planting just around the corner it is best to wait a few more weeks and use this time to prepare the soil and remove perennial weeds from the area. Mix some compost into the soil if tree roots are not in the way, or add a few inches of bed mix to raise the area a little and facilitate drainage. If you are adding bed mix over a large area beneath the branch spread of trees and shrubs, don't add more than 4 inches of the mix because burying a tree's roots with more mulch reduces the oxygen level at the roots and can stress a tree.

CARE

ANNUALS

If you still have summer annuals growing, continue to remove spent blooms on those that don't tidy themselves up by dropping old blooms. Sometimes the soil becomes crusted or compacted over time if there isn't a mulch layer on the soil surface. Take a hand cultivator and lightly—1 inch deep—scratch the soil surface to break it up, kill any young weeds getting a start, and provide better aeration for the roots. Don't cultivate too deeply or you will damage an annual plant's shallow root system.

EDIBLES

If okra plants have become too tall to harvest easily, cut some of them back to force side shoots and an early to mid-fall harvest. That way you'll have some still producing while the pruned plants are regrowing.

Keep all bare soil areas covered with mulch to deter weeds, hold in moisture, and moderate soil temperatures. Place a shade cover over newly seeded areas for a couple of weeks to help the seedlings get going in the hot weather. Row-cover fabric works well for this and, if covered around the edges, also serves to keep pests off of your tender new plants.

Remove suckers and water sprouts from fruit trees to allow maximum light in to the interior branches for good fruit bud formation, which is happening now for next year's crop.

LAWNS

Mow at least weekly with a sharp mower blade for a clean cut. Dull mower blades *tear* the ends of the grass blades (instead of cutting them), leaving a brown tip. The visual effect of a million or more brown tips is a less green lawn. So sharpening your mower blade can make your lawn greener.

PERENNIALS & ORNAMENTAL GRASSES

Prune ginger and canna stalks to the ground after the stalks' blooms fade. The plant will

■ *Butterfly ginger is a beautiful late-summer to fall bloomer. Cut spent bloom stalks back to the ground after they fade to tidy up the planting.*

■ *Keep the mower blade sharp to make clean cuts, which will result in a greener lawn. The blade on the right was cut with a dull blade.*

keep on growing and put its energies into more bloom stalks.

Shear back Gregg's sage (*Salvia greggii*), skeleton-leaf goldeneye (*Viguiera stenoloba*), and other perennial subshrubs back by a third. Then fertilize and water them well. These plants tend to bloom themselves into a less vigorous state, and it takes new shoot growth to produce more blooms. The plants may still have some blooms on them, making it difficult to bite the bullet and cut them back. But do it now and you'll be rewarded with lots of new growth and blooms in the coming months, far more than if you just left them as they are.

Trim back Mexican honeysuckle (*Justicia spicigera*) and hummingbird plant or Uruguayan firecracker plant (*Dicliptera suberecta*) here and there to shape the plant and encourage more compact growth. These plants can get rather floppy and irregular over time, and a little snipping here and there can really improve their appearance and keep them from flopping over on an adjacent plant.

ROSES

Cut repeat-blooming roses back by a third in late August to promote plenty of new growth on which the fall bloom show will appear. The more shoots

■ *Shear* Salvia greggii *and other perennial subshrubs and then provide a boost of fertilizer and water to promote new growth and prolific fall blooming.*

you promote, the more blooms your rose bush can produce. Follow pruning with fertilizer and water.

SHRUBS

Shear hedges to promote fresh new growth and more blooms. While it is common to shear many kinds of shrubs, if they are not part of a hedge consider more natural pruning techniques for a more natural look. Cut shoots growing out of bounds back to where they join another shoot, preferably back inside the canopy's exterior. This way when you are done pruning, the bush looks tidy but not sheared. Examples of bushes that look much better this way are Texas sage or cenizo (*Leucophyllum frutescens*), bush germander (*Teucrium fruticans*), abelia (*Abelia grandiflora*), azaleas, gardenias, camellias (*Camellia sasanqua* and *C. japonica*), Virginia sweetspire (*Itea virginica*), and butterfly bush (*Buddleia davidii*).

In late August cut butterfly bushes (*Buddleia davidii*) back by a third, fertilize, and blast spider mites according to instructions provided in the July Care section. This will stimulate more growth and a great early to mid-fall bloom show.

TREES

Remove any guy wires and stakes that were attached to trees you planted this past fall through spring season. The tree should be well established and the wires are no longer needed.

VINES & GROUNDCOVERS

Groundcovers such as ivy, jasmine, cast iron plant, and liriope that are looking bad after a summer of heat, drought, pest, or disease damage can be cut back now. Use a string trimmer or lawn mower, or in the case of cast iron plant, hand pruners, to remove the old growth. Then water well with an inch of irrigation to promote fast regrowth and you'll have an attractive groundcover area within a few weeks. Don't be afraid to rejuvenate such plantings when they are looking ragged.

Shear back star jasmine (*Trachelospermum jasminoides*) and other vigorous vines used to form a living wall in the landscape. This shearing will increase their density and keep them growing closer to the supporting fence or lattice.

Complete any minor pruning needed to spring-flowering vines this month in zones 8 to 9 to allow them time to set bloom buds on the remaining growth between now and mid- to late fall. Excessive pruning and fall pruning will reduce the amount of bloom buds for next spring.

WATER

ANNUALS, PERENNIALS & ORNAMENTAL GRASSES

Established annual and perennial flower will do fine with a half-inch of water twice a week. Newly planted flowers will need a little extra TLC by watering daily for a week after planting just enough to wet the top two inches of the soil. Then switch to every other day for another couple of weeks to keep their roots moist while they adjust to their new home and start to establish roots.

EDIBLES

Water vegetable and herb gardens twice weekly in the heat to keep roots hydrated. New transplants may need daily watering for a while. Just water enough to keep the soil moist but not soggy wet

Late summer to fall watering is important to help pecans fill the shell with plump kernels.

for extended periods of time. A 6-inch berm of soil around new transplants can help you soak the rootball and surrounding soil thoroughly when you water.

Water fruit trees enough to maintain moist soil to a depth of at least 10 to 12 inches. The species that bloom in spring are setting fruit buds now and dependable soil moisture is critical to good bud set and next year's production. If you had a lot of malformed "twin" fruit on your peach tree this year it was due to drought conditions in midsummer to mid-fall last year.

Pecans have hardened their nut shells and are filling the kernels for the remainder of the season. They need plenty of soil moisture to do this, or the shells will be at least partially hollow at harvest time.

LAWNS

Lawns need an inch of water a week during these hot summer months. Watch your turf for signs of drought stress and water as needed to alleviate it. St. Augustine takes on a "bluish" tint when it lacks water. Footprints don't bounce back up and the leaf blades roll up a bit when it is becoming drought stressed.

ROSES, SHRUBS & TREES

Water in fertilizer applications to roses to start dissolving the product and releasing the nutrients to the plant's roots. Water all woody

ornamentals planted since last fall according to March's Here's How to Irrigate New Shrubs and Trees to keep them going strong in the brutal heat of August.

VINES & GROUNDCOVERS

Water vines and groundcovers by applying 1 inch of water every week in the absence of rainfall. Annual vines and newly established perennial and woody vines (and groundcovers), especially those planted in full sun or in sandy soils, which don't hold moisture very well, may need two applications per week.

FERTILIZE

ANNUALS

Water new plantings with a complete soluble fertilizer at the stronger labeled rate. Then repeat this about a week later. After the plants have been in-ground for a few weeks use a dry granular fertilizer at a low to moderate rate.

Established plantings will benefit from an application of complete fertilizer this month to promote good vigor and continued bloom production. When practical, scratch the fertilizer into the surface inch of soil. Always water fertilizer in after applying it to prevent the nitrogen in the product from washing away in heavy rains or evaporating as a gas.

EDIBLES

Fertilize warm-season vegetables at a moderate rate this month. Hold off on fertilizing beans and peas unless the plants lack good green color, in which case a light application may be helpful. See Here's How to Fertilize Flowers, Ornamental Grasses, and Vegetables in April for help in knowing how much fertilizer to apply for light and moderate rates.

Stop fertilizing fruit and nut trees this month. They have plenty of nutrition to carry them through fall, and they need to slow their growth in the fall as they prepare for winter dormancy. This is especially true for figs and any other species, such as citrus or avocadoes, that might be only semi-hardy in your area.

LAWNS

There is no need to fertilize a home lawn in summer if you are returning the grass clippings. Nature is decomposing the clippings to release their nutrients into the soil.

PERENNIALS & ORNAMENTAL GRASSES

Work some compost or composted manure into the soil around your perennial plants, taking care not to disturb their roots or rhizomes. This will decompose slowly over the coming months, releasing nutrients to the growing plants while promoting lots of microbial activity in the soil.

Make a final fertilizer application of the season to ornamental grasses in zones 7 to 9 to invigorate them for more fall growth. Use the moderate rate in the chart Here's How to Fertilize Flowers, Ornamental Grasses, and Vegetables in April. Then hold off for the remainder of the growing season to allow the grasses to slow down and prepare for dormancy.

ROSES

Fertilize roses according to instructions provided in June. Repeat bloomers need a good feeding after they are cut back this month (see the Care section), followed by watering. Avoid excessive fertilization of roses that only bloom once per year, as they are setting bloom buds for next year in late summer to early fall and need only moderate nutrition and vigor at this time.

SHRUBS & TREES

Pushing a tree late in the growing season with nitrogen fertilizer can predispose it to injury from an early freeze, so now is the time to make a final application of fertilizer for the season to shrubs and trees that haven't yet reached the desired size. Then wait until late winter to spring to resume fertilizing.

VINES & GROUNDCOVERS

Don't fertilize vines and groundcovers for the remainder of the season. They have plenty of nutrients to carry them through fall. The spring bloomers are setting bloom buds in the coming weeks and excessive nitrogen fertilizing can adversely affect bloom production. An exception is a newly planted groundcover that you need to fill in fast.

■ *Cut back shrub roses in late August and then fertilize the bushes to encourage new growth for a bountiful bloom show in fall.*

These can get one more application this month before you stop for the remainder of this year.

PROBLEM-SOLVE

ALL

Woody weeds such as poison ivy and hackberry seedlings are difficult to eradicate. They will soon be storing up carbohydrates for fall so now is a good time to take action. Herbicides that are taken up by the foliage and moved down into the plant will be more effective if applied this month or next. Rather than spray them on a large area consider cutting the trunk and "painting" the product on the freshly cut surface to minimize the amount of product you apply. If you don't want to apply an herbicide then hand digging is another option. Wet the soil thoroughly a few days ahead of time to make digging easier.

ANNUALS, PERENNIALS & ORNAMENTAL GRASSES

Spider mites will soon be declining, but if you have a plant that is infested it is a good practice to blast them off with a hard spray of water directed upward from beneath the plant. Do this in early and mid-month and your mite problems should be done for the remainder of this growing season.

Fungal leaf spots or bacterial spots on foliage of your plants may be an indication that you are wetting the foliage too often (with irrigation), which promotes such disease problems. You can't control rainfall, but you can control how often you turn on the sprinkler. Water deeply when you water (see May, Here's How to Determine How Long to Water) and as infrequently as possible. An infrequent, deep soaking is better than frequent, light applications of water. If your annuals have been hard hit by such diseases it is probably better to pull them out and replant. If perennials are suffering, do some sanitation pruning by cutting out all diseased shoots and foliage, and then discard them in the trash. The plant will respond with fresh new growth.

EDIBLES

Several types of insects could be around to munch on your vegetable plants this month. One simple solution that avoids the need to spray is to cover plants with the lightest weight row-cover fabric (.5 ounce/square yard) sealing down the edges with soil or boards to screen out the pests. Check under the fabric every few days to make sure there were no pests present when you put the cover over.

■ *Floating row covers can be laid directly on plants or suspended on hoops above plants, which allows for better air circulation.*

■ *Chinch bugs usually start near a sidewalk or other masonry structure and are especially common in late summer. They suck the juices out of a St. Augustine lawn and can kill large areas of turf if not controlled.*

Otherwise you would just be locking them up in the cafeteria and away from their natural enemies.

LAWNS

Browning areas of the lawn may be a sign of a chinch bug infestation. These insects have their largest population explosion in late summer to early fall. The brown areas usually appear in sunny areas adjacent to driveways, curbs, or hardscape walkways. The browning gradually moves outward into the lawn. Dry soil and some diseases can also cause similar symptoms, so take a sample to your County Extension Office for diagnosis before treating with an insecticide. (See May, Here's How to Take a Turf Sample.)

If you catch the problem early you can prevent loss of turf, as these pests can kill St. Augustine grass. Early detection also minimizes the amount of pesticide you use since treatments need only be applied in and just beyond the affected turf area.

ROSES

Watch for blackspot and powdery mildew on roses. These diseases are better prevented than cured so resistant varieties are the first line of defense. If your roses are not naturally resistant, then treat preventatively with a labeled fungicide according to the instructions on the label rather than wait until much of the foliage is infected with these diseases. By then treatments are too late to be of much benefit.

SHRUBS

If azalea foliage is showing a yellowish brown speckled color, check the undersides of the leaves for

■ *Fall webworms are often just a nuisance but in large numbers can defoliate susceptible tree species such as pecan, mulberry, and wild cherry.*

lace bugs, which are in their second destructive generation of the year in Texas. Pyracantha shrubs and sycamore (trees) are likewise susceptible to other species of lace bugs, which can build up to problem levels during the course of a growing season (see May for more information on lace bugs).

TREES

Fall webworms are starting their most damaging generation of the year, which can severely defoliate susceptible species, including pecan, mulberry, persimmon, wild cherry, hickory, redbud, and sweetgum. Look for webbing over groups of leaves around the canopy of the tree. If the tree is not too large take a long pole and break up the webs every day or two, which will allow wasps in to eat the caterpillars, their favorite food. Larger trees can be protected by spraying if you are able to reach at least 75 percent of the canopy. Sprays of *Bacillus thuringiensis (B.t.)* are effective if applied when the caterpillars are still young, but it's not effective against older caterpillars.

Fine webbing on the trunks and major scaffold limbs of trees with tightly grouped "herds" of ⅛-inch-long insects beneath the webbing is an indication that bark lice have set up housekeeping on your landscape tree. These insects are not pests and, in fact, feed on fungi, algae, dead plant tissues, and other debris, cleaning up the tree's trunk as they develop through the summer. Think of them as an "entomological maid service" and ignore them. They will go away on their own by about mid-fall.

TO IMPROVE TURF DENSITY IN SHADE

Turfgrass needs sunlight to produce the carbohydrates needed to maintain growth and density. When an area becomes too shady the lawn will gradually become thinner. Here are some tips for improving turfgrass density in shady areas:

1. Set your mower on the highest setting that will still be aesthetically acceptable. Grass blades are "solar panels" and the longer the blade the more light it can capture.

2. Avoid unnecessary foot traffic in shady areas. This reduces wear and tear on the grass and minimizes soil compaction.

3. Thin out the canopy of trees a little to allow more light to reach the ground. A bright, dappled shade may be sufficient to maintain a fairly dense lawn.

4. Raise the "skirt" around the outer edge of a tree's canopy. This allows reflected light to come in from the sides and can help, especially in areas near the outer canopy.

5. Don't try to replace sunlight with extra water and fertilizer. That won't work. Provide enough water to the turf in shady areas to keep the soil moist and fertilize at low to moderate rates.

6. Rake up fallen leaves promptly. When trees drop their foliage, the turf under a deciduous tree can capture some sunlight and replenish its stored reserves if sunlight is allowed to reach the grass.

VINES & GROUNDCOVERS

If vines are wilting during the day and recovering in early evening they probably need a little extra watering. The demands of summer can be intense when temperatures rise into the triple digits and vines are often unable to pump water as fast as the foliage transpires it away, thus causing wilting even in moist soil. The key is to keep the soil moist without overwatering or keeping it soggy for extended periods of time.

September

Fall is the "second spring" in Texas. The weather starts to cool off and fall rains begin to arrive this month, especially along the coast where tropical storm season is still underway. Even though it is still very hot out, now that the worst of summer is over we can start the main fall planting season in flower and vegetable gardens. Don't miss out on the best gardening season of the year. Whether you start plants from seed, start your own transplants, or purchase plants from a local garden center, take advantage of the cooler morning hours to get your fall garden underway.

This is a big planning month as we renovate summer plantings for fall gardening and begin to prepare for winter gardening too. Take a stroll through your garden to look things over. Notice what is thriving and what is struggling to survive. Where would a flower bed be a nice addition? Where could a blooming shrub or a small blooming tree make a big impact? Fall planting season for woody ornamentals is around the corner. So planning now will pay off in better choices later and a more beautiful landscape next year.

This is a good time to notice fall color. I don't mean fall foliage but fall blooms. There are a number of plants that bloom in the late summer to fall season. Make some notes in your gardening journal and snap a few pictures as you visit botanical gardens or drive about town so you can make plans to add more fall bloomers to your landscape.

Cold weather is still months away, but now is a great time to plan for the addition of a small greenhouse or even a cold frame. Our Texas winters are very mild in most of the state and we can keep on gardening with a little extra protection for our plants. If you purchase one soon you can have it set up and ready to go before the first frost arrives.

PLAN

ALL

This month make some notes in your gardening journal as to how various plants fared over the long, hot summer. You may want to plan on moving some to better locations where the sun or shade is more to their liking or where watering is more readily available.

Early to mid-fall is a good time to take cuttings from cold-tender landscape plants to root and keep in a greenhouse or indoors over the winter. This is a good way to plan for winter and next year's planting of these plants. Select the section of new growth that is in between succulent and woody. These are called semi-hardwood cuttings. Remove the leaves from the bottom half, dip the bottom third in a rooting hormone and place in a moist rooting media. A 50:25:25 mix of perlite, peat, and vermiculite works well as a rooting mix, or you can use a 50:50 perlite-and-peat mix. Cover with a clear cover and place in a bright area but out of direct sunlight. Most species will root in month or two. Then pot them up and provide a little liquid fertilizer. This way you can make more plants and also carry a cold-tender species through the winter for spring planting.

ANNUALS

It will be time to transplant cool-season flowers in about a month in zones 6 to 7 and two months in zones 8 to 9. Now is a great opportunity to plan your cool-season flower beds. Remember that you don't need a flower bed to plant flowers. Include some in containers for versatile color options.

Containers are handy because you can always move them to a protected spot when a freeze threatens and then move them back out when it is over. (See December, Problem-Solve, for a tip on moving containers more easily.)

Since our freezes in much of Texas are infrequent, container flowers can carry on well into or even through the winter season.

■ *Vegetables aren't just for vegetable gardens but can be included in the landscape such as in this beautiful courtyard planting.*

FLOWERS THAT BLOOM IN THE FALL

The heat of summer is lessening as the days start to get shorter, triggering a new set of perennial plants to burst forth in a beautiful display of blooms. Here are a few great choices for the landscape. Remember that "perennial" is a relative term, so check a plant's hardiness for your zone when selecting perennials for your location.

Candy corn plant or cigar plant (*Cuphea micropetala*)

Chrysanthemum (*Chrysanthemum* spp.)

Copper canyon daisy (*Tagetes lemmonii*)

Fall aster (*Symphyotrichum oblongifolium*)

Firespike (*Odontonema strictum*)

Gregg's mistflower (*Conoclinium greggii*)

Mexican bush sage (*Salvia leucantha*)

Mexican mint marigold (*Tagetes lucida*)

Mexican sage (*Salvia mexicana*)

Mountain sage (*Salvia regla*)

Philippine violet (*Barleria cristata*)

White mistflower (*Eupatorium wrightii*)

■ *Philippine violet* (Barleria cristata)

EDIBLES

Fall is an excellent time to plant perennial herbs. If you are creating a new herb garden with a geometric design do some planning on graph paper so you can draw things out to scale. Then use stakes and twine to lay out pathways and planting areas so you can get an idea what it will look like. If you don't have room for a formal garden consider an herb border around a patio or outdoor sitting area. Or line a sidewalk or other pathway with herbs. Make a "shopping list" of the number of herbs of each type you'll need. Check around to see if there's a local herb society that is having a fall sale or a program where you can get information and inspiration for planning and planting.

PERENNIALS & ORNAMENTAL GRASSES

Fall planting season begins this month especially for gardeners in zones 6 to 7. Review your garden journal and notes from gardening lectures to consider some new perennials to replace ones that didn't perform well or were problem prone this past year. Plan some new perennial plantings to add more color to spring, summer, and fall. Start checking around for plant availability and also look online for less common species and varieties.

A few great plants to consider that put on a big show in the late summer to fall season include Mexican bush sage (*Salvia leucantha*), fall aster (*Symphyotrichum oblongifolium*), Philippine violet (*Barleria cristata*), angel's trumpet (*Brugmansia* spp.), Mexican mint marigold (*Tagetes lucida*), mountain sage (*Salvia regla*), copper canyon daisy (*Tagetes lemmonii*), and sweet autumn clematis (*Clematis terniflora*).

Don't forget bulbs when planning a garden. Choose types that naturalize in your area for the most return on your gardening dollar. Bulbs are great in that most appear for their big show and

■ *Mexican bush sage is one of several great fall-blooming perennials that can be planted this month to extend landscape color into the fall season.*

HERE'S HOW

TO ROOT-PRUNE A SHRUB OR TREE

1. Use a sharp shovel to cut down 10 to 12 inches in a 2- to 5-foot diameter circular area (depending on the size of the plant) around the tree or shrub. The wider the better for the plant's survival but the more difficult it will be to move the roots and soil later.

2. Make a cut downward with the shovel. Then skip a space about the width of the shovel and make another downward cut.

3. Repeat all the way around the plant.

4. Water the area within and just beyond the circle cut by the shovel. Water over the coming weeks as needed to keep this area evenly moist.

5. The tree will send out new roots from near the cut ends of the roots, increasing its ability to survive a move to a new location.

then disappear until the following year. This keeps the landscape ever-changing and therefore more interesting. Purchase your bulbs as soon as they arrive in local garden centers or buy them via mail order early in the month. You want to have the best selection possible and you can always store them at home for a few weeks until it is time to plant them outdoors.

ROSES, SHRUBS & TREES

If there are woody ornamentals that you plan to move this fall, October (zones 6 and 7a) and November (zones 7b to 9) are the months to do so. However, you can do some root pruning now to help prepare them for the move in the coming months. See Here's How to Root-Prune a Shrub or Tree on the previous page. Keep the area from the base of the plant out to just beyond the pruned roots moist to promote development of the new roots that will appear after root pruning.

VINES & GROUNDCOVERS

Sketch out a design for new groundcover beds to be planted in fall. Large sweeping curves are aesthetically pleasing and easier to mow around. To break up the "sea of green" in your landscape consider using groundcovers with variegated foliage (such as variegated liriope, Aztec grass, and variegated Asian jasmine) in shady areas, and species with silvery foliage (such as silver ponyfoot, lamb's ear, or woolly stemodia) in sunny areas with excellent drainage.

PLANT

ANNUALS

In zones 8b to 9 there is still time early this month to put in a planting of warm-season annuals for a fall show that will last up to the first frost, which won't come until about the holidays in these zones. Take advantage of the mild fall season and bring some extra color to your landscape. Always prepare the soil before you plant for best results.

Plant some new flowers this fall for a change of pace. Now that fall is just around the corner, some less heat-tolerant annuals such as calibrachoa and bacopa can be planted to extend the warm-season color show.

If you want to grow your own transplants of cool-season flowers such as snapdragons, stock, calendula, nasturtiums, and alyssum, you can start them this month indoors where it is cooler. After the seeds are up and have a true leaf, move the transplants to a shady spot under a tree to continue growing. Fertilize them weekly with a dilute soluble fertilizer at the low "constant-feeding" label rate. Gradually move them to a brighter area over a week or so until you are able to move them into morning sun about two weeks after they moved outdoors. In about six to eight weeks from seeding, the transplants will be large enough to set out in the garden and the weather will be much more favorable for them.

EDIBLES

This is the busiest planting month for vegetables of the entire fall season. Cool-season root crops (radish, turnip, beet, and carrot) and cole crops (broccoli, cauliflower, kale, and cabbage) are going out into the garden all month in zone 8b to 9, and early to mid-month for zones 6 to 8a. There is a short window for planting cool-season peas (snow, snap, and English types) in early September (zone 7), mid-September (zone 8), and mid- to late September (zone 9). The strategy is not to plant so early that they succumb to the sweltering heat or so late that the crop freezes before you are able to harvest it.

Leafy greens, including lettuce, arugula, and mustard, also start to go in this month in zones 6 to 8, and zone 9 with some sun protection, and especially after a cool front breaks the heat. Cool-season greens, such as spinach, are finicky about sprouting in hot soil, so a shade cover over the row is helpful. Another option is to start them as transplants in the outer shade of a tree and gradually move them to more sun after they are up and growing well to acclimate them to full sun in about four weeks when they can go into the garden. This technique also helps make the best use of garden space.

If you can find the plants locally or mail order them, this month and next are good times to plant strawberries in Texas. Fall-planted berries will grow much of the winter and when spring arrives they will be larger, stronger plants for a much more bountiful harvest than their spring-planted counterparts.

Mix fertilizer at a moderate to high rate into the soil prior to planting. The rates mentioned in April, Here's How to Fertilize Flowers, Ornamental Grasses, and Vegetables, will also be appropriate for strawberry plants. Then set strawberry plants or bare-root crowns at the same depth they were previously growing. This is especially important because strawberries planted too shallow or too deep won't thrive. Water the new plants with a soluble fertilizer and repeat the fertilizing twice more at seven-day intervals.

LAWNS

Now that a long summer season has taken its toll on our lawns there may be some areas that need to be replanted, or that should be transitioned from turf to groundcovers or other plants. With the

brunt of the heat letting up, it will require less watering to establish a turfgrass this month in all zones, and also next month in zones 7b to 9. Small areas of dead grass can be filled in with sections of sod or planted with plugs as mentioned in August. Before your new sod arrives, prepare the soil by loosening it with a spading fork, or a rototiller if tree roots are not in the way. Remove surface debris. Then lay the sod and press it into contact with the soil below. Water the area well right away before it has a chance to dry out, which would set it back.

PERENNIALS & ORNAMENTAL GRASSES

Now is a good time to plant chrysanthemums (mums) for fall decoration. The plants are about to bloom so select plants that have lots of buds with a few starting to open. All mums can be grown in a container or in the landscape, but the florist-type

■ *Plant strawberries in the fall for larger, more productive plants during their harvest season in early to mid-spring.*

■ *Western natives such as pink skullcap do best with minimal soil amendments and well-drained planting beds.*

mum won't generally naturalize as a perennial in the landscape. Select varieties touted for landscape use if you want more than a year of enjoyment out of a mum plant.

Begin planting perennials across the state this month. Gardeners in zones 8 to 9 can also do just fine by planting next month, but who can wait? Prepare the soil before you plant. If your beds are not prepared and you see a plant that you can't bear to leave at the garden center, then go ahead and bring it home. But set it to the side until you get its new home ready. The goal is for it to thrive and soil preparation is the most important key to success with any plant. Add an inch or two of compost to the soil and loosen the soil in the planting area.

Drought-tolerant perennials such as santolina or lavender cotton (*Santolina chamaecyparissus*),

blackfoot daisy (*Melampodium leucanthum*), and pink skullcap (*Scutellaria suffrutescens*) will do fine with just some soil loosening. Too much compost can make them not feel at home since they are from more arid regions with very low soil organic matter. If you plant them in muck and then overwater them they will succumb to root rots quickly.

Plant ornamental grasses into prepared beds, setting the grasses at the same level they were growing in the container. Firm the soil around the roots and water well at planting. Consider your layout for ornamental grasses. These plants can be used as focal points such as a variegated type of maiden grass (*Miscanthus* spp.) in the center of a planting bed of other lower-growing perennials. They can also make a type of "hedgerow" by planting one of the larger muhly species such as big muhly (*Muhlenbergia lindheimeri*) or bamboo muhly (*Muhlenbergia dumosa*) in a line of plants to mark a property border or form a low wall in the landscape.

Ornamental grasses are also useful in groupings. Low-growing species can be planted in small groups of three to five plants or mass planted to form a taller groundcover effect, rather like a mini meadow. Mexican feathergrass (*Nassella tenuissima*) works very well when mass planted as a taller groundcover. In shady areas inland sea oats (*Chasmanthium latifolium*) will fill in nicely, especially in moist soil areas. Gulf muhly (*Muhlenbergia capillaris*) also works well in a grouping. Plant it so that the morning or late-day sunlight shines through the plant so the burgundy-colored, wispy seedheads will be illuminated for a striking effect.

ROSES, SHRUBS & TREES

Although October and November are the ideal months to establish new woody ornamental plants you can plant this month if circumstances make it more convenient. Be ready to water the new plants in small daily to every-other-day doses as September can still be quite hot across the state.

VINES & GROUNDCOVERS

The weather is still hot but the brunt of summer is past and cooler temperatures are on the way, so it is fine to start fall planting, including groundcovers and vines. Choose species for the area considering drainage, ability to irrigate the area, sun or shade exposure, and, of course, cold hardiness for your area when choosing the best species to plant.

Transition areas where turf struggled due to sun and drought, or too much shade to drought-hardy or shade-loving groundcovers. Remove the turfgrass, mix in some compost if tree roots are not in the way and plant the groundcovers. If the turf is bermudagrass or a variety of *Zoysia japonica* use a broad-spectrum weedkiller to kill the grass plants two weeks before putting in the groundcovers or you'll be in for a long battle removing grass from the groundcover. If you don't want to use an herbicide, some diligent spading and hand removal will be in order and you may want to start a month earlier to allow several weeks to catch resprouts that you missed the first time.

Space groundcover plants at 50 (faster coverage) to 75 percent (economize on plants) of their mature width depending on whether faster coverage or saving money on plants is your primary goal. Water the area thoroughly a day or two prior to planting to soften the soil and make digging easier. Then set plants at the same depth they were growing in the container and water them in well after planting.

CARE

ALL

Take cuttings of plants you want to multiply, or frost-tender plants that you want to carry through winter indoors. Consider which plants would make good gifts for gardening friends, perhaps for the holidays, and start them as cuttings now. Gardeners always get excited about a new plant.

■ *Take cuttings of desirable plants now to root and make more plants for overwintering or sharing with friends as gifts during the upcoming holiday season. This rooting has been dipped in perlite.*

HERE'S HOW

TO ROOT CUTTINGS

1. Take a cutting about 4 inches long.

2. Remove the leaves from the bottom half of the cutting.

3. If the plant has large leaves, cut the remaining leaves in half, leaving only the half attached to the stem.

4. Dip the cut end in rooting hormone.

5. Place the cutting in a premoistened mix of 50 percent peat and 50 percent perlite, or 50 percent vermiculite and 50 percent perlite.

6. Cover the cuttings with a clear plastic cover or place in a plastic bag.

7. Place in a bright spot out of direct sunlight.

8. Moisten the rooting media as needed to keep it moist.

9. When new growth starts to appear, repot the plant into a larger container using potting soil.

Remove the lower leaves and dip the cuttings in a rooting hormone. Root the cuttings in a mix of half perlite and half vermiculite. Set a clear cover over the cuttings to allow light in and set in an area away from direct sunlight. For more on how to make root cuttings see Here's How to Make Root Cuttings, above.

Perhaps the easiest way to propagate a plant is by air layering. This technique roots the stem of a plant while it is still attached to the "mother plant," thus improving the chances of success significantly. To learn how to make an air layer see Here's How to Air Layer a Plant on the next page.

ANNUALS

Deadhead zinnias and blooms of other species that remain on the plant after the blooms fade. Remove yellowing or dead foliage to make the planting look better. If any plants you set out last month didn't survive, replace them with a new plant right away to keep the planting full and uniform.

HERE'S HOW

TO AIR LAYER A PLANT

1. Make two cuts through the outer bark of the plant's stem and remove the bark down to the inner wood. Dust the area with rooting hormone. Place moist sphagnum moss around the wounded area.

2. Place a plastic bag around the moss-covered wounded area, securing it above and below with twist ties.

3. Wrap aluminum foil around the plastic to exclude light from the area where roots will form.

4. Wet the moss periodically as needed to keep it moist.

5. Roots will form inside the plastic bag (within a few weeks).

6. Cut the stem off below the wounded area and repot the new air layer in a container of potting soil.

Annual color beds that are looking bad after the long hot summer with its maladies of insects, mites, and diseases should be pulled out rather than trying to rejuvenate them. Clear out the bed and start with new plants for a fresh new start. Your planting will be looking much better in a few weeks than it would have had you left the tired old plants in place.

Cool-season weed seeds such as henbit, carpetweed, and chickweed are germinating in early to mid-September in zones 6 to 7 and from mid- to late month in zones 8 to 9. Keep the soil surface covered with mulch to block out the light, and these weed seeds won't be able to get a foothold in your flower beds.

EDIBLES

Maintain a mulch cover of leaves, pine needles, or straw over the soil. Remember, "Wherever sunlight hits the soil, nature plants a weed!" In early September, shear back herbs that are looking rather ragged from a long, hot summer season. They will respond with fresh new growth to make a more attractive plant.

LAWNS

Remove the grass in turf areas you plan to transition to groundcovers. Bermuda and zoysia will need to be eradicated with an herbicide or they will be a persistent weed in the new groundcover beds. These herbicide products work best when the grass is actively growing, so if it has been dry, water the area well before applying the products. Wait two weeks and then rototill the area, mixing in a few inches of compost to prepare for planting next month. St. Augustine can simply be scraped from the soil surface with a flat shovel as it has no underground rhizomes from which to regrow.

PERENNIALS & ORNAMENTAL GRASSES

Divide and reset irises this month. Cut the ends of Louisiana and bearded rhizomes about 6 inches long to remove the old sections, leaving fresh new rhizome tissues. Remove any dead foliage and brush the cut ends in sulfur dust to control rotting of the cut surface. Reset them so that the top of the rhizome is at or just below the soil surface, spacing Louisiana iris 8 to 10 inches apart and bearded iris 12 to 16 inches apart. Then water them and apply a little leaf or pine straw mulch. If you need to prepare the bed after digging before you can replant, then wet the rhizomes and place them in a shady area with some moist mulch over the rhizomes to keep them from drying out until you can get them reset.

Begin dividing other spring-blooming perennials late this month and reset them in their beds or pot some up for sharing with your gardening friends.

■ *Divide and replant Louisiana irises and bearded iris this month, as well as many other spring- to summer-blooming perennials.*

Bulbs that bloom in late winter to spring can all be divided now if they have formed large clumps and blooming is not as prolific as it once was. Examples include daffodils and paperwhites (*Narcissus*), snowdrops (*Leucojum aestivum*), white cemetery iris (*Iris albicans*), and bearded iris (*Iris germanica*).

If perennials or subshrubs in zones 8 to 9 have old spent blooms, go ahead and prune the old blooms out now to clean up the planting and allow for one more bloom cycle before cold weather shuts them down. 'Powis Castle' artemisia is a great groundcover perennial but can become ragged with time. If it is not looking very good, go ahead and shear it back by half in early September. With some watering it will regrow fresh new foliage and look great through the fall. Don't shear the flowering perennial plants back in zones 6 to 7 since regrowth will be slowing with the arrival of

■ *Divide and reset groundcovers, including purple heart, now so they can establish and be ready for filling in next spring.*

fall and shearing won't allow time for adequate regrowth and reblooming.

Maintain a 2- to 3-inch mulch in perennial beds to protect the soil surface and deter weeds. Fallen leaves and pine needles both make excellent mulch. Bark and compost are also good mulching materials.

ROSES

If you didn't prune reblooming roses back by one-third in August you can still do so early this month in zones 8 to 9 to promote a better fall bloom show. Don't delay; they'll need time to regrow and set buds. In zones 6 to 7 just leave them alone and enjoy the fall blooms, but make a note to try pruning them back next August.

SHRUBS

Make a final shearing of hedges in early September for zones 6 to 8a. Red-tipped photonias sheared early in the month in all zones will put on new foliage that will take on the characteristic red color with the arrival of cooler weather.

VINES & GROUNDCOVERS

Don't prune spring-flowering vines such as crossvine, Carolina jessamine, and wisteria any more this season or you'll reduce next year's bloom production. Vines grown for foliage can be sheared one more time this month to maintain good density. Trim the edges of groundcover beds to maintain shape.

Once the first cool front passes through you can divide groundcovers to make more plants to expand the groundcover bed or to share with friends and family. While vining types can be trimmed to keep them in place, some species such as ferns and cast iron plants, or purple heart, can grow wider over time, reaching farther than you may want. Dig and divide the plants around the periphery to keep the planting in-bounds. It helps to water them well a day or two before digging to soften the soil and make the job easier.

WATER

ANNUALS

Keep newly planted annuals from August adequately moist. These plants have established some roots, but if a hot period arrives, which is not uncommon for September, they will need some supplemental watering to stay hydrated. The same is true for annuals being planted this month. If in doubt, dig down and feel the soil a few inches deep. That way you can determine if the roots are in moist or dry soil. Any plants still hanging on from summer have more extensive root systems and may only need watering once a week; twice if it gets really hot.

EDIBLES

Because it is still warm, vegetable gardens still need water once or twice a week to ensure that the roots never lack moisture.

LAWNS

Shorter days and slightly cooler temperatures decrease the amount of water a turf grass uses. In the absence of rainfall, apply ½ inch of irrigation per week.

New sod plantings need a light daily watering (about ⅓ inch) for a week. Then, switch to every other day for a week; then water twice a week with ½ inch of irrigation if there's no rain to do the watering for you.

PERENNIALS & ORNAMENTAL GRASSES

September usually brings the return of some periodic rainfall. Combined with some cloudy weather, a little break in the heat (usually), and days that are slowly getting shorter means our watering regimen can start to back off for established perennials. Watch your perennials for signs of wilting and water accordingly. You may be able to cut back to one watering per week now. Drought-hardy perennials can be kept a little on the drier side and will do fine. If the weather gets rainy make sure any automatic sprinkler systems are turned off or soggy conditions will develop that are very detrimental to these plants.

Perennials that have been in the ground for less than a month will still need fairly frequent watering to help them become well established. Water them twice a week in the absence of at least ½ inch of rainfall that week.

ROSES, SHRUBS & TREES

September often brings rainy weather to coastal and southeastern parts of the state as tropical storm season arrives. In the absence of rain, supplemental watering is needed for roses, other shrubs, and trees that have been in the ground less than a year, since the weather is still quite hot. Follow the chart Here's How to Irrigate New Shrubs and Trees in March for guidance on how much and how often to water them.

When watering established roses avoid wetting the foliage as this can promote blackspot fungus. Drip irrigation is the best way to water since it is the most efficient and doesn't wet the plants' leaves.

VINES & GROUNDCOVERS

If it hasn't rained in the past week, water groundcover areas with an inch of irrigation. As the weather cools our watering schedule can back off to every other week in the absence of rainfall.

FERTILIZE

ANNUALS

Fertilize new annuals with a soluble fertilizer when you water the new plants and again once a week for two more applications. Then switch to a dry granular product spread at a moderate to high rate. (See April, Here's How to Fertilize Flowers, Ornamental Grasses, and Vegetables.) Use a complete fertilizer product and scratch it into the soil surface before watering it in. Established annual plantings will benefit from a boost at a light to moderate rate. This will help them put on some new growth for more flowers in the weeks to come.

If the foliage in new plantings is starting to look yellow, especially on the new growth, it may be due to soggy soil conditions. If that is not the case, then provide an iron supplement to the beds at the rate on the product label. Iron can be applied in soluble fertilizer with extra iron or granular forms. If you can find a chelated form of iron, it will

■ *Fertilize cool-season greens and cole crops such as this red Russian kale to promote vigorous growth during the mild temperatures of early to mid-fall.*

provide longer benefits to the plants. Ask a local nursery professional what types of iron they carry. Take care when using iron to avoid getting it on masonry or sidewalks and driveways as it will leave a rust stain. If some does get on these surfaces just sweep or wash it off right away and there won't be a problem.

EDIBLES
Beans and peas should be fine without any fertilizing, especially if the soil they were planted in had plenty of composted organic matter in it. Fertilize squash, cucumbers, melons, tomatoes, peppers, and eggplant with a moderate application of a fertilizer with a 3-1-2 or 4-1-2 ratio of nutrients to give them a boost of nitrogen to promote strong growth and deep green foliage color. Give cole crops and greens the same feeding

to invigorate the plants. The larger your cauliflower and broccoli plants are when they start to produce their heads, the larger the heads will be.

There is no need to fertilize herbs for the remainder of the season except to give new transplants a boost with a soluble fertilizer product at planting and perhaps again a week later.

Provide citrus such as kumquats, satsumas, Meyer lemon, and limes with a light dose of a dry fertilizer or a soluble fertilizer this month to support the plant, which is putting a lot of energy into a crop of fruit that it is ripening for a fall harvest. Don't overdo it or fruit quality and cold hardiness can be adversely affected.

LAWNS

A final application of fertilizer can be made for lawns in zones 6 and 7a to provide the nutrients, including potassium, that are important in helping the turf build winter hardiness. (See April, Here's How to Fertilize a Lawn.)

PERENNIALS & ORNAMENTAL GRASSES

Fertilize new perennials with a soluble fertilizer at planting and twice thereafter at seven-day intervals. Then apply a moderate amount of a complete fertilizer and gently cultivate it into the soil surface followed by a good, soaking irrigation.

As with annuals, if new growth looks yellow check the soil for excessive moisture and consider an iron supplement.

Established perennials that were not fertilized in August can be fertilized in early September. Then hold off on additional fertilizing for the year since the soil has adequate nutrients for their needs as the growing season draws to a close in the coming months.

ROSES

In zones 8b to 9 give a little supplemental fertilizer to established roses that repeat bloom through the season. Apply ¼ cup per plant, unless a late August application was made. The plants are putting on a flush of new growth now for their big fall show, and they need good nutrition and vigor. Avoid excessive fertilization of roses that only bloom once a year, as they are still setting bloom buds for next year. Only moderate nutrition and vigor is needed at this time. Wait until late winter or early spring to fertilize newly planted roses in zones 6 to 8a to avoid triggering excessive vigor that might be killed by an early freeze. New transplants in zones 8b to 9 can be provided a light fertilizing by working 1 tablespoon into the soil surface around each bush and then watering well.

SHRUBS & TREES

Hold off on fertilizing shrubs and trees with commercial fertilizer products for the remainder of the fall and winter seasons. These plants need to slow growth and start preparing for dormancy. Late-season flushes of growth are more likely to suffer cold injury when freezing weather arrives. This is especially important with species that are only marginally hardy in your area.

Provide an iron supplement to plants with berries, such as hollies and pyracantha, if new growth is turning yellow or has green leaf veins with yellowing between the veins. Follow the instructions on the product for rate of application. Iron products can cause rust stains on masonry so avoid getting them on sidewalks or white rock walls and walkways. If you do, just sweep the product off into the adjacent beds.

VINES & GROUNDCOVERS

There is no need to provide additional fertilizer to vines or groundcover beds for the remainder of the season. The nutrients in the soil are adequate for the little growth that will occur in the coming months and pushing the plants into late-season growth is not recommended since tender growth is more likely to be damaged by the cold.

PROBLEM-SOLVE

ALL

Deer are shedding the velvet on their antlers in some parts of the state. They like to rub them on trees and bushes to aid in the process and in doing so can do serious injury to woody ornamental landscape plants. Their rubbing removes the bark and cambium layer, essentially girdling the tree, and in some cases breaking off branches and even knocking over very young trees.

If you live in an area where deer wander into landscapes take action to protect your plants from deer. This is not an easy task and sometimes the deer feed on or rub antlers on our plants despite our efforts, but there is often a way to reduce or avoid the damage. See Here's

■ *Brown patch or large patch is a common problem on St. Augustine lawns in the early to mid-fall season as temperatures cool off a little and rainfall is more plentiful.*

How to Protect Landscapes from Deer in July for ideas on ways to reduce the damage deer can cause to landscape plants.

We are nearing the end of hurricane season, but even without a tropical storm we can have windstorms that break off limbs and even uproot trees. If you lose a major limb there is little to do but cut it off as cleanly as possible. Such damage usually leaves a nasty wound in which the bark is stripped down the trunk and the interior wood is left exposed to decay organisms. Such wounds may never fully heal and are often the weak point on the trunk or limb from that point forward. This poses a liability to you and a threat to people and property.

It is best to hire a certified arborist to come and evaluate your tree and make recommendations for the best course of action. The International Society of Arboriculture has an online service to help you find a local certified arborist who specializes in the type of work you need done. The web address for this resource is www.isa-arbor.com/findanarborist/arboristsearch.aspx.

Fall is a great time to control fire ants, and the benefits will carry over into next spring. Use potato chips or unwashed tuna can lids to check for ant activity, and only put bait out when you see ants on these oily attractants. It is usually best to apply baits late in the day. Use fresh bait and follow the label carefully as to how much and where it can be applied.

ANNUALS, PERENNIALS & ORNAMENTAL GRASSES

Caterpillar outbreaks are fairly common this time of the year. Watch your plants for early signs of caterpillar feeding. Sprays containing *Bacillus thuringiensis (B.t.)* are a low-toxicity way to control caterpillars but are most effective when caterpillars are young, becoming less effective as the larvae near the time to spin their cocoons and transform into moths or butterflies.

Plants that suddenly show signs of wilting will likely have a root problem. This may be due to insect larvae such as grubs or wireworms feeding on the roots, or soggy wet conditions that have led to a root rot. Gently lift an affected plant with a spade and examine its roots and soil around them for pests. Treatment for these pests is generally not needed as they don't usually occur in enough numbers to harm established plants. But new plants with their limited root systems are more adversely affected, and a treatment may be in order if many roots are affected. Since these pests are usually not evenly distributed in an area, just treat plants that show symptoms, following the label carefully.

If the roots have a brown, water-soaked appearance, a root rot is most likely involved. Soggy soil is usually the predisposing factor, so allowing the soil to dry out is the best remedy. Perennials may be salvaged if the damage is not too extensive. Cut away rotting roots, dusting the remaining rootball or underground plant parts with sulfur and resetting the plants in drier soil conditions. Consider replanting them in a container where you can control the moisture in the root area. After a few weeks you will know whether the plant is recovering and with any luck the soil will be drier and ready for them to be replanted in their beds.

EDIBLES

The break in the heat that usually comes this month seems to signal to pests that it is time to move back into our gardens. Be on the lookout for caterpillars, aphids, beetles, and other pests so you can take early action before the damage is significant and when your effective options include the least toxic products. Remember also that just because a plant has a little pest damage it doesn't mean that spraying is necessary.

Powdery mildew loves mild temperatures and high humidity. Other foliage diseases proliferate when foliage is wet. September brings such conditions to our gardens. Watch for powdery mildew on susceptible plants, including squash and peas, and take action promptly to spray a preventative product labeled for the affected crop. There are both organic and synthetic options for controlling such diseases.

LAWNS

If large patch (brown patch) has been an annual problem in your St. Augustine lawn, you may be overwatering and overfertilizing. Once the large, brown, circular areas appear with the arrival of cool temperatures and fall rains it is too late for treatments to be of much benefit. A preventative spray can be applied in late September and again two to three weeks later, but the best approach is to avoid pushing the lawn into early fall growth with extra water and fertilizer.

Chinch bugs, which were in their peak at the end of summer, are decreasing in numbers now. Therefore additional treatments to the areas where they turned grass brown are no longer needed.

ROSES

Watch for early signs of powdery mildew and blackspot on roses and treat promptly with a labeled fungicide. If you have a variety that is prone to the disease then be proactive to treat it at the interval recommended on the label. This will prevent these diseases from destroying the foliage that is needed to ensure a great fall bloom cycle.

TREES

Fall webworms are at their peak this month and next. Trees are resilient and able to lose some foliage with no significant weakening of the plant. However, if 50 percent or more of the foliage is lost just prior to the dormant season, the tree will be significantly weakened. Control these pests earlier rather than later after the damage is done. See August for control comments.

October

Fall is for planting. Experienced gardeners know that fall gives the best return on planting shrubs and perennials. Plants established in the fall have several months to establish roots during our mild winter season.

Use October to establish trees and shrubs or to move trees and shrubs to another location in the landscape. Their chance of survival will be greater and by the time next spring arrives they will have a big head start on spring-planted perennials and woody ornamentals.

Find a place to tuck in some herbs this month. Fall planting gives perennial herbs a head start too. They can be mixed in with perennial flowers, tucked away in the corners or at the end of a vegetable row, or planted in containers. Fragrant and flavorful, herbs deserve a spot in any garden.

Fall is for roses too. Repeat-blooming roses are putting on their second big show of the year this month. Notice roses growing around town and note the ones that appeal to you most. Fall is as good—or better—a time for planting roses as spring. Whenever possible, choose varieties that are naturally disease resistant to take some of the not-so-fun parts out of growing roses. There are many exciting new roses on the market that promise increased disease resistance, attractive landscape plants, and stunningly beautiful blooms.

Fall is also for bulbs. When shopping for bulbs remember that many types won't naturalize in your part of the state but can put on a beautiful "one-shot" show anyway. Most types of tulips, Dutch hyacinth, and crocus fall into this category. There are many other bulbs that will naturalize, providing years of blooming returns on your investment. Check with a local botanical garden or other gardeners with bulb plantings to find the best choices for your area.

The vegetable garden is also a busy place in the fall. Don't let this wonderful season get away without investing in some long-term beauty and bounty in your landscape and gardens.

PLAN

ALL

Frosts and freezes are likely this month in zones 6 to 7 but are not that far away for the rest of the state. Make plans to protect your plants from the cold now while supplies are readily available. The night before a freeze there is usually a run on supplies at garden centers and home-improvement stores that may leave you and your plants out in the cold.

Some good supplies to have on hand are frost covers (including spunbond polyester fabrics or even old sheets, plastic sheeting, and tarps), support structures to hold the covers (PVC pipe, 2x4s), heat sources (portable light fixtures, a string of Christmas lights, heating cable, empty milk jugs), extension cords, and three-way connectors.

If you have valuable landscape or orchard plants that will need protection, such as a beautiful tropical hibiscus or citrus tree growing in the ground, you may want to go ahead and build a wood frame structure to be assembled and placed around it to hold a tarp on a freezing night. PVC pipe (¾-inch or 1-inch) bent into very large hoops or larger PVC pipe (2- or 3-inch diameter) connected with L and T connectors can be cut to size so it is ready to be put together like Tinker Toys before a freezing night.

Stockpile bags of leaves as soon as they fall to use as a thick mulch over tender perennials to protect the crown of the plant during a hard freeze. See Here's How to Protect Plants from Freezes later in this chapter for more tips on protecting all types of landscape plants when a freeze threatens.

ANNUALS

The planting season for cool-season flowers is arriving in zones 7 to 8. Consider the cool-season options and check on local availability to plan your flower plantings. If you are planting a large area with annuals check out Here's How to Estimate the Number of Plants Needed to Fill an Area in August for help determining how much to buy.

As you plan how you will protect plants during a cold snap, remember that the Texas climate, which is fairly mild in most of the state, takes just a few freezes to damage plants. If you can cover plants even for a night or two, you can continue to have great color into winter. Warm-season flowers are much more susceptible to cold and may not be salvageable when a hard freeze is on the way. Cool-season flowers, on the other hand, are much easier to keep going with a little extra protection on a freezing night.

■ *Hinckley's columbine is a great choice for Texas landscapes and performs well in dry shade locations with good drainage.*

■ *Disease-resistant roses such as 'Belinda's Dream' are a beautiful way to create a more easy-care landscape.*

EDIBLES

Frosts can begin this month in zone 6 and by the end of the month, gardeners in zone 8a may be experiencing their first frost of the season.

Make plans for what to do next in the beds where warm-season crops are growing. These will be taken out by the first frost and can either be planted with a cold hardy crop, sown with an overwintering green manure crop (such as cereal rye, ryegrass, clover, or vetch), or left fallow for the winter. See comments in the Care section in June for instructions on how to use leaves and other organic materials to prepare soil for a fallow period.

PERENNIALS & ORNAMENTAL GRASSES

This is prime planting season for perennials. Visit some local garden centers to see what they carry as you complete your plans for planting. Planning before you plant is always a good idea. Not all perennials are well adapted to your area, and not all adapted ones are available locally. It is better to leave a space or two open while you locate the plants you want. There is always the spring season for planting if you don't find them this fall. Check mail order sources if local sources don't have a plant you are looking for.

Try some new perennials that you haven't grown before. Have you tried columbines? They are a beloved flower, but the "Colorado" kind melts in our Texas heat. There are two native species that do fine as short-lived perennials: red columbine (*Aquilegia canadensis*), native to the Edwards Plateau, or Hill Country region, and Hinckley's columbine (*Aquilegia chrysantha* var. *hinckleyana*), native to the Big Bend area. Both do well in most areas of Texas if provided with good drainage and planted from seed or transplants in the fall season.

ROSES, SHRUBS & TREES

There is still time to plan and prepare the site for woody ornamental plants you want to plant this fall. Draw out your new planting beds to create a pleasing and functional design. Order bed mix or compost to build up or improve the soil and then shop around for the species or varieties that are best suited to the site and your aesthetic preferences.

VINES & GROUNDCOVERS

Complete plans to establish groundcover beds prior to planting. Draw them out on paper or use garden hoses to lay out the beds so you can create aesthetically pleasing curves that are easy to mow. Consider drainage, sun exposure, and foliage color as you create a beautiful, low-care carpet for your landscape.

PLANT

ANNUALS

We have many options for cool-season color. Depending on your area of the state you may be limited to the hardiest species, which include pansies, violas, and flowering cabbage and kale. Farther south the options open up to include cyclamen, primroses, dianthus, or sweet William (*Dianthus barbatus*), snapdragon, stock, calendula, alyssum, nasturtium, and lobelia. If you are willing to protect them during a hard freeze, even these less hardy cool-season flowering plants can go on through the winter in zone 9 and parts of zone 8.

The weather has cooled off enough in all zones to plant cool-season flowers. Pansies and violas don't like heat, so if you are in zone 9 and the weather is

■ *Use a garden hose to lay out groundcover or flower beds to help visualize the design and create sweeping curves.*

still fairly warm you might wait until early next month to plant them.

Prepare the soil with compost and set your flowering plants out on the bed to check spacing and make sure the colors are arranged like you want them. Then plant and water annuals with a soluble fertilizer solution. Mulch the beds after planting to prevent cool-season weed seeds from getting a start.

Biennials are plants that start their life cycle one season and finish it the next. We basically treat them as annuals. Our state flower, the bluebonnet, is an example of a biennial. Now is the time to plant seeds of several biennial species, including bluebonnets, poppies, and larkspur, in zones 8 to 9 where the winters are not too severe. Sweet peas, although not a biennial, also do best in these zones if they're fall seeded. Many gardeners wait to plant them until late winter or spring, but fall planting is a far superior option in areas that don't get the bitter cold of more northern zones. Seeded outdoors now, these species will sprout in the coming weeks and spend the winter as a small plant (that you might overlook as a weed). Then in

■ *Snapdragons are one of many cool-season flowering annuals for fall-to-winter color in the landscape. A mix of colors is best when viewed up close, such as along a walkway or beside a patio.*

■ *Larkspur and poppies, like other biennial flowers, bloom in spring but are seeded out in the garden in fall.*

■ *Before removing plants from their containers, place them in the prepared garden to see how they will look together. Experiment with different groupings until you find an arrangement that pleases you.*

spring, as the days get longer, they take off growing rapidly and bloom beautifully in March and April.

A week prior to planting biennial seeds, lightly apply fertilizer (see April, Here's How to Fertilize Flowers, Ornamental Grasses, and Vegetables), and mix it 4 inches into the soil. After planting there is no need to fertilize again.

Plant wildflowers in all zones this month. If the soil is not moist, water a couple of days before planting to wet the soil deeply. Then on planting day break up the soil surface with a hoe or rake for small areas or a rototiller for larger areas. There is no need to rototill deeply; a couple of inches is fine. Then scatter seeds at the rate specified on the packet, and rake again lightly to barely cover the seeds. Water with a sprinkler to settle the soil, and then water as needed every day or two to maintain moist soil at the surface where the seeds are germinating.

EDIBLES

Plant cool-season crops, including cole crops, root crops, and greens, in zones 7b to 9 this month. Sooner is better than later to allow them as much time as possible before the first freeze arrives to slow their growth and development. Be prepared to protect them against cold in the northern zones should a hard freeze arrive early. It is generally best to start all cool-season crops from transplants rather than seeds at this point in the season since seeds take longer to reach a size or maturity where they can be harvested. An exception would be "baby greens," which are just regular greens that are harvested while still young, so they are quite fast from seeding to harvest.

A PVC hoop structure or other support for row covers can extend the growing season in all areas of the state and keep you in fresh greens and other vegetables. Another technique is to plant in containers, especially ones that are easy to move. A wheelbarrow filled with potting soil and with holes drilled into the bottom for drainage makes an excellent portable garden. Set it in the sun during the day and move it to a protected area such as a garage when a freeze is forecast.

There isn't a better month of the year for planting perennial herbs, including thyme, chives, marjoram, mint, salad burnet, rosemary, chamomile (though not "German chamomile"), lemon balm, oregano, feverfew, fennel, garden sage, rue, pineapple sage (zones 8 to 9), culinary ginger (zones 8b to 9), lemon grass (zone 9), and bay laurel (a shrub, hardy to zone 8b). October has mild temperatures and usually some rainfall to make for perfect conditions to help the new plants become established quickly. Water your new plants with a soluble fertilizer and mulch them well to protect the roots and deter cool-season weeds.

This is the best month for strawberry planting also. See comments in the Plant section in September for information on how to prepare the soil and plant strawberries. If you can find container-grown fruit plants in your area, this month is a good time to plant them. Lean the plant over and slide it out of its container. Look for circling roots and cut any that you find. Then plant it, setting the top

■ *Fall is a great season for planting perennial herbs, including pineapple sage, which doubles as a beautiful flowering plant.*

of the rootball at, or just above, the soil line. Water the plant as you refill the hole with soil to settle the soil and ensure good root-to-soil contact.

LAWNS

This is the last call for planting sod in zones 7b to 8, but in zone 9 the sodding season can extend into November. The newly laid sod will need time to establish before winter cold arrives and with the arrival of shorter days and cooler temperatures growth and establishment will slow considerably.

Overseeding is not usually recommended since the overseeded species stresses our warm-season turfgrasses, especially during the transition period in early spring. Bermudagrass can tolerate overseeding as can zoysia, but St. Augustine cannot. If you have new construction or lost most of your lawn this past year, overseeding can provide a winter lawn until you are able to replant a warm-season lawn next spring.

If you plan to overseed your lawn this year, mid- to late October is the time to purchase and plant the seeds in zones 6 to 7a. First, mow the lawn as low as possible and rake the area so the seeds can reach the soil surface. Then scatter seeds of annual ryegrass at a rate of 10 to 12 pounds per 1,000 square feet.

Water the area well and don't allow it to dry out during seed germination and establishment. Fertilize a few weeks after the seeds emerge.

PERENNIALS & ORNAMENTAL GRASSES

October is a big month for the group of plants we refer to in general as bulbs (see What Is a Bulb? below). Bulbs that bloom in late winter to spring such as daffodils and paperwhites (*Narcissus*), snowflakes (*Leucojum aestivum*), spring starflower (*Ipheion uniflorum*), Spanish bluebells (*Hyacinthoides hispanica*), species tulips (*Tulipa praecox* and *T. clusiana*), grape hyacinth (*Muscari neglectum*), naked ladies (*Lycoris squamigera*), yellow spider lilies (*Lycoris aurea*), Chinese ground orchid (*Bletilla striata*), Byzantine gladiolus (*Gladiolus communis* subsp. *byzantinus*), white cemetery iris (*Iris albicans*), and bearded iris (*Iris germanica*) can all be planted now. You can also plant spring- to summer-blooming bulbs, including daylily, oxalis, rain lily (*Zephyranthes* and

WHAT IS A BULB?

The term "bulb" is often used in a generic sense to describe a group of different plants that have fleshy storage structures that grow at or below the soil surface. These structures have everything that the plant needs to survive and grow. There are five types of structures in the group of plants sometimes referred to as bulbs: true bulbs, corms, rhizomes, tubers, tuberous roots, and fleshy roots.

True bulbs have a basal plate that is actually the plant's stem and fleshy storage leaves called "scales." Tulips, daffodils, hyacinth, lilies, garlic, and onions are examples of bulbs.

Corms are a solid swollen stem base with a basal plate from which roots develop. If you cut a corm in half you won't find the rings or scales but rather the stem's solid storage tissue. Examples of corms include gladiolus, crocus, freesia, and crocosmia.

Rhizomes are a specialized type of stem that grows horizontally below the ground. Bearded iris, cannas, and gingers are types of rhizomes.

Tubers are swollen underground stem tissues without a basal plate. Caladiums and the common garden potato are examples of tubers.

Tuberous roots are swollen roots that contain buds near the end toward the plant's base from which shoots can grow. Dahlias, tuberous-rooted begonias, and sweet potatoes are examples of plants with tuberous roots.

Fleshy roots are plants with swollen storage roots that must be left connected to a section of the plant's base, which contains the buds for regrowth of a new plant. Daylilies are a common example of a plant with fleshy roots.

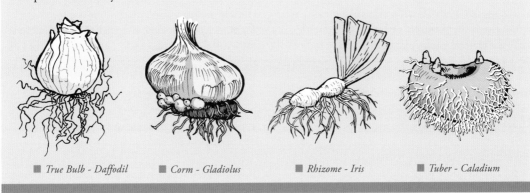

■ *True Bulb - Daffodil*   ■ *Corm - Gladiolus*   ■ *Rhizome - Iris*   ■ *Tuber - Caladium*

OCTOBER

■ *Fall is the time to plant spring-blooming bulbs, including these Byzantine gladiolus, which naturalize in many areas of the state.*

Habranthus), spider lily (*Hymerocallis* spp.), Louisiana iris, Hill Country rain lily (*Cooperia pedunculata*), and fortnight lily or African iris (*Dietes iridioides*).

Set true bulbs and rhizomes at the proper depth for the species. Your local garden center can advise you on the species it sells. Bearded iris rhizomes are set so the top of the rhizome is barely covered with soil. As a general guide, plant bulbs so the top of the bulb is two to three times as deep as the bulb is tall. A bulb-planting tool comes in handy if you are planting more than a handful of bulbs. Press the soil around the bulb to eliminate air pockets. Mulch all bulb plantings and water them.

If you'd like to start bulbs indoors for forcing, October is the time to get them started. Some bulbs, including hyacinth and tulips, require a pre-chilling period of twelve weeks or more with temperatures around 35 to 45°F, during which they develop roots in the pots in preparation for growth and blooming. This is difficult to achieve in our climate since it's just too warm outside in mid- to late fall to chill them in pots outdoors.

Amaryllis and paperwhites don't require pre-chilling and can be planted when you purchase them. Place them close together to fill a container for a full floral display. Add potting soil so that the tip of the bulb is barely showing above the soil. Water them in well and place in a shady spot outdoors until you see new growth emerging. Then bring them inside to enjoy the blooms, which will appear about two to three weeks after planting, depending on the species and variety.

If you want to plant tulips and hyacinths out in the garden now is the time to purchase the bulbs and chill them. This chilling is necessary for the blooms

184 ■ October

to develop inside the bulb. Place them in a crisper bin, but remove any other fruit, especially apples as they give off ethylene gas, which can cause the blooms to be malformed. Leave them in the bin until it is time for planting in late December.

This month is prime time for planting perennials of many types. Plants established now have all winter to settle in and develop roots in preparation for spring. They will be far ahead of their spring-planted counterparts. A money-saving tip is to choose a plant one pot size smaller in fall than you would have planted in spring. By the time next summer arrives the two plants will be virtually indistinguishable due to the head start that fall planting provides, and you'll have a few extra dollars to spend on more plants.

When planting perennial transplants it is best to scatter a light to moderate amount of fertilizer in the beds and mix it 4 to 6 inches deep prior to planting. There is no need to fertilize again until next spring when new growth begins.

If you have perennials that need to be moved, this month is a good time to do so. Perhaps they are in too much sun or not enough, or maybe you have other plans for that area. Dig the plants up and reset them in their new location right away, placing the plants at the same depth they were previously growing. Firm soil around the roots and provide a good soaking with a hose to settle the soil in around the roots. If the perennial clump is too large to carry, either divide it or slide it onto a tarp and drag the tarp to the new location. You can move a lot of weight with much less effort this way.

ROSES
February gets all the attention when it comes to roses, but October is the best month for planting container-grown roses. Consider your site before choosing the best type and variety for the planting spot. Remember that roses need sun: no sun, no blooms. There are hundreds of varieties available to purchase in many types, including miniatures, groundcovers, hybrid teas (for long-stem cut flowers), shrubs, and ramblers and climbers. Choose your varieties wisely. Some bloom only once in the spring while others repeat in flushes of bloom from spring to fall. Some are disease

resistant, and some require a full-time gardener standing by with a spray wand to fend off diseases. Some are fragrant, while others are not.

Build a raised planting bed if drainage is at all questionable. See comments in Shrubs & Trees below for advice on preparing the soil and planting.

SHRUBS & TREES
Fall is the best planting season of the year for woody ornamental plants. This month and next are a prime time to plant roses and other shrubs and trees in your landscape. By planting in the fall your plants will have more than six months to establish roots before the hot weather arrives next year, with its stressful demands for moving moisture from the roots to the aboveground parts of a plant.

Choose species and varieties that are adapted to your region and to the planting site (sun/shade, wet/dry, high pH/low pH). Consider the mature size of the plants you choose. If planting the shrub beside a walkway or under a window, select a species or variety that will reach a mature height or width that does not overgrow its area. This will save you a lot of work in years to come trying to prune it into a smaller size than it wants to become.

Do you want a hedge to block a view? Sit or stand where you will view the hedge and note how high it needs to be. A 6- to 8-foot hedge is often plenty large, depending on the view you want to block. Evergreen foliage is important if you are blocking a view but also adds interest to the winter landscape. Do you want flowers in spring, summer, or fall? If you are planting a tree, how large does it need to be to shade the area? Remember that it is more difficult to have flowers in the shade than in a sun to part-sun location. Some species cast a lighter shade than others. Is it located on the south or west side of the home where shade will save on energy bills?

Successful planting depends on attention to a few basic techniques. See Here's How to Plant Container-Grown Shrubs and Trees in November for details on planting a woody ornamental plant. Don't just dig a small hole and fill it in with compost around your new plant. Remember that the plant will be extending its roots far beyond the hole. Filling a planting hole with compost can cause roots to stay within the planting hole and can create an "underground bathtub" of poor drainage during rainy periods, especially in a clay soil.

Amend the soil in as large of an area around the shrub as is practical by mixing 3 to 4 inches of compost into the top 6 inches of soil. If the area tends to drain poorly purchase a bed mix from a local soil and compost supplier to raise the planting area 10 inches.

When soil preparations are done, dig the planting hole twice as wide as the plant but no deeper than the

■ *Build a raised berm of soil at least twice as wide as the plant's rootball to help provide deep soakings when you water the plant. This will improve its chances of survival after planting and especially during hot weather next year.*

HERE'S HOW

TO PLANT A BAREROOT HEDGE

1. Prepare the ground thoroughly by digging a trench about 2 feet wide. Amend the soil as needed and return the soil loosely to the trench. Cover the garden with 2 to 3 inches of shredded bark mulch. Hedgerow shrubs must be spaced at consistent intervals. Divide the length of your trench by the number of plants you have to determine how far apart to space the shrubs and place the shrubs in their spots. Make sure the spacing is within the guidelines for your shrub type.

2. Pull back the mulch and dig the holes wider and deeper than the largest roots. Make a firm cone of soil in the bottom of each hole.

3. Hold the plant upright so the crown is slightly below the soil line, and spread the roots out over the soil cone. Add soil as needed to keep the plant's crown at the correct depth. Make sure to fill in the hole completely with soil to avoid air pockets where the roots may dry out.

plant's rootball. Set the plant in the hole at the same depth it was in the container and use the soil from the hole to refill in around the plant. Don't add fertilizer into the planting hole since some products can burn the tender roots and the new plant won't need supplemental fertilizing until spring.

Build a raised berm of soil around the plant, making the berm at least 6 inches wider than the rootball all the way around the plant. Fill the berm with water to thoroughly soak the rootball and surrounding soil. This berm will be your key to proper watering of your new plant and will be expanded in size next spring. Finish with a 3-inch layer of mulch over the soil surface to protect from erosion, crusting, and to deter weeds.

This is a good month for moving a woody ornamental shrub or tree in zones 6 to 7. It is also fine to wait until next month. See directions in Here's How to Move a Woody Ornamental Plant in November. If you root-pruned a plant that is to be moved this fall water the base of the plant to just beyond the pruned roots to promote development of the new roots that are growing.

VINES & GROUNDCOVERS

This is one of the best months of the year for planting perennial and woody vines and groundcovers. The heat of summer is past, temperatures are still mild, and rain often falls, making it an ideal environment for a new plant.

Groundcovers that struggled through the summer with too much sun or excessive shade can be transitioned to a more appropriate species for the sun, shade, or drought conditions. Water a couple of days prior to planting if the soil is dry. This makes it easier to dig and plant your new plants. Water plants well to settle the soil around the roots. Don't fertilize now as the plants don't need it and it will mostly be a wasted effort. The new plants won't be growing much above ground this fall, but they will be expanding their root systems. When next spring arrives they will be ready to take off like a rocket.

CARE

ALL

Air layering is one of the easiest ways to propagate new plants from ones you already have. It involves rooting a section of stem while it is still attached to the plant, which increases your chances of success. Perhaps you have a bay tree or other plant that may

■ *Divide spring-blooming bulbs, including paperwhites and daffodils, to make more plants. Then reset them in their new locations or share a few with friends.*

HERE'S HOW

TO DIVIDE PERENNIALS

1. Dig the perennial and shake off loose soil. Use a sharp spade or long knife to cut through the clump.

2. Divide the plant into individual plants or small groups of plants. Replant or pot up divisions for later planting or sharing with friends.

not be hardy in your area. Do an air layer to create a new plant to take indoors in case the "mother plant" outdoors gets killed this coming winter. (See September, Here's How to Air Layer a Plant.)

If you took cuttings last month to start new plants for holiday gifts, pot them up and begin to water with a dilute fertilizer solution this month. Keep them growing with regular watering so they'll be ready to take to a friend's house when you visit during the holiday season.

ANNUALS, PERENNIALS & ORNAMENTAL GRASSES

Deadhead annuals and perennials that don't drop their spent flowers. Cut back to the first set of leaves below the blooms.

Divide spring- to early summer-blooming bulbs and spring-blooming perennials, including daffodils and paperwhites (*Narcissus* spp.), bearded iris (*Iris* spp.), amaryllis (*Hippeastrum* × *hybrida*), spring star flower (*Ipheion uniflorum*), Chinese ground orchid (*Bletilla striata*), Hinckley's columbine (*Chrysantha*

var. *hinkleyana*), ox-eye daisy (*Chrysanthemum leucanthemum*), Shasta daisy (*Leucanthemum* x *superbum*), coreopsis (*Coreopsis grandiflora*), purple coneflower (*Echinacea angustifolia*), Indian blanket (*Gaillardia* spp.), wild foxglove (*Penstemon cobaea*), oxalis (*Oxalis crassipes*), prairie phlox (*Phlox pilosa*), moss pink (*Phlox subulata*), Louisiana phlox (*Phlox divaricata*), mealy cup sage (*Salvia farinacea*), yarrow (*Achillea millefolium*), and sweet violet (*Viola odorata*).

Work an inch of compost into the soil in the beds and reset the divisions at the level they were previously growing. Water the newly set divisions well to settle the soil in around their roots. Take care not to allow the roots of perennials to dry out during division and replanting so they are not set back.

Dig and store caladium tubers for planting next spring and summer. Dig the plants and allow them to dry for a week. Then remove the dead foliage and brush away any soil. Store in dry peat or sawdust in a cool, dry area where temperatures will remain above 55°F.

EDIBLES

Pull freeze-sensitive vegetables after the first freeze ends their growing season. Replenish mulch in all vegetable beds to help insulate roots and deter seeds of cool-season weeds from germinating.

Stop pruning fruit trees for the season. They need time to go into dormancy and won't be putting on more growth at this point in the season. The next time to prune will be in mid- to late winter.

LAWNS

Cooling temperatures mean that mowing season is coming to a close. Winter weeds are germinating this month throughout the state. Pre-emergence weed control products must be applied prior to the weed seeds germination in order to be effective. After they sprout a post-emergence product will be needed to control them. Remember to water the pre-emergence product into the soil surface according to the label or it won't be effective.

If your lawn is rather thin and lacks vigor topdress with ½ inch of finely screened compost (which most of the time is purchased as finely screened when topdressing a lawn). This will cover bare spots in the turf to minimize weed seed germination, and it will decompose as the weather warms in spring, releasing its nutrients to the growing turf.

ROSES

Deadhead roses to remove unsightly spent blooms and keep the bushes attractive. As a general guide, when deadheading roses cut back to the first leaf with five leaflets.

SHRUBS

In zones 8b to 9 you can make a final shearing for the season on hedges early in the month. With growth slowing and the potential for freezing weather around the corner additional shearing is usually not needed or recommended.

VINES & GROUNDCOVERS

Provide a final trimming to edge your vining groundcover beds. If you are having problems with turfgrass and groundcovers mixing, consider installing metal edging to line the beds. Then it will be easier to cut between the two plantings with a string trimmer.

■ *Thin radishes, carrots, turnips, and other root crops to at least twice as wide as the variety's normal root width to allow them plenty of room to grow.*

Tie any vines that have wandered off their trellis to the trellis or wind them through to give them support and tidy up the arbor or trellis area. On woody vines, trim back any broken shoots or those in the way of pedestrian traffic by cutting them back to where they join another branch or the trunk of the plant. That way there won't be any sticks poking out that may be dangerous to passing pedestrians.

WATER

ANNUALS, PERENNIALS & ORNAMENTAL GRASSES

Water as needed to maintain moist soil. In most of Texas, periodic rainfall and cooling temperatures allow us to cut back on watering to one-third or less of the summer rate. If, however, your area is experiencing a drought it is important not to allow perennials to dry out during this time as they are growing well in the mild temperatures and are preparing for winter. Drought stress now will result in weaker plants when they resume growth in the spring.

EDIBLES

Vegetable gardens should need half the water they normally use now that the weather is cooling off. Dig down a few inches and feel the soil before

HERE'S HOW

TO PROTECT PLANTS FROM FREEZES

Often the temperature drops to a killing cold level for only a few hours just prior to sunrise, making it very practical to protect a marginally hardy plant through one of the few really cold spells your area receives. This doesn't mean you can grow date palms in Dalhart, but it does allow you to stretch a plant's zone a bit farther than otherwise possible.

1. Place a tarp, blanket, or plastic sheeting over the plant. A PVC pipe frame or arches of bent PVC pipe can be used to keep a heavy tarp from crushing a tender plant or to prevent the material from contacting outer foliage where it can "cold burn" the foliage during a freeze.

2. Drape the tarp or plastic to the ground and secure it with stones or soil to seal in dead air space and to prevent air movement within the covered area during windy conditions. Don't wrap the cover around the plant as this excludes the heat from the soil or from a heat source and leaves the trunk and base of the plant unprotected.

3. If desired for extra heat, put a source of heat beneath the cover such as incandescent bulbs. Don't allow the lights to be too close to leaves and stems or damage can occur. A string of Christmas lights with the larger bulbs that give off a small amount of heat can also be used.

4. Check cords and connections for safety. Make sure the connections and lights are protected from rain and away from dry grass or mulch.

5. Mound soil up 1 foot high against the trunk of grafted trees such as citrus to protect the graft union. Should the entire tree be killed the plant can resprout from above the graft. Remove the soil mound when the danger of freezing weather is past.

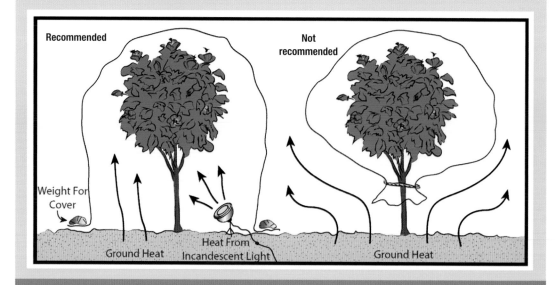

Recommended
Not recommended
Weight For Cover
Ground Heat
Heat From Incandescent Light
Ground Heat

watering. If it is moist to the touch you can hold off a little longer and maybe rain will arrive and do the job for you. If it is a little dry to the touch then water ½ inch.

Water new strawberry plants every two or three days to get them off to a good start. Sprinkler irrigation is fine for the first few weeks, as the plant is just starting to develop roots and drip irrigation's wetting pattern may not be sufficient.

LAWNS

Water only if it hasn't rained at least ½ inch in the past ten days. Your lawn is slowing growth and its water needs are reduced in the cooler weather of fall.

ROSES, SHRUBS & TREES

Water established woody ornamental plants only as needed to keep the soil slightly moist. It is best if these plants are slowing growth now in preparation for dormancy and the cold weather that is just around the corner.

VINES & GROUNDCOVERS

Water vines and groundcovers only if it hasn't rained in the past two or three weeks.

FERTILIZE

ANNUALS

Warm-season annuals are looking great now and growing well in the mild days of fall. It is a good idea to fertilize them with a light application of a complete fertilizer such as a turf-type product to provide a boost of nitrogen to sustain new growth and more blooms. Cool-season annuals are putting on early growth and will also benefit from a light to moderate application of the same type of fertilizer. The goal is to get them growing fast to fill in and have plenty of plant area for a full coverage of blooms while temperatures are still mild.

EDIBLES

Fertilize cool-season crops, except for beans and peas, with a moderate application of fertilizer. The soil microbial activity will be slowing as the weather cools off and some supplemental fertilizing can be helpful. If you use an organic product, double the rate to account for lower nutrient content and less microbial activity to release the product's nutrients. The bonus is that the nutrients won't wash away as readily as with a more soluble product and

■ *Fertilize cool-season color plants such as dianthus to keep the plants growing and blooming their best.*

you'll have a longer period of nutrient availability that will carry your plants into late winter.

Don't fertilize herbs or fruit plants this month. The exception is strawberries, which will benefit from a moderate application. The rates mentioned in Here's How to Fertilize Flowers, Ornamental Grasses, and Vegetables in April will also be appropriate for strawberry plants.

PERENNIALS & ORNAMENTAL GRASSES

The preplant fertilizer application you gave your new perennials will be adequate for them until next spring. Established perennials will be shutting down soon and have adequate nutrients in the soil to carry them on into winter without additional feeding. The late-season bloomers—including Mexican bush sage (*Salvia leucantha*), fall aster (*Symphyotrichum oblongifolium*), and Copper Canyon daisy (*Tagetes lemmonii*)—won't be pushed into more blooms with fertilizer at this point, and in fact the Copper Canyon daisy already has a tendency toward a lanky, floppy growth habit.

ROSES

Hold off on fertilizing roses, except in zones 8b to 9, to avoid stimulating succulent new growth that would be susceptible to an early freeze. In zones 8b to 9 apply ¼ cup of a 3-1-2 ratio fertilizer per bush to established roses and 1 tablespoon per bush to new transplants. Then water it in well. This will sustain them for another eight weeks of blooming in these warmer areas of the state.

SHRUBS

If hollies, pyracantha, or other berry-producing shrubs are showing chlorosis on the young foliage, feed the shrubs an iron supplement according to label instructions.

VINES & GROUNDCOVERS

Don't fertilize groundcovers or vines this late in the season. They have plenty of soil nutrients to support limited growth and the plants are busy storing carbohydrates as they prepare for winter dormancy.

PROBLEM-SOLVE

ANNUALS, PERENNIALS & ORNAMENTAL GRASSES

Hungry caterpillars are looking for their last meal before transforming into a cocoon for overwintering. Check your plants periodically, and if there are only a few of these pests, just pick them off and destroy them. If their numbers appear to be large, then a spray of *Bacillus thuringiensis* (B.t.) should take control of the situation.

In the southern parts of the state the mild temperatures and humidity that follow rainfall can create the perfect environment for powdery mildew. The disease is especially fond of shady locations. Catch it early and it can be prevented with less toxic sprays of products such as horticultural oil or potassium bicarbonate.

EDIBLES

Loopers are fond of our cole crops and leafy greens. A spray of *Bacillus thuringiensis* (B.t.) applied early will control them well. The key is to check your plants so you can know when a problem is just getting started. Aphids can also be a problem, but a spray of insecticidal soap is an effective, low-toxicity option for shutting them down.

LAWNS

Large patch (or brown patch) begins to appear in St. Augustine lawns when the temperatures become milder and some rainy periods develop. This disease shows up as circular brown areas, usually with yellowing grass at the outer edge of the circle, and often with some regreening of the interior. The fungus rots the leaves off of the runners but doesn't kill the grass. Sprays to manage it must be applied before it appears and are of little effect after the large circular patches appear. It is best managed by avoiding excessive nitrogen applications, which can make the turf more susceptible to the fungus. When the weather warms up in spring, the brown areas will regreen as the grass blades fill back in.

■ *Large patch or brown patch is common on cool, wet conditions and while unsightly doesn't kill St. Augustine grass. The brown circular areas will re-green in the spring when warm weather returns.*

If your lawn was damaged by take-all patch this year, consider applying a topdressing of sphagnum peat moss to the lawn to deter the disease. Break up the compressed peat moss product into a fine, fluffy material and then spread it about ½ inch deep across the lawn. Then water the area with ½ inch of irrigation.

ROSES

Continue to check roses and treat as needed for blackspot and powdery mildew damage to the foliage. Petal blights can cause petals to turn brown, even before the blooms open. Preventative sprays can be helpful, but in most cases gardeners simply prune out the affected blooms.

Roses with powdery mildew problems may be in a bit too much shade. A move to a sunnier location can help lessen the disease incidence. Another option is to plant a different, less susceptible variety in that location. Fall is a great time to plant roses.

SHRUBS

Milder temperatures may bring on a recurrence of powdery mildew on susceptible plants (see April,

Problem-Solve). This disease is better prevented than cured, so take early action to prevent damage to a plant's foliage.

Check hollies for yellow foliage, a sign of nutrient deficiency. Plants carrying a heavy load of berries often show such symptoms. Apply a complete fertilizer and an iron supplement according to label rates and water it in to speed the movement of nutrients to the plants' root systems.

TREES

Twig girdler damage appears in fall and winter as fallen branches in the landscape that are about pencil-sized or a little larger that look like they were cut with a knife or small saw. Twig girdlers of various species are usually seen on pecans and persimmons in Texas but can attack many species, including citrus, elm, hackberry, hickory, huisache, mimosa, red oak, retama, rose, Texas ebony, walnut, and various fruit trees. The insect's eggs and larvae are in the fallen branches, so gather and put them in the trash to reduce reappearance of these pests. Their damage is usually minimal and doesn't require spraying.

November

This month is when we really begin to experience fall weather. The temperatures are cooling off considerably and frosts are starting to arrive in much of the state. That means the end of warm-season flowers and vegetables. We can clean out these areas and replant with cool-season plants to carry our gardens on through the winter in all but the most northern areas, where it gets cold enough at some point in the winter to shut down most flowers and vegetables.

It is still a wonderful time to plant new woody ornamentals, including shrubs, roses, trees, and woody vines. Don't wait until spring if you can find the plants you want. Get them in the ground now for a great head start. It is also still a good time to move any if they are not thriving.

Prior to planting *anything*, take time to prepare your soil. These plants are long-term investments and good soil preparation is critical to success. If the area drains poorly it should be evident in the cooler, often rainy days of fall. See Here's How to Evaluate Soil Drainage later in this chapter. Bring in some bed mix to create a raised bed and, when possible, redirect runoff so plant roots don't drown during rainy periods.

November is the official start of "leaf season," when the first freezes arrive along with the annual deluge of foliage. Don't let a good thing pass you by. Leaves are a free, natural source of plant nutrients. In fact, the fallen leaves from a tree contain about 75 percent of the nutrients the tree took up during the year.

Collect your leaves, and your neighbors', as a valuable source of mulch or recycle them by making compost to release their nutrients back into your garden soil. You can even use a mulching mower to mulch them down into your lawn where they help cover the soil surface and deter cool-season weeds. That is a *lot* easier than raking.

Enjoy the wonderful temperatures this month, which make outdoor gardening a pleasure.

PLAN

ALL

Continue to collect bags of leaves from your yard and from neighbors. These will help protect tender perennials in the winter and are useful for composting and mulching in the months between now and next leaf season. There is always a need for more leaves, especially when next summer arrives. Stockpile them in a large heap or crush them in a grinder to save space. If you have the space, a large section of wire mesh can be used to create a giant circular leaf bin 6 to 8 feet (or more) across to stockpile leaves. As the leaves settle you can add more to the bin so that in the end you can put a *lot* of leaves in even a moderate-sized holding bin.

Some leaves can be left in their bags for a while, but the bags will start to break down in the sunlight over a few months. They also will catch rainfall, thus becoming a breeding ground for mosquitos in the warmer seasons if the bags are not rolled over to dump the water after a rain.

Purchase row-cover fabrics of the heavier weight (about 1.5 ounce per square yard) for use in frost protection. Consider your flower and vegetable beds when planning the purchase. There are also individual plant covers on the market that work well in protecting small shrubs. It is best to have these ready to go well before a freeze is forecast than to scramble around the day before a blue northern blows into town.

ANNUALS

Plan some new cool-season color containers for decorating the landscape and home exterior for the holidays. Choose a variety of container sizes and types, grouping them together. Remember to select colors that are pleasing when combined. Some examples of great combinations are yellow or orange with blue; red or pink with silver, gray, or lavender; and white with any color. It is too late to start them from seeds so shop around for transplants and get them started right away.

EDIBLES

Complete the process of getting any areas of the garden that won't be planted prepared for a fallow season over the winter. See the June Care section for instructions on how to prepare soil for a fallow period by mixing leaves and other organic materials into the soil and using them as a blanket of mulch.

Winter-planting season is not too far away and often the weather at that time is not suited for soil preparations. Take advantage of good weather this month to prepare the soil for fruit planting in late winter. Build up raised planting beds using a quality bed mix in areas where the soil's drainage is poor to questionable. A raised bed about 10 to 12 inches high is usually needed, as the soil will settle over time. If possible, prepare a bed as wide as a tree's or shrub's mature root spread. Improving this wide area of soil will ensure faster growth during the first few years while the plant is reaching its productive, mature stage.

PERENNIALS & ORNAMENTAL GRASSES

Tuck a few bulbs in here and there throughout the landscape, especially along pathways or adjacent to sitting areas for a series of pleasant surprises through the year. If you are planting bulbs for viewing at a distance, perhaps from the street or out a picture window, then long lines or large groupings should be used for sufficient effect.

Consider the height of the bulb and the height of surrounding plants. It would be a shame to have a bulb's beautiful flower hidden behind a taller perennial plant. Also consider the bloom time as you plan your bulb plantings. Use a variety of different species to create a parade of blooms from late winter or early spring to fall.

SHRUBS

Make plans to protect shrubs that are cold tender in your area from a hard freeze. This may require building a temporary PVC structure around the plant to hold protective tarps on a cold night or simply purchasing some tarps and lights for a little extra warmth. See Here's How to Protect Plants from Freezes in October.

■ *Include cool-season color plants in your fall gardening plans, combining colors that look great together.*

PLANT

ANNUALS

Plant annuals in landscape beds in zones 8 to 9 where the weather is still mild enough to allow them to become well established before a hard freeze arrives. Fertilize the new plants with a soluble product at planting. Then mulch the beds to moderate soil temperatures and deter weeds. Ornamental kale, ornamental cabbage, pansies, and violas are the most cold-tolerant of our cool-season color plants. Dusty miller also is fairly cold hardy. It combines well with both light blue and light burgundy varieties of violas and pansies.

You can still seed wildflowers in zones 8b to 9 in early November, but don't delay. Break up the soil surface with a rake and scatter seeds. Then lightly rake the area and water to settle the soil into contact with the seeds for best germination success.

Keep watering with a light sprinkling every day or two until seedlings are up and on their way.

EDIBLES

Cool-season vegetables can still be planted in zones 8 to 9 if you are able to provide cold protection from a hard freeze. Choose transplants rather than seeds now that the weather has cooled, which slows growth, and to be better prepared for the freezes that are to be expected soon in most of Texas.

There is still time to plant perennial herbs and container-grown fruit trees, vines, and bushes. Set these plants at or just above the level at which they were previously growing in their container as they need good drainage for their roots; most won't tolerate being planted too deep. Check the roots of fruit plants before setting them in the ground to make sure they are not circling their container. Circling roots *won't* unwind in the soil but just grow larger as the trunk grows larger, resulting in the potential for the root to strangle the trunk (girdling) a few years after planting. Cut these roots with hand pruners or slice vertically through the rootball in three places to sever circling roots.

Remove plant tags. If the plastic tags are left around the trunk, especially if covered with soil or mulch (where the sun can't photodegrade them), they can strangle the tree, within the first year or two of growth.

LAWNS

Early November is the time to overseed lawns in zone 7b. In zones 8 to 9 wait until mid-month and late month, respectively. See the comments in October for more information on whether or not overseeding is a good decision and instructions on how to prepare and plant the area.

PERENNIALS & ORNAMENTAL GRASSES

You can still plant paperwhite and amaryllis bulbs indoors this month for forcing into bloom. Forcing bulbs is a great way to enjoy flowers on a dreary winter day. They also make great gifts even for nongardeners. Plant so the tip of a bulb is just above the surface of the potting soil, filling the container with bulbs for best effect. Then water them. Place in a cool location where temperature will be below 50°F most of the time until new growth appears. Another option is to set the bulbs in a container that holds water and fill in around them with pebbles to hold the bulb upright. Add

■ *Spring-blooming bulbs, such as Johnson's amaryllis, can be planted now for a great show next spring.*

water to reach just the base of the bulbs. They will grow roots down into the water and bloom beautifully in a few weeks.

There is also time to plant perennial bulbs in garden beds outdoors this month. See October for a list of fall-planted bulbs to get you off to a great start. For the best effect, plant groups of bulbs in clusters or drifts. Bulbs are great for surprising you when they pop up for their showtime each year.

November is a great time to plant other perennials that are dependably hardy in your area. Semi-hardy perennials can also be planted but will need a little extra protection if a hard freeze arrives early. Take advantage of any mild days and good weather to get these plants established so that when spring arrives they will have a great head start on the season.

If you have purchased or been given perennial plants that you don't have beds prepared for you can move them into a larger container and overwinter them in a bright, shady location or a spot with some morning sun. This gives you time to prepare the soil for spring planting and the plants can continue to establish rather than become pot-bound.

ROSES, SHRUBS & TREES

November is one of the best months for planting container-grown roses and other woody ornamentals. Their roots will grow whenever soil temperatures are in the mid-40s to 50s or above, which is all winter in some parts of the state and most of the winter even in northern areas of Texas. Fall planting gives the head start your plants need, and fall-planted woody ornamentals will significantly outpace and outperform their spring-planted counterparts. See Here's How to Plant Container-Grown Shrubs and Trees later in this chapter for advice on getting your plants off to a successful start and fast growth in the coming years.

Berry-producing plants provide color for late fall and winter and are a source for indoor decorations too. Consider which berry-producing plants would be good additions to your landscape and plant them now for years of enjoyment. Some examples are beautyberry and many types of holly, including yaupon holly and pyracantha.

November is the best month to move a shrub or young tree. The key is to get as much of the root system as you can without making the resulting rootball too heavy to move. Wider is better than deeper as you dig your plant for transport to its new home. If you root-pruned the plant in September, dig about 6 inches wider all the way around the plant to get some of the new roots that have grown as a result of the pruning. See Here's How to Move a Woody Ornamental Plant near the end of the chapter for details on how to transplant a shrub or tree.

If you are not able to plant at the same time as you have to move a shrub or tree, there are two techniques that will allow you to hold a plant for many weeks until its new planting spot is ready.

1. Choose the largest container you can find and cut the roots to fit. Place the dug-up shrub or tree in a container and add a soil-and-compost mixture, making sure to fill in well around all the roots. Trim the top of the plant back by at least half and place the container in a spot with good light but not mid- to late-day sun. Water it thoroughly and daily to keep the soil moist.

2. Heel it in for temporary holding until its planting site is ready. Move the plant to a site with good light but protection from the hot mid- to late-day sun. Mound a mix of soil and compost around the plants as you water the roots and soil well. If the plant was moved on a plastic tarp, you can also add the soil mix around the plant on the tarp and pull the tarp up around the base of the plant to hold in moisture. Take care not to overwater; just keep the roots moist.

VINES & GROUNDCOVERS

This is a great month for establishing vines and groundcovers throughout the state but especially in zones 7 to 9. The weather has cooled and there's usually rain to help things along. Prepare the soil by mixing in some compost prior to planting unless, in the case of groundcovers, there are tree roots that make such soil mixing impractical to impossible. In such cases simply work some compost in as you dig individual planting holes for the groundcovers. Firm the soil around the plants and water the area well to settle soil around the roots. Wait until next spring to start fertilizing.

■ *Plants that produce berries bring color to the cool-season landscape. Now is a great time to establish these and other cool-season woody ornamentals.*

CARE

ALL

If newly rooted cuttings are growing and starting to get leggy, pinch the tips back to encourage bushier, more compact growth.

If you have more leaves than you can shred, compost, or stockpile, use them as mulch. There are always places around the landscape that can use more mulch and leaves can be quite attractive, especially if shredded first to create a nice uniform appearance. Walkways are another place to put extra leaves. A thick covering of leaves makes an excellent all-weather walkway material and will sink down as you tread across it so more leaves can be added. This walkway then becomes a type of composting pathway so later you can pull back the surface leaves and harvest some of the rich leaf mold or compost near the soil surface.

There are many plants that are not dependably hardy in your area of the state. Yellow bells (*Tecoma stans*), pride of Barbados (*Caesalpinia pulcherrima*), gingers of various types, firebush (*Hamelia patens*), and bananas are examples of such plants. A deep mulch can protect a plant's base or crown and be the difference between losing or saving it during a winter freeze.

If you are not able to place protective covers over shrubs and small trees that are marginally hardy, such as Mexican olive or anacahuita (*Cordia*

HERE'S HOW

TO PLANT CONTAINER-GROWN SHRUBS AND TREES

1. Mix compost into a large area as deeply as is practical.

2. Dig a hole twice as wide but only as deep as the rootball of the plant.

3. Slide the plant out of the container and check for circling roots. Cut roots circling the container with a box cutter. Check for plastic nursery tags and remove them.

4. Set the plant in the hole and check that it is at the proper depth.

5. Loosen the surrounding soil.

6. Build a soil berm to aid in watering during the coming months.

7. Soak the rootball and surrounding soil well by filling the berm with water.

TO EVALUATE SOIL DRAINAGE

1. Dig a post hole about 24 inches deep.

2. Fill the hole with water.

3. Check back periodically to see how long it takes for the water to drain out of the hole:

    Less than 8 hours = great drainage
    8 to 24 hours = good drainage
    24 to 36 hours = fair drainage
    More than 36 hours = poor drainage

boissieri), satsuma mandarins, kumquats, and figs, you can save the plant from death by mounding up some soil or compost about a foot high around the trunk during a night where temperatures are forecast to drop to killing lows. This will protect the base from which the plant can resprout when the weather warms again. Don't leave the soil against the trunk for extended periods, only for the duration of the killing cold spell.

ANNUALS

Be ready to cover annual beds during frosts and freezes to keep their growth from being slowed or set back. This will ensure a much better bloom display as we move into the winter season.

Fall-planted annuals and biennials such as poppies, sweet peas, and larkspur have sprouted and are sitting out the winter as small plants in preparation for their big growth push and bloom in early spring. Carefully remove cool-season weeds, which can be competitive with these flowers for light, moisture, and nutrients. Hand pulling or a careful, shallow hoeing will do them a lot of good. Place a

little finely ground mulch around them to shade the soil and help protect against crusting while deterring more weed growth.

EDIBLES

Maintain mulch around vegetable, herb, and fruit plants to deter weeds and moderate soil temperatures over the late fall through winter season.

Don't prune fruit trees, vines, or shrubs this month. It is better for the plants if you wait until mid- to late winter to prune.

Pecans are entering their harvest season. Good luck in the race against the squirrels. Collect and store them promptly for best quality. You can store them in the shell or shelled. For maximum storage life, store them in the freezer where they will keep for over a year.

LAWNS

Grass-mowing season is over in most of the state this month, but leaf season is arriving. As leaves begin to fall from deciduous trees, one way to collect them fast is to mow with a bagging attachment. The bag contents are great for mulching or composting. If you have a lot of leaves, bagging can be slow and tedious. Try mowing without the bag to shred and blow the leaves into a central pile for easier gathering. Use a tarp to transport a lot of leaves easily across the yard to gardens and shrub beds that could use a little extra mulch.

VINES & GROUNDCOVERS

There isn't much to do in the way of tending vines this month except to remove any dead or damaged branches. Groundcovers likewise are preparing for dormancy and need no special care. However, if practical it is a good idea to rake or blow fallen tree leaves out of groundcover beds to prevent them from building up and shading the plants, most of which are evergreen and continue to gather light even in the late fall through winter season.

PERENNIALS & ORNAMENTAL GRASSES

Dig and divide Shasta and ox-eye daisies that are not blooming as well anymore or if the clumps are getting large and you want to plant some in other areas. These plants should be divided every couple of years. Other perennials mentioned in

HERE'S HOW

TO MOVE A WOODY ORNAMENTAL PLANT

1. Dig in a circular area around the plant to be moved, digging about 6 inches or more outside the area where roots were cut, if pre-pruning of roots was done earlier in the fall.

2. Dig down about 10 inches and then under the plant. Getting a wider section of roots is more important than digging deeper. The more soil you end up moving the more difficult it will be to carry the extra weight.

3. Lean the plant away from the cut side and slide a tarp underneath the roots and soil.

4. Repeat the digging down and under on the other side.

5. Slide the roots and soil onto the tarp.

6. Either drag the tarp to move the plant to its new location or have two to four people grab corners to lift and carry it.

7. Reset the plant in a hole at the same depth in its new location.

8. Firm the soil around the roots and water the area well to settle the soil around the roots.

October can also be divided and reset this month, but do so earlier rather than later if you live in zones 6 to 7.

Perennials spending the winter in containers are a little more susceptible to freeze injury than the same species growing in the ground. Roots in containers get colder than those of in-ground plants. So place containers in an unheated, protected location such as a garage, or group them close together against the south or southeast side of a home or an outbuilding. Just watch that the rain running off the roof doesn't land in the pots and wash out the soil. Should we have a really cold snap you can cover the entire group of plants with a tarp for added protection.

Don't cut back perennials when a frost burns the tops. Wait until a freeze kills the top back before cutting them back. Gardeners in zones 7 to 8a will likely receive their first freeze of the year this month. See the note about cutting back the tops of perennials in the December Care section.

WATER

ANNUALS, EDIBLES, PERENNIALS & ORNAMENTAL GRASSES

Supplemental watering should only be needed during droughts or if the soil is dry to the touch at a depth of a few inches below the surface. Now that temperatures have dropped, rainfall should be adequate to keep the soil adequately moist. Water newly set transplants and young seedlings as needed to maintain moist soil.

LAWNS

Water only in the absence of rainfall for several weeks in zones 6 to 8. Cool temperatures slow water use dramatically. In zone 9, water every other week as long as temperatures are warm.

ROSES, SHRUBS & TREES

Water only as needed to prevent drought stress. Some drying out of the soil is fine as deciduous plants go into their winter dormancy in most of the state this month. Berry-producing shrubs such as yaupon, possumhaw and other hollies, pyracantha, nandina, and beautyberry are an exception. Continue to maintain moderate soil moisture to support these plants that are carrying loads of berries into the cool-season.

VINES & GROUNDCOVERS

Watering is seldom needed this month unless your area is in an extended drought, in which case watering every few weeks will suffice since temperatures have cooled off considerably and there are little demands on the plants for moisture.

FERTILIZE

ANNUALS & EDIBLES

Fertilize cool-season vegetables with a moderate application of a fertilizer high in nitrogen, such as a turf-type fertilizer with a 3-1-2 or 4-1-2 ratio of nutrients. Supplement this with an equal amount of potassium magnesium sulfate in the acidic, sandy soils of East Texas. For an added boost, fertilize new transplants with a soluble plant food at the higher label rate and repeat the application twice more at seven-day intervals.

Herbs and fruit trees won't need supplemental fertilizing this month.

PROBLEM-SOLVE

ANNUALS, EDIBLES, PERENNIALS & ORNAMENTAL GRASSES

Continue to periodically patrol plants for pests. In warmer areas aphids and caterpillars are still quite active and are best stopped early before they can do any significant damage.

LAWNS

If you have the large brown circles that large patch (brown patch) causes in St. Augustine lawns it is too late to treat. When the weather warms in spring the areas will recover and become green again.

TREES

Trees defoliated by fall webworms may be pushing out another set of leaves now. There is nothing you can do at this time except make a note to give them extra TLC next spring and summer as they try to rebuild lost carbohydrate reserves.

December

The holidays can be a hectic time, so gardening often gets put on hold for other things. Our landscapes offer bounty of a different type this time of the year. Evergreens are great for making decorations, including berry-bearing plants such as pyracantha, yaupon, and other hollies. Some types of berries are poisonous, so check before using berrying plants in homes where small children might be visiting. Let your imagination run as there are many other plants that are nice additions to arrangements, including Southern magnolia foliage, pine cones, and spent seedheads from various tall-stemmed flowers.

You may have started some cuttings earlier in the year that would make nice gifts this month. If not consider purchasing a plant for gardening friends. Books, tools, and bird feeders also make wonderful gifts.

Take advantage of inclement weather to take care of your pruning tools. Clean any rust off of the blades with a wire brush and lubricate them with oil to halt the rust and make pruning a little easier. Sharpen the cutting blades so they'll be ready to go next month when pruning season begins. Put your mower and other power equipment to bed for the winter by draining the gas tank and running it until it stops to remove the gas from the lines.

December is a good month for garden planning. When the weather is cold and rainy put the time to good use by enjoying the inspiration of old seed catalogs, books, and magazines along with educational web sites to begin to dream about the next gardening season to come.

Some ways to enjoy the winter weather ahead include setting out bird feeders to bring birds up close to enjoy on a cold winter day and forcing some bulbs indoors where you can enjoy their beauty and fragrance.

It will soon be time to start seeds indoors for late winter and early spring planting. Why not build or buy a seed-starting setup to try your hand at growing your own transplants this coming year?

PLAN

ALL

Whether purchasing tools for yourself or as gifts for friends remember that quality tools are often the least expensive in the long run. Cheap tools don't last and it's often frustrating to get them to work well. Invest in well-made hoes, rakes, hand pruners, loppers, saws, and power equipment for years of use and enjoyment.

Mowing season is over so prepare your lawn mower and other power equipment for winter. Drain the gas tank and then run the engine until the remaining gas is used up. Clean up the interior housing, removing dirt and clumps of dried grass.

HERE'S HOW

TO RECYCLE LEAVES

1. **Use as mulch**
   A mower is a fast, easy way to gather leaves. You can use your grass catcher or simply blow the leaves toward the center of the yard as you mow, which chops them up somewhat. Then gather them on a tarp for easy transporting to areas that need mulch.

2. **Use in composting**
   Shredding the leaves speeds the decomposition process, but even unshredded leaves and pine needles will decompose in time.

3. **Use to amend soil**
   Leaves can be mixed into the soil in areas that won't be planted for a month or more. It helps if the leaves or pine needles are shredded somewhat first, but it is not required. Spread leaves 2 to 4 inches deep over the soil surface. Run a rototiller over the leaves, mixing them into the soil. You can also use a spading fork to turn them under the soil.

Don't make the layer too deep or it will be difficult to mix them into the soil well. If you want to mix more leaves into the soil rather than adding too thick of a layer at one time, simply repeat the process doing a few inches each time. You can add some high nitrogen fertilizer to the soil if you'd like to speed the decomposition, but it isn't necessary.

■ *Gather and stockpile fallen tree leaves and pine needles for use in composting and mulching all year long.*

If the blade wasn't sharpened recently, remove it and have it sharpened so you'll be ready when mowing season starts up again. At that time the places that sharpen blades may have a bit of a backup. Consider buying a second blade so you can always have a sharp spare on hand. Sharp blades make cleaner cuts and put less strain on the motor.

EDIBLES

Plan your garden changes for next year, the best gardening year ever. Spring comes early for gardeners in zone 9 so it pays to plan out any new beds or planting design changes now. Store trellises, stakes, and tomato cages for winter. There is still a lot of gardening to be done in zones 8b to 9, so if you don't have winter supplies such as hoop tunnels, cold frames, or heavier weight row-cover fabric (1.5 ounces/square yard) make plans to purchase them now to continue enjoying the harvest of fresh vegetables on through the winter season.

Place mail orders for fruit and nut tree varieties not available from local sources for planting in mid- to late winter. Early ordering helps ensure that the varieties you want will still be in stock. Make sure to check into whether or not the kind of fruit you are planting needs a second variety for cross-pollination before you place your orders. See Here's How to Select Fruit Trees for Pollination.

ROSES, SHRUBS & TREES

Pruning chores are best put off until mid- to late winter, but if you live in zone 6 and you've had several hard freezes, you can prune your woody ornamentals if circumstances prevent delaying the chore.

VINES & GROUNDCOVERS

If you didn't get some new groundcover beds installed this past fall and time is limited now to get out and plant, you can use this time to plan

SELECT FRUIT PLANTS FOR POLLINATION

Some fruit trees are able to pollinate themselves while others require a separate variety for cross-pollination in order to set a full crop of fruit successfully. The chart below will guide you in whether or not a second fruit variety is usually needed.

Apple	Yes
Blackberry	No
Blueberry	No*
Citrus	No
Fig	No
Grape	No
Jujube	No*
Loquat	No
Pear, Asian	Yes**
Peach	No
Persimmon	No
Plum	Yes**
Pomegranate	No
Strawberry	No

* Fruit yield improved with cross-pollination.
** A few varieties are self-fruitful.

the areas. These are long-term investments in your property, and groundcovers, along with lawns, are the carpets of the landscape. It makes sense to spend some time designing aesthetically pleasing beds and to include more than one species in the landscape for interest and variety.

PLANT

EDIBLES

Plant cool-season vegetables as transplants in zone 9 and spinach, lettuce, and other greens grown as "baby greens" in zones 8 to 9. Fertilize them at planting with a soluble fertilizer. Cover them with a row cover whenever frosts or freezes threaten.

PERENNIALS & ORNAMENTAL GRASSES

Remove bulbs such as tulips and hyacinths that have been in storage in the refrigerator for chilling and plant them outdoors in late December. Stagger plantings for a longer bloom show starting as early as mid-December in all zones and continuing on until late December in zone 9 and early to mid-January in zones 6 to 8. A general guideline for planting is to set them so that the top of the bulb is about three times as deep as the bulb is tall. Wet the soil thoroughly. They will start to root and in a few weeks new growth will emerge and they'll bloom. The length of the bloom period depends on the species, variety, and especially on weather conditions. Warm periods during blooming result in shorter bloom times.

ROSES, SHRUBS & TREES

Now is still an acceptable time to plant container-grown woody ornamentals. Make sure to firm the soil around the roots, watering well afterward to remove air pockets and settle the soil. Mulch the new plant with 3 inches or more of bark, shredded leaves, or other organic mulch materials to moderate soil temperature extremes around the new plant's root system.

■ *Take tulips and hyacinths out of their refrigerated storage for planting late this month. A mass of tulips can provide eye-popping color in a landscape bed.*

■ *Remove dried fruit "mummies" in fruit trees since they often harbor disease spores that can affect next year's crop.*

VINES & GROUNDCOVERS

You can still plant vines and groundcovers across the state, especially in zones 7 to 9 where temperatures remain quite mild for most of the winter season.

CARE

ANNUALS

Pull out annuals that were killed or severely burned back by a frost or freeze. Clean out any weeds and debris in the beds to prepare for putting in the next color planting. Annuals that are still alive but no longer blooming well can also be pulled to prep for the next set of annuals to be planted. You can skip adding compost in this transition as it won't be decomposing much over the winter and you'll be adding more for the spring transition to warm-season color.

In zone 9b and the southern parts of zone 9a there are so few freezes, and they are so short, that you can grow tropical color plants, which are normally considered annuals, as perennial plants with some protection. If you'd like to carry your tropical color through the winter, take steps to protect the plants against the first frost, which usually happens this month in your zone. These plants are extra sensitive to cold so don't wait for a freeze. Protect them even if a frost is forecast. (See October, Here's How to Protect Plants from Freezes.)

EDIBLES

Sheet mulching is a good way to protect soil over winter while building it into a richer soil for growing plants. See the comments on sheet mulching in the June Care section and take advantage of the winter season to prepare soil for a fallow rest in beds that are not planted.

Check fruit trees, vines, and bushes for dead, dried fruit, called "mummies," on the plants. Remove them along with any fallen fruit. Also prune out dead branches on the plants. This includes pear trees, which may have had fire blight that killed the ends of branches last spring. Make your cuts a few inches past the dead area into healthy wood. Dip the pruners in isopropyl alcohol between cuts to avoid spreading diseases. All this "picking and pruning" is to sanitize the planting to remove potential sources of disease infection when spring arrives.

LAWNS

Keep fallen leaves raked off of the lawn surface. St. Augustine and to a lesser degree most other turf species continue to capture sunlight and slowly build reserves during mild winter periods. If left shaded by a blanket of leaves, these areas will decline.

PERENNIALS & ORNAMENTAL GRASSES

After the first freeze kills back the top growth of perennials you have two options. The first is to

■ *Remove fallen leaves from the lawn to allow sunlight to reach the grass.*

■ *Ornamental grasses, such as this bamboo muhly, can be an attractive feature in the winter landscape if left unpruned until just prior to the spring season.*

■ *You can build a screening tray out of 2x4s and ½-inch hardware cloth to screen compost into a fine-textured product for adding to bare areas in groundcover beds, or for use in other parts of the landscape and garden.*

leave it over the winter as this dead material provides a little protection for the crown of the plant. The second option is to cut back the plants to a few inches above the ground and then mulch heavily to protect the crown. A 6-inch layer of leaves will suffice for hardy perennials. For marginal perennials provide at least this much mulch and be ready to also toss a blanket or sheet over them on a bitter cold night.

Ornamental grasses can be quite attractive in the winter with their tan color and seed heads that get frosted on a cold morning. You can prune them back now but if possible consider waiting until late winter and enjoy their unique contribution to the winter landscape. See comments in the January Care section regarding how to cut back perennial grasses.

ROSES, SHRUBS & TREES

Check mulch around established woody ornamental plants. A 3-inch depth of mulch is desirable to block out the sun, which deters weeds from establishing from seed. Mulch also moderates soil temperature extremes. Bark nuggets, decomposed bark, shredded branches, decomposed manure, and leaves (including pine needles) all make excellent mulches. Research has shown that pine needle mulches only lower soil pH very slowly and very little, so don't be afraid to use them even in eastern parts of the state with acidic soil conditions. A little lime will easily counteract their acidifying effect and in most areas of the state some acidifying is desired.

VINES & GROUNDCOVERS

Consider adding a thin layer of mulch over groundcover areas that are bare due to new plants that haven't filled in yet or older plantings that are thinning due to too much shade or droughty conditions. Use a screened mulch or compost rather than leaves or bark and spread it about an inch or so deep to cover the soil and deter weeds. Make a note to revisit the beds next spring to either fill in with new plants or to revamp them with a better-adapted species for the growing conditions in that site.

WATER

ANNUALS, PERENNIALS & ORNAMENTAL GRASSES

Water perennials this month only if your region is experiencing a drought or if you're getting new transplants established. Annuals will usually receive adequate rainfall to keep the plants healthy, but if not, be prepared to irrigate periodically, especially in the warmer parts of the state.

EDIBLES

Water growing vegetables only if the soil is dry a few inches below the surface. Cool temperatures and winter rains should make watering unnecessary or infrequent in most areas of the state.

LAWNS

Water turf in zones 8 and 9 if it hasn't rained in the past two or three weeks and the soil a couple of inches below the surface is getting dry to the touch.

FERTILIZE

ANNUALS

Fertilize annual color beds this month with a turf-type fertilizer that is high in nitrogen. The soil is cooling off and microbial activity is less as a result. Organic matter and most organic fertilizers are not releasing nutrients as fast so some supplementing is helpful in maintaining good health on hardy cool-season annuals.

EDIBLES

Vegetable beds that were not fertilized last month can be given a light to moderate application of fertilizer this month.

PERENNIALS & ORNAMENTAL GRASSES

There is no need to fertilize perennials this month. Wait until spring when new growth begins.

ROSES, SHRUBS & TREES

If you have access to well-decomposed manure or compost the plants will benefit from a 1-inch layer on the soil surface around the plants. Pull back the

■ *Fertilize cool-season flowers to maintain good vigor and to promote more bloom production.*

Deer can become more of a problem in our landscapes when their food supply in the wild is reduced during the winter season. They get braver as they get hungrier.

mulch, apply the manure or compost, and then cover it with a 3-inch mulch of leaves, pine needles, bark, or shredded branch trimming. This simulates a "forest floor" environment where roots thrive as the organic matter slowly releases nutrients over time.

VINES & GROUNDCOVERS

Now that the plants are entering dormancy no fertilizer is needed and, in fact, will only be washed away in winter rains (potentially contributing to water pollution in streams, lakes, and aquifers). If you have access to aged (well-decomposed) manure or compost you can spread it over the area an inch thick to mulch the soil surface. It will slowly decompose over the coming months to release its nutrients gradually into the soil for the plants to use.

PROBLEM-SOLVE

ALL

Move container-grown flowers and vegetables to a protected location when a freeze is forecast. Don't hurt your back in the process. A hand truck or dolly will move a very heavy container with little effort. Just slide the dolly under the edge of the container and then take a rope or strap to go around the dolly and container to hold the container up against the dolly. Then off you go.

Deer may be getting hungry and therefore braver as freezes take away much of their browse out in the wild. If you live in an area where deer damage is common take preventative measures to protect your plants from damage. (See July, Here's How to Protect Landscapes from Deer.)

ANNUALS

Freeze damage causes plant tissues to turn to mush and then brown. If you didn't protect a planting of annuals or if the cold outpaced your protective measures then assess the degree of damage. If there is only some tip burn on the foliage or some minor burn of some leaves it will probably be worth leaving them in so that they can regrow and recover. If the damage is significant and the aesthetic appeal is gone, then pull and replace the plants. Cold damage is erratic in zones 8 to 9 but frequent in zones 6 to 7. In these more northern zones it may be best to leave the bed fallow for the remainder of winter. Cover the soil surface with a layer of mulch to prevent erosion, crusting, and cool-season weeds.

EDIBLES

Warmer areas of the state where vegetables are still growing fairly rapidly will also likely have pests showing up to feed on them. Take action when you see pests arriving. If you are not sure whether an insect is a pest or not, or if a discolored area on a plant leaf is a disease, take a sample to your County Extension Office for assistance in diagnosis and advice on whether or not control measures are needed.

ROSES

Once your roses have gone through a freeze or two, any leaves remaining on the plants that show signs of fungal disease spots can be pulled off and all fallen foliage raked up and discarded to reduce the incidence of infection when the new growth appears in spring.

Frost-Freeze Data for Texas Cities

Credited to the National Oceanic and Atmospheric Administration's (NOAA) National Climatic Data Center.

Obtained through the Office of the State Climatologist, Texas

City	First Fall Freeze	Last Spring Freeze	City	First Fall Freeze	Last Spring Freeze
ABILENE	12-Nov	24-Mar	CROCKETT	24-Nov	9-Mar
ALICE	17-Dec	5-Feb	DALHART	17-Oct	25-Apr
ALVIN	6-Dec	20-Feb	DALLAS	25-Nov	8-Mar
AMARILLO	24-Oct	15-Apr	DEL RIO	4-Dec	19-Feb
ARLINGTON	22-Nov	9-Mar	DENTON	12-Nov	24-Mar
AUSTIN	6-Dec	19-Feb	EAGLE PASS	8-Dec	14-Feb
BAYTOWN	12-Dec	9-Feb	EL PASO	14-Nov	17-Mar
BEAUMONT	6-Dec	21-Feb	ELGIN	28-Nov	5-Mar
BEEVILLE	10-Dec	18-Feb	FLATONIA	6-Dec	24-Feb
BIG SPRING	16-Nov	22-Mar	FLORESVILLE	22-Nov	12-Mar
BLANCO	13-Nov	22-Mar	FORT DAVIS	30-Oct	8-Apr
BOERNE	14-Nov	20-Mar	FORT STOCKTON	18-Nov	17-Mar
BRADY	11-Nov	26-Mar	FORT WORTH	26-Nov	6-Mar
BRENHAM	1-Dec	2-Mar	FREDERICKSBURG	9-Nov	26-Mar
BROWNSVILLE	30-Dec	8-Jan	FREEPORT	22-Dec	31-Jan
BROWNWOOD	7-Nov	29-Mar	GALVESTON	28-Dec	3-Feb
CANYON	22-Oct	16-Apr	GEORGETOWN	26-Nov	7-Mar
CARRIZO SPRINGS	3-Dec	22-Feb	GLEN ROSE	22-Oct	8-Apr
CARTHAGE	19-Nov	14-Mar	GOLDTHWAITE	13-Nov	21-Mar
CHILDRESS	7-Nov	1-Apr	GOLIAD	26-Nov	2-Mar
CLEBURNE	11-Nov	24-Mar	GONZALES	1-Dec	28-Feb
COLLEGE STATION	2-Dec	26-Feb	GREENVILLE	18-Nov	19-Mar
CONROE	1-Dec	28-Feb	HARLINGEN	30-Dec	13-Jan
CORPUS CHRISTI	19-Dec	2-Feb	HOUSTON	8-Dec	18-Feb
CORSICANA	25-Nov	6-Mar	HUNTSVILLE	3-Dec	28-Feb

City	First Fall Freeze	Last Spring Freeze	City	First Fall Freeze	Last Spring Freeze
JUNCTION	7-Nov	25-Mar	NEW BRAUNFELS	25-Nov	9-Mar
KAUFMAN	16-Nov	20-Mar	ORANGE	26-Nov	28-Feb
KERRVILLE	8-Nov	29-Mar	OZONA	7-Nov	29-Mar
KILLEEN	21-Nov	11-Mar	PALESTINE	12-Nov	24-Mar
KINGSVILLE	13-Dec	5-Feb	PARIS	17-Nov	18-Mar
LAMPASAS	15-Nov	22-Mar	PLAINVIEW	1-Nov	5-Apr
LAREDO	14-Dec	3-Feb	PLEASANTON	29-Nov	27-Feb
LIBERTY	4-Dec	24-Feb	ROBSTOWN	21-Dec	2-Feb
LLANO	10-Nov	24-Mar	SAN ANGELO	11-Nov	26-Mar
LONGVIEW	18-Nov	17-Mar	SAN ANTONIO	1-Dec	1-Mar
LUBBOCK	2-Nov	4-Apr	SAN SABA	18-Nov	13-Mar
LUFKIN	20-Nov	10-Mar	SEALY	5-Dec	22-Feb
LULING	23-Nov	9-Mar	SHERMAN	19-Nov	17-Mar
MADISONVILLE	14-Nov	17-Mar	STEPHENVILLE	11-Nov	27-Mar
MARFA	25-Oct	16-Apr	SUGAR LAND	16-Dec	6-Feb
MARSHALL	22-Nov	11-Mar	SULPHUR SPRINGS	13-Nov	21-Mar
MASON	10-Nov	27-Mar	TEXARKANA	19-Nov	16-Mar
MATAGORDA	10-Dec	15-Feb	TYLER	19-Nov	14-Mar
MATHIS	20-Dec	4-Feb	UVALDE	28-Nov	1-Mar
MC KINNEY	7-Nov	28-Mar	VICTORIA	6-Dec	22-Feb
MEXIA	24-Nov	10-Mar	WACO	21-Nov	13-Mar
MIDLAND	10-Nov	29-Mar	WAXAHACHIE	17-Nov	19-Mar
MOUNT PLEASANT	7-Nov	28-Mar	WEATHERFORD	5-Nov	31-Mar
MULESHOE	20-Oct	23-Apr	WESLACO	28-Dec	18-Jan
NACOGDOCHES	16-Nov	19-Mar	WICHITA FALLS	10-Nov	28-Mar

Spring Vegetable Planting Guide

Vegetable	Zone 6	Zone 7	Zone 8	Zone 9A	Zone 9B
Asparagus	After March 1	After Feb. 15	After Feb. 1	After Jan. 15	NR*
Beans, lima bush	May 1–May 15	Apr. 15–May 15	March 15–Apr. 15	March 1–Apr. 1	Feb. 15–Apr. 1
Beans, lima pole	May 1–May 15	Apr. 15–May 15	March 15–Apr. 15	March 1–Apr. 1	Feb. 15–Apr. 1
Beans, snap bush	Apr. 15–May 15	Apr. 1–May 5	March 5–May 1	Feb. 10–Apr. 15	Feb. 1–March 15
Beans, snap pole	Apr. 15–May 1	Apr. 1–May 1	March 5–Apr. 15	Feb. 10–March 15	Feb. 1–March 15
Beets	March 1–June 1	Feb. 15–May 20	Feb. 1–March 1	Jan. 15–Apr. 15	Jan. 1–March 1
Broccoli	March 1–June 15	Feb. 15–March 20	Feb. 1–March 1	Jan. 15–Feb. 25	Jan. 1–Feb. 15
Brussels sprouts	Feb. 15–Apr. 1	Feb. 15–March 10	NR*	NR*	NR*
Cabbage	March 10–Apr. 15	Feb. 15–March 10	Feb. 1–March 1	Jan. 15–Feb. 10	Jan. 1–Feb. 1
Carrots	March 10–Apr. 15	Feb. 15–March 10	Jan. 15–March 1	Jan. 15–Feb. 10	Jan. 1–Feb. 1
Cauliflower (transplants)	March 1–Apr. 15	Feb. 15–March 10	Feb. 1–March 1	Jan. 15–Feb. 15	Jan. 15–Feb. 15
Chard, Swiss	March 1–June 1	Feb. 15–May 1	Feb. 1–March 10	Jan. 15–Apr. 1	Jan. 1–Apr. 1
Collards	March 1–May 1	Feb. 15–Apr. 10	Feb. 1–March 25	Jan. 15–March 15	Jan. 1–March 15
Corn, Sweet	Apr. 1–May 20	March 15–May 1	Feb. 25–May 1	Feb. 15–March 15	Feb. 1–March 15
Cucumber	Apr. 15–June 1	Apr. 1–May 15	March 5–May 1	Feb. 1–Apr. 10	Feb. 1–Apr. 1
Eggplant	May 10–June 1	Apr. 10–May 1	March 15–May 1	Feb. 20–Apr. 1	Feb. 1–March 15
Garlic (cloves)	Jan. 1–Jan. 15	NR*	NR*	NR*	NR*
Kale	March 1–May 1	Feb. 15–Apr. 10	Feb. 1–March 25	Jan. 15–March 15	Jan. 1–March 15
Kohlrabi	March 1–Apr. 15	Feb. 15–March 1	Feb. 1–March 1	Jan. 15–Feb. 15	Jan. 1–Feb. 15

Vegetables	Zone 6	Zone 7	Zone 8	Zone 9A	Zone 9B
Lettuce	March 1–May 15	Feb. 15–May 1	Feb. 1–March 15	Jan. 15–March 15	Jan. 1–March 1
Muskmelon (cantaloupe)	May 1–June 1	Apr. 10–May 1	March 15–May 1	Feb. 20–Apr. 15	Feb. 1–Apr. 1
Mustard	March 1–May 15	Feb. 15–May 1	Feb. 1–Apr. 1	Jan. 15–March 15	Jan. 1–March 1
Onion (plants)	March 1–Apr. 15	Feb. 15–March 10	Feb. 1–March 1	Jan. 15–Feb. 10	Jan. 1–Feb. 1
Parsley	March 1–Apr. 15	Feb. 15–March 10	Feb. 1–March 1	Jan. 15–Feb. 10	Jan. 1–Feb. 1
Peas, English	Feb. 15–March 15	Feb. 15–March 1	Feb. 1–March 1	Jan. 15–Feb. 1	NR*
Peas, Southern	Jan. 1–June 15	Apr. 20–May 15	March 25–May 20	March 15–Apr. 15	March 1–Apr. 15
Pepper (transplants)	May 10–June 1	Apr. 10–May 1	March 15–May 1	Feb. 20–March 10	Feb. 1–March 10
Potato	March 15–Apr. 7	March 10–Apr. 1	Feb. 15–March 1	Jan. 15–Feb. 15	Jan. 1–Feb. 1
Potato, sweet (slips)	May 15–June 15	Apr. 25–May 15	Apr. 10–May 15	March 15–May 10	March 1–Apr. 15
Pumpkin	May 15–June 1	Apr. 25–May 20	Apr. 1–Apr. 20	March 10–May 1	March 1–Apr. 1
Radish	March 1–Apr. 1	Feb. 15–May 20	Feb. 1–May 1	Jan. 15–Apr. 15	Jan. 1–Apr. 1
Spinach	March 1–Apr. 1	Feb. 1–March 1	Jan. 1–Feb. 15	Jan. 1–Feb. 15	Jan. 1–Feb. 1
Squash, summer	May 1–June 1	Apr. 10–May 1	March 5–May 1	Feb. 10–Apr. 10	Feb. 1–Apr. 1
Squash, winter	May 1–May 15	Apr. 1–Apr. 25	March 5–May 1	Feb. 10–Apr. 10	Feb. 1–Apr. 1
Tomato (transplant)	May 10–June 1	Apr. 10–May 1	March 15–Apr. 10	Feb. 20–March 10	Feb. 10–March 10
Turnip	March 1–June 1	Feb. 15–May 20	Feb. 1–March 10	Jan. 15–Apr. 15	Jan. 1–March 1
Watermelon	May 10–May 15	Apr. 10–May 1	March 15–May 1	Feb. 20–Apr. 1	Feb. 1–Apr. 1

*Not recommended

Fall Vegetable Planting Guide

Vegetable	Zone 6	Zone 7	Zone 8	Zone 9A	Zone 9B
Beans, Lima bush	July 15	July 25	Aug. 20	Sept. 1	Sept. 15
Beans, snap bush	July 15	Aug. 1	Sept. 1	Sept. 10	Oct. 1
Beets	Aug. 15	Sept. 1	Oct. 15	Nov. 1	Dec. 15
Broccoli (seed)	July 15	Aug. 1	Sept. 1	Oct. 1	Nov. 1
Broccoli (transplants)	Aug. 1	Aug. 20	Sept. 20	Oct. 20	Nov. 20
Cabbage (seed)	July 15	Aug. 1	Sept. 1	Oct. 1	Nov. 1
Cabbage (transplants)	Aug. 1	Aug. 20	Sept. 20	Oct. 20	Nov. 20
Carrots	July 15	Aug. 15	Nov. 10	Nov. 20	Dec. 15
Cauliflower (seed)	July 15	Aug. 1	Sept. 1	Oct. 1	Nov. 1
Cauliflower (transplants)	Aug. 1	Aug. 20	Sept. 20	Oct. 20	Nov. 20
Chard, Swiss	Aug. 1	Aug. 15	Oct. 1	Oct. 20	Dec. 15
Collards	Aug. 1	Aug. 15	Oct. 10	Oct. 20	Dec. 15
Corn, sweet	July 1	Aug. 10	Aug. 20	Sept. 10	Sept. 20
Cucumber	July 15	Aug. 1	Sept. 1	Sept. 10	Oct. 1
Eggplant (seed)	July 1	June 15	July 1	July 10	Aug. 1
Eggplant (transplants)	June 25	July 10	July 25	Aug. 10	Sept. 1
Garlic (cloves)	July 15	Aug. 15	Oct. 15	Nov. 15	Dec. 15
Kale	Aug. 1	Aug. 15	Oct. 10	Oct. 20	Dec. 15
Kohlrabi	Aug. 15	Sept. 1	Sept. 10	Oct. 1	Nov. 1
Lettuce, leaf	Sept. 1	Sept. 15	Oct. 10	Nov. 1	Dec. 1
Mustard	Sept. 1	Oct. 1	Nov. 1	Dec. 1	Dec. 15
Onion (seed)	NR*	NR*	Nov. 1	Dec. 1	Dec. 15
Parsley	Sept. 15	Oct. 1	Oct. 10	Nov. 1	Dec. 1
Peas, Southern	June 15	July 1	Aug. 1	Aug. 15	Sept. 1
Pepper (seed)	June 1	June 15	July 1	July 15	Aug. 1
Pepper (transplants)	June 25	July 10	July 25	Aug. 10	Sept. 1
Potato	NR*	Aug. 1	Sept. 1	Oct. 1	NR*
Pumpkin	June 1	July 1	Aug. 1	Aug. 10	Sept. 1
Radish	Sept. 1	Oct. 1	Nov. 25	Dec. 1	Dec. 15

Vegetable	Zone 6	Zone 7	Zone 8	Zone 9A	Zone 9B
Spinach	Aug. 15	Sept. 1	Nov. 15	Dec. 1	Dec. 15
Squash, summer	Aug. 1	Aug. 15	Sept. 10	Oct. 1	Oct. 10
Squash, winter	June 15	July 1	Aug. 10	Sept. 1	Sept. 10
Tomato (seed)	June 1	June 15	July 1	July 15	Aug. 1
Tomato (transplants)	June 25	July 10	July 25	Aug. 10	Sept. 1
Turnip	Sept. 1	Oct. 15	Nov. 1	Dec. 1	Dec. 15

*Not recommended

Texas Chill Hour Map

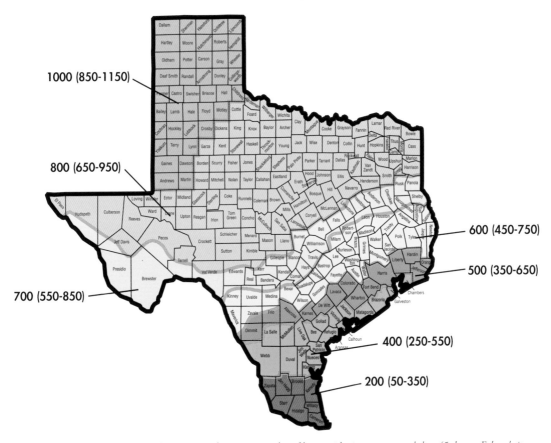

1000 (850-1150)

800 (650-950)

700 (550-850)

600 (450-750)

500 (350-650)

400 (250-550)

200 (50-350)

■ *Some plants, especially bulbs and fruit trees, need a certain number of hours with air temperatures below 45 degrees Fahrenheit. Make sure that your area has enough chill hours to ensure the plant's survival.*

Glossary

Acidic soil: On a soil pH scale of 0 to 14, acidic soil has a pH below 7, which is considered neutral. Acidity can range from very acidic, such as 5.0, to only slightly acidic, such as 6.5.

Aerial roots: Root-like structures that grow from vines that aid them in attaching to walls, trellis structures, tree trunks, and other objects.

Afternoon sun: A garden receiving afternoon sun typically has full sun from 1to 5 p.m. daily, with more shade during the morning hours.

Alkaline soil: On a soil pH scale of 0 to 14, alkaline soil has a pH higher than 7.0. Many plants native to central and western Texas or the desert southwest thrive in slightly alkaline soils.

Annual: A plant that germinates (sprouts), flowers, and dies within a year.

Bacillus thuringiensis (B.t.): An organic pest control ingredient based on naturally occurring soil bacteria, often used to control harmful caterpillars such as cutworms, leaf rollers, and webworms. Other strains of this bacterium are effective against fungus gnats or some leaf-feeding beetles.

Balanced fertilizer: A fertilizer containing equal percentages of nitrogen, phosphorus, and potassium, such as 20-20-20.

Balled and burlapped (B&B): Plants that have been grown in field nursery rows, dug up with their soil intact, wrapped with burlap, and tied with twine. Most of the plants sold balled and burlapped are large shrubs and trees.

Bare root: Plants dug and shipped without soil around their roots. Roses and fruit trees are often sold as bare-root plants in mid- to late winter.

Bed mix (or landscape bed mix): A mix of topsoil, sand, compost, composted bark, or other materials that is used to build a raised planting bed, especially in areas where the native soil is shallow or otherwise unsuitable for optimum plant growth.

Beneficial insects: Insects that perform valuable services such as pollination and pest control. Examples are ladybugs, lacewings, hover (syrphid) flies, parasitoid wasps, and many types of bees.

Biennial: A plant that begins growth one year and then blooms and dies during its second year.

Bolting: The process in which a plant switches from vegetative growth to producing flowers and seeds. Bolting often occurs quite suddenly with changes in the day length, and an annual plant usually dies shortly after bolting.

Bottom watering: Placing a tray with seeds or young transplants into a shallow tray of water to allow the water to gently "wick" up into the seed-starting mix to wet it thoroughly. This is an efficient way to water and doesn't dislodge seeds or knock over young seedlings as a spray of water can.

Broad-spectrum weed killer: A product that kills different types of weeds rather than just grasses or broadleaf weeds. Examples include glyphosate or horticultural vinegar.

Brown materials: A part of a well-balanced compost pile, brown materials include high-carbon materials such as brown leaves and grass, woody plant stems, wood chips, and sawdust.

Bud: A compact growth on a plant branch that will develop into a leaf, flower, or shoot.

Bulb: A bulb is a plant with a large, rounded underground storage organ formed by the plant stem and leaves. Examples are tulips, daffodils, and hyacinths. Bulbs that flower in spring are typically planted in fall. Sometimes other types of storage structures such as corms are generically referred to as "bulbs."

Bush: *See* shrub.

Cane: A stem on a blackberry, raspberry, or blueberry plant. Vigorous rose stems can also referred to as canes.

Central leader: The term for the center or main trunk of a fruit tree.

Chilling hours: A term usually used in fruit growing to describe the time needed to break down the chemicals that inhibit bud growth so the leaf and flower buds can emerge in the spring. Chilling hours accumulate over the winter when temperatures are primarily in the 40 to 50°F range.

Chlorosis: Loss of color as foliage turns from green to yellow due to a lack of certain nutrients, such as iron.

Cole crops: A term for the group of vegetables that include broccoli, cabbage, kale, kohlrabi, collars, cauliflower, and Brussels sprouts. Most of the members of this group have bluish-green foliage.

Common name: A name that is generally used to identify a plant in a particular region, as opposed to its botanical name, which is standard throughout the world; for example, the common name for *Echinacea purpurea* is "purple coneflower."

Compost tea: A solution made by steeping compost in water to soak some of the nutrients, microbes, and other compounds out of the compost for use in watering plants or spraying on their foliage.

Complete fertilizer: A fertilizer that contains all three of the major nutrients: nitrogen, phosphorus, and potassium.

Compound leaf: A leaf made up of several leaflets attached to a petiole, which in turn attaches to the plant stem. Common examples of compound leaves include pecans, Texas mountain laurel, bluebonnets, yellow bells (*Tecoma stans*), and roses.

Contact herbicide: A type of herbicide that only kills the part of the plant that it contacts, such as the leaves or the stems.

Container: Any pot or vessel that is used for planting; containers can be ceramic, clay, steel, or plastic, or something whimsical such as an old boot, bucket, or wheel barrow.

Container garden: A garden created by growing plants in containers instead of in the ground.

Container grown: A plant that is grown and sold in a pot or container.

Containerized: A bare-root plant that has been potted up for sale, as opposed to one grown in a container.

Cool-season annual: A flowering plant, such as snapdragon or pansy, that thrives during cooler months.

Cool-season vegetable: A vegetable, such as spinach, broccoli, or peas, that thrives during cooler months.

Cover crop: A crop grown specifically to enrich the soil, prevent erosion, suppress weeds, and in some cases help control pests and diseases. Examples included clover, vetch, and cereal rye.

Cross-pollinate: The transfer of pollen from one plant to another plant.

Crown: The base of a perennial plant or grass plant, from which regrowth emerges. The term "crown" is also used for the overall canopy of a tree.

Cultivator: A tool used for loosening the soil surface to break up crusting and destroy small weeds. Hand cultivators are usually composed of three curved tines attached to a short handle. Larger cultivator tools may be attached to long handles with stationary or rotary tines, or to a set of two handles with a rolling wheel for working the soil while walking down a row of plants.

Dappled shade: A bright shade created by high tree branches or tree foliage, where patches of sunlight and shade intermingle.

Day-neutral plant: A plant that flowers when it reaches a certain size or age, regardless of the day length.

Deadhead: To remove dead flowers in order to encourage further bloom and prevent the plant from going to seed.

Deciduous plant: A plant that loses its leaves seasonally, typically in fall or early winter.

Dibble or dibber: A tool consisting of a pointed wooden stick with a handle. Used for poking holes or shallow furrows in the ground to plant seeds, transplants, and small bulbs.

Dividing: A technique consisting of digging up clumping perennials, separating the roots, and replanting.

Dormancy: The period when plants stop growing and deciduous plants cast off their foliage; this happens naturally and seasonally, usually in winter.

Drip line: The ground area under the outer circumference of tree branches.

Evergreen: A plant that keeps its leaves year-round, instead of dropping them in the winter season.

Expanded shale: A product made from shale that is fired in a kiln, causing it to expand, leaving it porous and lightweight. It is used to improve drainage of heavy clays, heavy potting soils, or bed mixes. Expanded shale is also known as "haydite."

Fallow: Left unplanted. Soil that is fallow is often plowed and then left to rest for a period of time before replanting.

Fertilizer grade: The fertilizer grade (also called "fertilizer analysis") is represented by the three numbers—representing nitrogen (N), phosphate (P2O5), and potash (K2O)—with dashes between the numbers, that is usually printed on the front of a fertilizer bag. These three numbers represent the percentage of nitrogen, phosphorus, and potassium by weight. For example, an 8-2-4 fertilizer contains 8 percent nitrogen, 2 percent phosphate, and 4 percent potash by weight.

Fertilizer ratio: The relative amounts of each of the three major nutrients, nitrogen, phosphorus, and potassium, in that order. For example, a 3-1-2 ratio fertilizer would have three times as much nitrogen as phosphorus (phosphate), and twice as much potassium (potash) as phosphorus. (see "fertilizer grade" for comparison).

Floating row covers: *See* row-cover fabric.

Floricane: A second-year cane on a blackberry or raspberry shrub. Floricanes are fruit bearing.

Forcing: Growing bulbs (typically indoors) in containers of water, pebbles, or growing media to get them to produce blooms.

Four-inch pot: The 4-inch-by-4-inch pots that many annuals and small perennials are sold in. Four-inch pots can also be sold in flats of eighteen or twenty.

Frost: Ice crystals that form on plant surfaces when the air temperature falls to near or below freezing (32°F). Plant surfaces can lose heat faster than the air, resulting in frost forming on their surfaces even when the air temperature is above freezing.

Full sun: Areas of the garden that receive direct sunlight for six to eight hours a day or more, with little to no shade.

Fungicide: This describes a chemical compound used to control fungal diseases.

Garden fork: A garden implement with a long handle and short tines, used for loosening and turning soil.

Garden lime: A soil amendment that raises soil pH.

Germination: This is the process by which a seed initiates growth into a plant.

Graft union: The place on a fruit tree trunk where the rootstock and the scion have been joined.

Grafted tree: A tree composed of two parts: the top, or scion, which bears fruit, and the bottom, or rootstock.

Granular fertilizer: A dry, pellet-like form of fertilizer rather than a liquid or powder.

Grass clippings: The parts of grass that are removed when mowing, clippings are a valuable source of nitrogen for the lawn or the compost pile.

Green materials: An essential element in composting that includes grass clippings, kitchen scraps, and manure, and which provides valuable nitrogen for the composting process.

Hand pruners: An important hand tool that consists of two sharp blades that perform a scissoring motion. They are used for light pruning, clipping, and cutting branches ½ inch or less in diameter.

Hardening off: Acclimating seedlings and young plants grown in an indoor environment to the outdoor environment to prepare them for transplanting outdoors. This is done by leaving them outdoors for longer periods of time over the course of a week or two.

Hardiness zone map: A map listing the average annual minimum temperature ranges for the various areas of North America. This information is helpful in determining appropriate plants for the garden.

Haydite: *See* expanded shale.

Heading cut: Cutting off the end of a branch in an area not adjacent to a side branch. *See* thinning cut (for comparison).

Hedging: The practice of trimming a line of plants to create a solid mass for privacy or to define garden areas. Heading cuts are used in the process of shearing a plant to create a hedge.

Heel in: To mound up soil, a soil and compost mix, or moist sawdust over the root system of a bare root or newly dug plant to keep the roots moist until it can be planted in its new location.

Heirloom: Definitions vary but generally refers to a plant variety that has been in cultivation in an area for at least fifty years.

Herbicide: A substance used for destroying or controlling weeds. Herbicides are available in organic and synthetic forms.

Hill: A grouping of seedlings as opposed to a row of seedlings. Melons, squash, and cucumbers are often planted in hills. Note that the term "hill" does not mean that the soil in the area is raised.

Holdfast: A root-like structure that anchors a vine to a structure or tree trunk. These are often modified tendrils with discs on the end that adhere like miniature suction cups to a wall, trellis structure, or another plant.

Host plant: A plant grown to feed caterpillars that will eventually transform into butterflies.

Hybrid: Plants produced by crossing two genetically different plants, hybrids often have desirable characteristics such as disease resistance.

Insecticide: A substance that is used for destroying or controlling insects that are harmful to plants. Insecticides are available in organic and synthetic forms.

Irrigation: A system of watering the landscape, irrigation can include in-ground automatic systems, soaker or drip hoses, or hand-held hoses with nozzles.

Jute twine: A natural-fiber twine used for gently tying plants to stakes or other supports.

Kneeling pad: A padded, weather-resistant cushion used for protecting knees while performing garden tasks such as weeding and planting.

Landscape bed mix: *See* bed mix.

Landscape fabric: A synthetic material that is laid on the soil surface to control weeds and prevent erosion.

Larva: The immature stage of an insect that goes through complete metamorphosis. For example, a caterpillar is a butterfly or moth larva.

Larvae: This is the plural of larva.

Leaflet: The leaf-like part of a compound leaf. Individual leaflets are often mistakenly called leaves, but they differ in that while they are attached to the compound leaf's petiole, true leaves are attached to the plant's stem.

Leaf rake: A long-handled rake with flexible tines on the head, used for easily and efficiently raking leaves into piles, or removing loose, lightweight surface debris from the soil.

Liquid fertilizer: Plant fertilizer designed for use in a liquid form. Some types are highly soluble granules (soluble fertilizer) that are dissolved in water, and some types are sold in a liquid form.

Long-day plant: Plants that flower when the days are longer than their critical photoperiod. Long-day plants typically flower in early summer, when the days are getting longer.

Loppers: A manual gardening tool used with two hands to prune branches of ½ to 3 inches in diameter with a scissoring motion.

Morning sun: Areas of the garden that have an eastern exposure and receive direct sun in the morning hours.

Mulch: Any type of material that is spread over the soil surface around the base of plants to suppress weeds and retain soil moisture.

Nematode: Microscopic, wormlike organisms that live in the soil; some nematodes are beneficial, while others are harmful to plants.

Naturalized: Plants that are introduced into an area, as opposed to being native to it, but which establish and continue to return each year or to grow for years to come.

Nectar plant: Flowers that produce nectar that attracts and feeds butterflies or hummingbirds.

New wood (new growth): The current season's growth on plants, it is characterized by a greener, more tender form than older, woodier growth.

Nonselective herbicide: *See* broad-spectrum weed killer.

Nozzle: A device that attaches to the end of a hose and disperses water through a number of small holes to create a spray that covers a wider area, often also with a smaller droplet size.

Old wood: Old wood is growth that grew during the previous season or before. Some fruit plants produce on last year's growth.

Organic: Derived from naturally occurring materials instead of synthetic materials. To be organic a product must not just be natural but also be approved by the USDA's organic-certification program.

Part shade: Areas of the garden that receive three to six hours of sun a day are in part shade. Plants requiring part shade will often require protection from the more intense afternoon sun.

Part sun: Areas of the garden that receive three to six hours of sun a day are in part sun. Although the term is often used interchangeably with "part shade," a "part sun" designation places greater emphasis on the minimal sun requirements.

Perennial: A plant that lives for more than two years, usually dying back in winter and returning from the roots or crown in spring.

Pesticide: A substance used for destroying or controlling insects that are harmful to plants. Pesticides are available in organic and synthetic forms.

pH: A figure designating the acidity or the alkalinity of garden soil, pH is measured on a scale of 1 to 14, with 7.0 being neutral. Less than 7 is acidic and more than 7 is alkaline.

Pinch: Removal of the tender new growth at the tips of plant shoots with your fingers or hand pruners to promote bushier growth and increased blooming.

Pitchfork: A hand tool with a long handle and sharp metal prongs, a pitchfork is typically used for moving loose material, such as mulch or hay.

Pollination: The transfer of pollen from the male pollen-bearing structure (stamen) to the female structure (pistil), usually by wind, bees, butterflies, moths, or hummingbirds. This results in fertilization and is required for fruit production with most but not all types of fruit.

Post-emergent herbicide: A weed killer that destroys weeds after they have sprouted and are growing.

Potting soil: A mixture used to grow flowers, herbs, and vegetables in containers. Potting soil provides proper drainage and sometimes extra nutrients for healthy growth.

Powdery mildew: A fungal disease characterized by white powdery spots on plant leaves and tender stems. This disease is worse during times of mild temperatures and high humidity and when plants have poor air circulation.

Pre-emergent herbicide: A weedkiller that works by preventing weed seeds from sprouting.

Primocane: A first-year cane on a blackberry shrub. A primocane doesn't produce fruit.

Pruning: This is a garden task in which a variety of hand tools are used to remove dead or overgrown branches to increase plant fullness, health, and productivity.

Pruning saw: This hand tool for pruning smaller branches and limbs features a long, serrated blade. Pruning saws sometimes feature a curved blade and only cut in the pulling motion.

Ratio of nutrients: *See* fertilizer ratio.

Rhizome: An underground horizontal stem that is a storage organ for the plant, similar to the function of a bulb. Examples of plants that produce rhizomes include bearded iris, butterfly ginger, and canna.

Rootball: The network of roots and soil clinging to a plant when it is lifted out of the ground or removed from the container in which it was growing.

Rootstock: The bottom part of a grafted fruit tree. Rootstocks are often used to create dwarf fruit trees, or to impart pest or disease resistance.

Rotary spreader: A garden tool that distributes seed and herbicides in a pattern wider than the base of the spreader. Rotary spreaders are used for activities such as applying fertilizer and spreading fire ant bait.

Row-cover fabric: A lightweight material made of spunbond polyester fabric that is used to protect plants. The lightest types (.5 ounce/square yard) protect plants from pests like a screen, while the heaviest types (1.5 ounce/square yard) provide about 4 to 8 degrees of cold protection. Plants can be left to grow under the lightweight types, while the heavier types are removed after the danger of frost is past.

Runner: A stem sprouting from the center of a strawberry plant, creating a new plant at its tip. Runners typically produce fruit in their second year.

Scaffold branch: Horizontal branch emerging from the trunk that forms the main structure of a tree.

Scientific name: This two-word identification system consists of the genus and species of a plant, such as *Ilex opaca*, the scientific name for American holly.

Scion: The top, fruit-bearing part of a grafted fruit tree.

Seed-starting mix: A soilless blend of perlite, vermiculite, and peat moss. Seed-starting mix is fine textured and is specifically formulated for growing plants from seed.

Selective herbicide: An herbicide that is selective for either grasses or broadleaf plants, killing or preventing the seed germination of one of the other types of weed.

Self-fertile: A plant that does not require cross-pollination from another plant in order to produce fruit.

Semidwarf: A fruit tree grafted onto a rootstock that restricts growth of the tree to one-half to two-thirds of its natural size.

Shade: Garden shade is the absence of any direct sunlight in a given area. Shade can vary from deep, dark shade to very bright shade. Some plants can tolerate a bright shade but not necessarily a deep shade.

Short-day plant: A plant that flowers when the length of day is shorter than its critical photoperiod. Short-day plants typically bloom during fall, winter, or early spring.

Shredded hardwood mulch: A mulch consisting of shredded wood that interlocks, resisting washout and suppressing weeds.

Shrub: This woody plant is distinguished from a tree by its multiple trunks and branches and its shorter height of usually less than 15 feet tall.

Shrub rake: This long-handled rake with a narrow head fits easily into tight spaces between plants.

Sidedress: To sprinkle fertilizer along the side of a plant row.

Slow-release fertilizer: A form of fertilizer that releases nutrients at a slower rate throughout the season, requiring less-frequent applications.

Soil knife: This garden knife with a sharp, serrated edge is used for cutting twine, plant roots, turf, and other garden materials, or to break up soil for setting out transplants.

Soil rake: This tool has a long handle and rigid tines at the bottom. It is great for moving a variety of garden debris, such as soil, mulch, leaves, and small stones.

Soil test: An analysis of a soil sample that determines the level of nutrients (to identify deficiencies) and the soil pH.

Soluble fertilizer: A term usually used to refer to a product designed for mixing in water and then applied to plants as a drench. There are synthetic soluble fertilizers and organic products used in this way, such as fish emulsion and seaweed, or compost tea.

Spur: This is a small, compressed, fruit-bearing branch on a fruit tree.

Standard: Describing a fruit tree grown on its own seedling rootstock or a nondwarfing rootstock, this is the largest of the three sizes of fruit trees.

String trimmer: A hand-held tool that uses monofilament line instead of a blade to trim grass.

Subshrub: A plant that has semi-woody above-ground parts that may partially die back but not generally all the way to the ground. These are often grouped with perennials rather than shrubs.

Succulent: A type of plant that stores water in its leaves, stems, and roots and is acclimated for arid climates and soil conditions.

Sucker: A rapidly growing upright shoot that originates from the base of a tree or a woody plant. If the plant is a grafted rose or fruit tree, these sprouts usually originate from below the graft union. Suckers are unproductive, divert energy away from the desirable tree growth, and should be removed by cutting them off as close to where they attach to the trunk as possible.

Summer annual: Annuals that thrive during the warmer months of the growing season.

Systemic herbicide: A type of weedkiller that is absorbed by the plant and taken into the roots to destroy all parts of the plant.

Taproot: An enlarged, tapered plant root that grows vertically downward.

Thinning: The practice of removing excess vegetables (root crops) to leave more room for the remaining vegetables to grow. Thinning also refers to the practice of removing small fruit from fruit trees so that the remaining fruits can grow larger.

Thinning cut: Cutting off the end of a branch in an area just above or outside where a side branch is attached. *See* heading cut (for comparison).

Top-dress: To spread fertilizer or compost on top of the soil (usually around fruit trees or vegetables); or to spread compost, peat moss, or other fine-textured organic matter over a lawn.

Transplants: Plants that are grown in one location and then moved to and replanted in another; seeds started indoors and nursery plants are two examples.

Tree canopy: A tree's outer layer of growth, consisting of its branches and leaves.

Tropical plant: A plant that is native to a tropical region of the world and thus acclimated to a warm, humid climate and not frost or freeze hardy.

Trowel: This shovel-like hand tool is used for digging or moving small amounts of soil.

True leaves: Most seedlings produce a pair of "seed leaves" or cotyledons when they first sprout and then begin to produce "true leaves," which appear more like the normal leaves of the species.

Variegated: The appearance of differently colored areas on plant leaves, usually white, yellow, or a brighter green.

Warm-season annual: A flowering plant, such as zinnia or marigold, that thrives during warmer months.

Warm-season vegetable: A vegetable that thrives during the warmer months. Examples are tomatoes, okra, and peppers. These vegetables do not tolerate frost.

Watering wand: This hose attachment features a longer handle for watering plants beyond reach, providing a spray of smaller droplets.

Water sprout: A rapidly growing vertical shoot that emerges from a scaffold branch in a tree. These shoots do not usually bear fruit but can shade out the interior of the tree, making other branches less fruitful. The sooner you remove them the better for the tree and its future production.

Weed and feed: A product containing both an herbicide for weed control and a fertilizer for grass growth.

Weeping: A growth habit in plants that features drooping or downward curving branches.

Wood chips: Small pieces of wood made by cutting or chipping; wood chips are used as mulch in the garden.

Woody ornamentals: Landscape shrubs (including roses), trees, and woody vines that don't die back to the ground like perennials but have a woody aboveground structure that persists from year to year.

Index

Photo Credits

Contech Enterprises: pp. 135

Cool Springs press: pp. 67 (right), 73, 84, 123, 134, 150 (bottom), 156 (bottom), 169, 181 (bottom), 186 (bottom three), 200 (all), 201

Katie Elzer-Peters: pp. 88, 99 (top), 102 (both)

Skip Richter: pp. 14, 16, 19 (all), 20 (both), 21 (all), 22, 23, 24, 25, 28, 31, 32, 35, 37 (both), 38, 39, 40, 43, 44 (all), 47, 50, 52, 53, 54 (all), 55, 56, 57, 58, 59 (both), 61 (both), 62, 63 (both), 64, 65, 67 (left), 68, 70, 72, 73 (left), 75, 76 (both), 77, 78 (all), 79, 80 (both), 82, 87, 89, 90, 92, 93, 95, 96, 97, 98, 99 (bottom), 101, 103, 104 (both), 105, 106, 107, 108, 110, 112, 114, 115, 116, 117, 118, 119 (all), 120, 121 (both), 122 (both), 125, 126, 130, 131, 133, 136 (all), 137, 139, 140, 141, 142 (all), 144, 146 (both), 148, 149, 150 (top), 152 (both), 153, 154, 155, 156 (top). 157, 158, 160, 161, 162 (both), 164, 165, 166, 167 (all), 168 (all), 170, 172, 174, 176, 178, 179, 1180 (both), 181 (top), 182, 184, 186 (top), 187, 188 (both), 189, 190, 191, 193, 194, 197, 198, 199, 202 (all), 204, 206 (all), 207, 208, 209, 210 (both), 211, 212, 213

Shutterstock: pp. 6

Meet Skip Richter

Robert "Skip" Richter is a horticulturist, gardening educator, garden writer, and avid horticultural photographer. Skip received his master's degree in horticulture from Texas A&M University and has gone on to manage Master Gardener programs in Montgomery, Travis, and Harris counties, where he currently coordinates more than 320 volunteers. He helped develop a variety of environmental gardening programs, including the Texas A&M AgriLife Extension Service's "Don't Bag It" yard waste recycling program, the "Composting for Kids" educational web page, and the "Grow Green" environmental education program. He loves teaching gardeners about beneficial insects and natural gardening techniques.

Skip serves as a contributing editor for *Texas Gardener* magazine and appeared weekly on the "Central Texas Gardener" television program for more than a decade. He has created more than 150 brief gardening videos, which appear on his YouTube channel. Skip has gardened in the brush country of south Texas, the rocky hills of the Missouri Ozarks, the acid sands of the East Texas piney woods, the semi-arid climate and high-pH soils of central Texas, and the humid, hot climate and black clays of southeast Texas.

Skip is an avid outdoorsman and loves reading and woodworking as well as spending time in his garden. This is his first book for Cool Springs Press.